The Local Church in Evangelism

An Independent-Study Textbook
by Randy Hurst

Third Edition

**Berean School of the Bible,
a Global University School**

1211 South Glenstone Avenue
Springfield, MO 65804 USA

1-800-443-1083
Fax: (417) 862-0863
E-mail: berean@globaluniversity.edu
Web: www.globaluniversity.edu

GLOBAL UNIVERSITY

Randy Hurst serves as communications director for Assemblies of God World Missions in Springfield, Missouri. An appointed missionary-evangelist with AG World Missions, he served as a resident missionary in the Samoan Islands for four years. He has since ministered in evangelism for more than twenty years in the United States and more than fifty other countries. He taught at Open Bible College in Des Moines, Iowa, and Central Bible College (CBC) in Springfield, Missouri. He earned a B.A. in Bible from CBC, and an M.A. in intercultural communication from the Assemblies of God Theological Seminary, Springfield, Missouri. Randy has done additional graduate study at Concordia Seminary in St. Louis, Missouri.

Global University
Springfield, Missouri, USA

© 2005, 2006, 2010 Global University
All rights reserved. First edition 2005
Third edition 2010

Scripture quotations are taken from the New American Standard Bible®, Copyright © 1960, 1962, 1963, 1968, 1971, 1972, 1973, 1975, 1977, 1995 by The Lockman Foundation. Used by permission. (www.Lockman.org)

Scripture quotations marked (NIV) are taken from the Holy Bible, NEW INTERNATIONAL VERSION®. NIV®. Copyright© 1973, 1978, 1984 by International Bible Society. All rights reserved throughout the world. Used by permission of International Bible Society.

PN 03.15.01

ISBN 978-0-7617-1459-0

Printed in the United States of America by Gospel Publishing House, Springfield, Missouri

Table of Contents

Digital Course Options 7
How to Use Berean Courses 8
Course Introduction: The Local Church in Evangelism 12

UNIT 1	*THE GREAT COMMISSION*	
Chapter 1	**Defining the Great Commission** 16	
Lesson 1.1	The Great Commission in Mark and Matthew	
Lesson 1.2	The Great Commission in Luke/Acts and John	
Chapter 2	**Analyzing the Great Commission**..26	
Lesson 2.1	The Comprehensive Nature of the Mission	
Lesson 2.2	The Inclusive Nature of the Mission	
Chapter 3	**The Great Omissions** 36	
Lesson 3.1	Why?—Divine Authority and Human Condition	
Lesson 3.2	How?—The Promised Empowerment	
UNIT 2	*JESUS AND PERSONAL EVANGELISM*	
Chapter 4	**Jesus' Teaching**..46	
Lesson 4.1	The Parables	
Lesson 4.2	The Soils	
Lesson 4.3	The Sower	
Lesson 4.4	The Character of the Believer	
Chapter 5	**Jesus' Example** 60	
Lesson 5.1	The Opportunity	
Lesson 5.2	The Focus	
Lesson 5.3	The Message	
Chapter 6	**Jesus' Promise** 72	
Lesson 6.1	The Promise of Power	
Lesson 6.2	The Nature and Purpose of the Spirit's Power	
Lesson 6.3	Seeking the Spirit	
UNIT 3	*THE APOSTLES IN EVANGELISM*	
Chapter 7	**Evangelism in Peter's Preaching**...86	
Lesson 7.1	Peter's Message in Acts	
Lesson 7.2	Peter's Message in Mark	

Chapter 8   **Evangelism in Paul's Teaching** 96
- Lesson 8.1   Comprehensive Witness
- Lesson 8.2   The Spiritual Harvest Process
- Lesson 8.3   Paul's Principles

Chapter 9   **Paul's Evangelism Practices** 108
- Lesson 9.1   Pray for Open Doors
- Lesson 9.2   Share Christ Clearly
- Lesson 9.3   Be Wise with Outsiders
- Lesson 9.4   Make the Most of Opportunities
- Lesson 9.5   Speak with Grace
- Lesson 9.6   Respond Individually

Chapter 10   **Motivation for Evangelism** 128
- Lesson 10.1   Motivation Levels
- Lesson 10.2   Maintaining Motivation

        UNIT 4   *PASTORAL LEADERSHIP IN EVANGELISM*

Chapter 11   **The Pastor's Role in Evangelism** 138
- Lesson 11.1   Modeling and Motivating Evangelism
- Lesson 11.2   Mobilizing and Maintaining Evangelism
- Lesson 11.3   Partnering and Planting in Evangelism

Chapter 12   **Evangelism in the Pulpit** 152
- Lesson 12.1   The Power of the Preached Word
- Lesson 12.2   Preparation for Proclamation
- Lesson 12.3   Call to Decision

Chapter 13   **From Decision to Disciple** 166
- Lesson 13.1   Initial Follow-Up
- Lesson 13.2   Discipling
- Lesson 13.3   Components and Means of Discipling

Chapter 14   **World Missions** 180
- Lesson 14.1   Our Worldwide Mission
- Lesson 14.2   World Missions in the Local Church

Chapter 15   **The Church in Mission** 190
- Lesson 15.1   The Redemptive Mission of the Church
- Lesson 15.2   Fulfilling the Mission

Appendix A 201
Glossary 209
Reference List 213

Essential Course Materials 215
Service Learning Requirement Assignment and Report Form 217
Unit Progress Evaluation Instructions 221
Unit Progress Evaluations 223
Answer Keys 239
Test Yourself Quizzes 241
Unit Progress Evaluations 242
Forms 243
Round-Tripper 245
Request for Printed Final Examination 247

Digital Course Options

This printed independent-study textbook (IST) represents only one of the ways you can study through Global University's Berean School of the Bible (BSB). Global University offers electronic delivery formats that allow you to complete courses without using printed material.

You may choose one or more of these course delivery options with or without the printed IST.

Digital Courses

- <u>Online Courses</u>. Complete your entire ministry training program online with fully interactive learning options.

  You can complete your chapter reviews, unit progress evaluations, and final exam online and receive instant results, even if you use print or other digital study versions.

- <u>Logos Bible Software</u>. Purchase an entire digital library of Bibles and Bible reference titles and the Berean courses specifically created to function inside these digital library environments.

- <u>Electronic courses</u>. Check Global University's website for additional electronic course versions (for e-readers and other devices) and their availability.

Enrollment Policies and Procedures

Enrollment policies and procedures are provided in the most current Berean School of the Bible Academic Catalog. An electronic version of the catalog is available at the Global University website.

Contact Global University for Enrollment Information

Phone: 1-800-443-1083 (9 a.m. to 6 p.m., CST, Monday–Friday)

Spanish language representatives are available to discuss enrollment in Spanish courses.

E-mail: berean@globaluniversity.edu

Web: www.globaluniversity.edu

Fax: 417-862-0863

Mail: 1211 S. Glenstone Ave., Springfield, MO 65804

How to Use Berean Courses

Independent study is one of the most dynamic and rapidly growing educational methods. Although different from traditional classroom study, the goal is the same—to guide you, the student, through a systematic program of study and help you gain new knowledge and skills. Berean courses are independent-study courses. Some students may participate in a Berean study group, where a facilitator enhances the learning experience for a group of Berean students. Other options include studying the courses online and/or purchasing digital study tools made possible through Berean's partnership with Logos Bible Software.

All Berean courses are printed in a comprehensive independent-study textbook (IST). The IST is your teacher, textbook, and study guide in one package. Once you have familiarized yourself with the course components, explained below, you are ready to begin studying. Whether you are studying for personal growth or working toward a diploma, the Berean faculty, advisers, and student service representatives are available to help you get the most out of your Berean program.

General Course Design

- Each course is based on course objectives.
- Each course is composed of several units.
- Each unit is composed of several chapters.
- Each chapter is composed of two or more lessons.
- Each lesson contains one or more lesson objectives.
- Each lesson objective corresponds to specific lesson content.

Course Objectives

Course objectives represent the concepts—or knowledge areas—and perspectives the course will teach you. Review these objectives before you begin studying to have an idea of what to focus on as you study. The course objectives are listed on the course introduction page.

Unit Overview

A unit overview previews each unit's content and outlines the unit development.

Chapter, Lesson Content, Lesson Objectives, and Numbering System

Each *chapter* begins with an introduction and outline. The outline presents the chapter's lesson titles and objectives. Chapters consist of short lessons to allow you to complete one lesson at a time (at one sitting), instead of the entire chapter at one time.

The *lesson content* is based on lesson objectives.

Lesson objectives present the important concepts and perspectives to be studied in the course.

Each chapter, lesson, and objective is uniquely numbered. This numbering system is designed to help you relate the lesson objective to its corresponding lesson content. Chapters are numbered consecutively throughout the course. Lessons are numbered within each chapter with a two-digit decimal number. For example, Lesson 2 in Chapter 3 is numbered 3.2. The first number is the chapter (3), the second number is the lesson (2) within the chapter.

Lesson objectives are tagged with a three-digit decimal number. For example, Chapter 1, Lesson 1, Objective 1 is identified as Objective 1.1.1. Chapter 1, Lesson 2, Objective 3 is Objective 1.2.3. The first number is the chapter, the second is the lesson, and the third is the objective. The numbering system is to assist you in identifying, locating, and organizing each chapter, lesson, and objective.

What to Look for in the Margins

Left margins contain numbers for units, chapters, and lessons. In addition, margins contain two learning tools—*lesson objectives with their respective numbers* and *interactive questions* that focus on key principles. Read, understand, and use these two learning tools to study the lesson text.

Interactive questions relate to specific lesson content and specific lesson objectives. Interactive questions, along with lesson objectives, will help you learn the concepts and perspectives that are tested in exam questions. Interactive questions are numbered consecutively within each chapter. Once you understand what the interactive question is asking, search for the answer as you study the lesson's related content section. You can compare your responses to our suggested ones at the back of each chapter.

Lesson objectives present the key concepts. These tips on using lesson objectives will help you master the course content and be prepared for exams:

- Identify the key concept(s) and concept perspectives in the objective.
- Identify and understand what the objective is asking you to do with the key concept(s).
- Think of the objective as an essay test question.
- Read and study the lesson content related to the objective and search for the answer to the "essay test question"—the objective.

Lesson Titles and Subheads

Lesson titles and subheads identify and organize specific lesson content.

Key Words

Key words are presented in **boldface** print and defined in the glossary of this IST; they are words that are used with a specific meaning in the lesson.

Reference Citations

Outside sources are documented using in-text citations in parentheses. These sources are compiled in more detail in the Reference List at the end of the IST.

Test Yourself

The Test Yourself section concludes the chapter with multiple-choice questions based on the lesson objectives, interactive questions, and their supporting lesson content. Test Yourself answer keys are in the Essential Course Materials at the back of this IST.

Glossary and Reference List

A *glossary* (which defines key words) and *reference list* (works cited in each chapter) follow the last chapter of the IST.

Recommended Reading Textbook

An optional textbook is recommended for use with each course. The textbook recommended to accompany this course is listed on the course introduction page. Some courses may provide additional suggested reading lists following the *reference list*.

Essential Course Materials in the back of this IST contain the following:

- Service Learning Requirement (SLR) Assignment and SLR Report Form
- Unit Progress Evaluation (UPE) Instructions and UPEs
- Answer Keys for Test Yourself quizzes and UPEs
- Forms: Round-Tripper (as needed) and Request for a Printed Final Examination (if needed)

Two Requirements to Receive a Course Grade:
To receive a grade for this course, you must:

1. Submit your SLR Report Form. The instructions for the SLR assignment are in the Essential Course Materials at the back of this IST. The report is required, but not graded.
2. You must also take a closed-book final examination. Your course grade is based on the final exam. The Berean School of the Bible grading scale is 90–100 percent, A; 80–89 percent, B; 70–79 percent, C; and 0–69 percent, F.

Checklist of Study Methods

STUDY METHODS	√	If you carefully follow the study methods listed below, you should be able to complete this course successfully. As you complete each chapter, mark a √ in the column for that chapter beside each instruction you followed. Then continue to study the remaining chapters in the same way.
1. Read the introduction in the Independent-Study Textbook (IST) to learn how to use the IST.		
2. Study the Table of Contents to familiarize yourself with the course structure and content.		

CHAPTERS	1	2	3	4	5	6	7	8	9	10	11	12	13	14	15	16	17	18
3. Pace yourself so you will study at least two or three times each week. Plan carefully so you can complete the course within the allowed enrollment period. Complete at least one lesson each study session.																		
4. Read Scripture references in more than one translation of the Bible for better understanding.																		
5. Underline, mark, and write notes in your IST.																		
6. Use a notebook to write additional notes and comments.																		
7. As you work through each chapter, make good use of reference tools, such as a study Bible, a comprehensive concordance, a Bible dictionary, and an English dictionary.																		
8. Complete all interactive questions and learning activities as you go.																		
9. In preparation for the Test Yourself, review the objectives for each lesson in the chapter and your notes and highlights to reinforce the key principles learned in the chapter.																		
10. Discuss with others what you are learning.																		
11. Apply what you have learned in your spiritual life and ministry.																		
UNIT EVALUATIONS																		
Review for each Unit Progress Evaluation by rereading the																		
a. lesson objectives to be sure you can achieve what they state.																		
b. questions you answered incorrectly in Test Yourself.																		
c. lesson material for topics you need to review.																		

Student Planner and Record

*This chart is for you to record your personal progress in this course. Be sure to keep it **up to date** for quick reference.*

In the boxes below, record the unit number, the date you expect to complete each chapter, the date you *do* complete the chapter, and the date of review.

Unit Number	Chapter Number	Expected Completion Date	Actual Completion Date	Date Reviewed
	1			
	2			
	3			
	4			
	5			
	6			
	7			
	8			
	9			
	10			
	11			
	12			
	13			
	14			
	15			
	16			
	17			
	18			

UNIT EVALUATIONS	Date Completed
Unit Evaluation 1	
Unit Evaluation 2	
Unit Evaluation 3	
Unit Evaluation 4	
Unit Evaluation 5	
Unit Evaluation 6	

WRITTEN ASSIGNMENTS & FINAL EXAM	Date Completed
Service Learning Requirement (SLR) Report	
Final Examination	
SLR report & closed-book final exam materials submitted (The SLR report does not apply to the internship courses.)	

The Local Church in Evangelism

Evangelism is not a special gifting the Holy Spirit gives only to a few members of the Body. It is a command of our Lord, and the privilege and responsibility of every believer.

Students enrolled in Berean courses may be training for ministry or enriching their personal Bible studies. This course is designed to primarily help anyone seeking ministerial credentials with the Assemblies of God. If you are, or plan to be, a youth pastor, children's pastor, music minister, or business administrator in a local church, evangelism should be part of your ministry.

While this course is applicable to anyone engaged in part-time or full-time ministry, it is primarily designed for senior pastors of local congregations. Without the senior pastor's leadership, all ministries of the church will lack direction, focus, and motivation.

If you are preparing for credentialed ministry, you may approach this course in one of two ways:

1. You can study to acquire the knowledge needed to pass examinations as a qualification for obtaining Assemblies of God credentials.
2. You can place your life and ministry before the Lord and allow the content of the course to influence what kind of minister you will be. Particularly if you pastor a congregation, you can determine that you will do everything you can, with the Spirit's enablement, to lead your church to reach the spiritually lost of your community and make an impact on the lost of this world.

Good books on the topic of evangelism abound. Many have helpful ideas. But the most important resource concerning evangelism is the Bible. Any study of evangelism must be rooted in God's revelation. The truth of His inspired Word is both timeless and timely—not a fad or trend. It remains supremely relevant in every culture, generation, and local church.

Many evangelism courses cite a variety of books by various authors concerning evangelism. This course is limited in such references. Instead, you will find hundreds of Bible references concerning evangelism, because the primary source for this independent-study textbook is the Bible.

Even from a practical standpoint, it is critical that evangelism be based on the Scriptures, because committed believers in whom the Holy Spirit dwells will be more highly motivated by God's Word than by the exhortation of even the most effective human teachers.

Most of this course is based on New Testament passages that are essential to the theology of evangelism and have relevant and practical applications—especially to personal evangelism. The Bible tells us to evangelize, but it also tells us how to evangelize. The Bible is not just another resource book. It is God's inspired revelation of His will both to individuals and to the church.

Some books on evangelism take a more pragmatic approach, supporting various methods of evangelism with scriptural proof texts. But in this course, especially the first three units, evangelism is approached from an expository base.

These primary Scripture passages are examined:

- The Great Commission in Matthew, Mark, Luke, John, and Acts
- The Parables in Matthew 13, Mark 4, and Luke 8 (especially the Parable of the Sower)
- Jesus' encounter with the Samaritan woman in John 4
- Peter's preaching in Mark and Acts
- Paul's teaching in Romans, 1 and 2 Corinthians, Colossians, and 1 Thessalonians

By taking an expository approach, this course pursues a comprehensive and integrated approach to evangelism and discipleship which avoids over-compartmentalizing the two concepts. Chapter 13 is devoted to discipleship, but the subject of discipleship is interwoven in eleven of fifteen chapters.

Units 1 through 3 are designed to provide foundational truths concerning evangelism that pastors can teach to a congregation. Many of the lessons are presented homiletically to provide sermon structures and can be adapted to preach in various settings.

The final unit presents a variety of issues concerning pastoral leadership in evangelism and missions. Some chapters and lessons in Unit 4 could justify entire courses; they are overviewed here to acquaint students with the subjects.

Throughout this course you will discover some duplication when a particular concept, truth, or Scripture needs to be reemphasized in a different context. By the congruous nature of God's Word, certain aspects of evangelism will be repeated as they reappear in various Scripture passages. To avoid repetition would eliminate a vital part of the intended emphasis and sacrifice the reinforcement of a major truth God's Word repeatedly emphasizes.

The purpose of this course is to offer the opportunity to study the Scripture passages that are especially relevant to principles and practices of evangelism. As a result you will be better motivated and equipped to enter into the Holy Spirit's work of proclaiming the gospel, making disciples, and seeing Christ's kingdom established.

Above all, evangelism must be

- Bible-based
- Spirit-empowered
- Christ-centered

At the beginning of this course, consecrate yourself to whatever ministry God has called you to lead. Through it, you can make an impact on the spiritually lost of your community and the world. Make your calling a matter of personal prayer and commitment before you begin the first lesson. If you do, this course will result not only in the acquisition of *information* but also in the *formation* of your life and ministry.

Course Description **MIN123 The Local Church in Evangelism (5 CEUs)**

The local church is the provenance of evangelism for reaching its community and the world. After a foundational, biblical theology of the Great Commission and the Holy Spirit's role in evangelism, this course proposes a comprehensive and integrated approach to evangelism in the local church that avoids over-compartmentalizing evangelism and discipleship. It focuses on a variety of evangelism methods, the evangelistic purpose of an organized fellowship of churches, and pastoral leadership in evangelism. The largest portion of the course is devoted to the evangelistic responsibility of all believers and practical biblical instruction concerning effective personal evangelism.

In addition to using your Bible, we recomment that you also use *The Master Plan of Evangelism, Second Edition, abridged*, by Robert E. Coleman to enhance your learning experience.

Course Objectives

Upon completion of this course, you should be able to

1. Identify the central message and primary purpose of evangelism.
2. Identify the source of evangelism's power and the believer's ability to evangelize.
3. Describe the relationship between evangelism and discipleship.
4. Define the church's role in world ministry.
5. Explain a theology of evangelism and the theological role of believers in evangelism.
6. Explain the value of personal evangelism to the church's outreach mission.
7. Identify the role of pastoral leadership in the effectiveness of church evangelism.
8. Identify key aspects and characteristics of evangelism.

BEFORE YOU BEGIN

Successfully completing this course requires that you apply content you study in a ministry activity. The instructions for this Service Learning Requirement (SLR) are found in the Essential Course Materials in the back of this IST. Please take time now to become familiar with these instructions so that you can be planning your SLR activity throughout your study of this course.

UNIT 1

The Great Commission

Any study of evangelism needs to be based upon God's inspired Word. The apostle Paul wrote, "Oh, the depth of the riches both of the wisdom and knowledge of God! How unsearchable are His judgments and unfathomable His ways!" (Romans 11:33). [All Scripture quotations are from the *New American Standard Bible* unless otherwise noted.]

Because the judgments of an infinite and holy God are unsearchable and His ways unfathomable, we can only know about God what He has chosen to reveal to us. People cannot worship and serve Him as they conceive Him to be or wish Him to be but only as He truly is. God is known by experience, but that experience must be rooted in His revealed truth.

A study of evangelism should begin by examining our Lord's instructions to His disciples in the final weeks of His life on earth. His parting words have come to be known as the Great Commission.

The Great Commission is more than a simple statement or command. It is an expression of the mission to which Jesus committed His first followers, and it extends to His church today.

If asked to quote the Great Commission, most Christians probably would quote a portion of Mark 16:15: "Go into all the world and preach the gospel to all creation." Or a portion of Matthew 28:19: "Go therefore and make disciples of all the nations."

But Jesus used more than one occasion to direct His disciples to proclaim His message in all the world. Each of the four Gospels concludes with a command or teaching concerning the mission to which Jesus committed His followers.

When all four Gospels and the early part of Acts are studied in their entirety, there is a continuity that also presents the comprehensive and inclusive nature of the mission as well as why it is essential to the church and how it can be accomplished.

Chapter 1   Defining the Great Commission

Lessons
1.1   The Great Commission in Mark and Matthew
1.2   The Great Commission in Luke/Acts and John

Chapter 2   Analyzing the Great Commission

Lessons
2.1   The Comprehensive Nature of the Mission
2.2   The Inclusive Nature of the Mission

Chapter 3   The Great Omissions

Lessons
3.1   Why?—Divine Authority and Human Condition
3.2   How?—The Promised Empowerment

CHAPTER 1

Defining the Great Commission

Henry Martyn was born in 1781 in Cornwall, England. He planned to study law, but while attending Cambridge he heard of William Cary's missionary work in India. He became a chaplain for the East India Company and prepared to sail for India. He left behind his family, friends, and Lydia, the woman he deeply loved and planned to marry. On the journey, he wept as he recalled his loved ones. He wrote in his diary, "My feelings were those of a man who should suddenly be told that every friend he had in the world was dead."

While in India, Martyn established many schools and translated the New Testament into Hindustani. Tuberculosis had killed his parents and sister, so when the disease threatened his life, doctors recommended a sea voyage to restore his health. He left India for Persia (modern Iran), where he translated the New Testament and Psalms into Persian and Arabic. He was the only Christian where he lived, and he suffered great discouragement. Even then he put his trust in God. During this time in his life, he wrote, "I cast all my care upon Him who has already done wonders for me, and I am sure that, come what will, it shall be good, it shall be best. I try to live on from day to day, happy in His love and care." Suffering frequently from fevers, he finally headed home to England, traveling through Turkey. He never reached his destination, dying en route at Tocat, Turkey. He was buried by strangers and unbelievers, far from any of the places where he had lived or ministered. He was only thirty-one.

What motivated a man to such a life of hardship and sacrifice? Henry Martyn and countless others have been compelled by the commands and teaching of our Lord concerning the greatest cause on earth, to proclaim the message of Christ and make disciples in all the world—the Great Commission.

Lesson 1.1   The Great Commission in Mark and Matthew

Objectives
1.1.1   *Explain the multiple sources needed in order to fully describe the Great Commission.*
1.1.2   *Explain the issues that suggest a later date for the composition of the Great Commission in Mark.*
1.1.3   *Identify the various verb forms in the Great Commission in Mark and Matthew.*
1.1.4   *Describe three common elements in the Mark and Matthew passages.*

Lesson 1.2   The Great Commission in Luke/Acts and John

Objectives
1.2.1   *Describe the relationship between Luke and Acts.*
1.2.2   *Summarize the content of the gospel message.*
1.2.3   *Distinguish the unique nature of the Gospel of John.*
1.2.4   *Explain the central role of preaching in fulfilling the Great Commission.*

Lesson 1.1

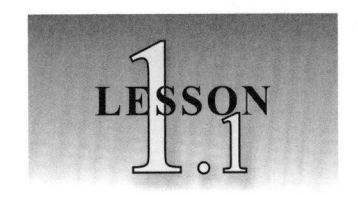

1.1.1 OBJECTIVE
Explain the multiple sources needed in order to fully describe the Great Commission.

1 Does the familiar command in Mark 16:15 fully express the Great Commission?

1.1.2 OBJECTIVE
Explain the issues that suggest a later date for the composition of the Great Commission in Mark.

2 What do textual differences between the final verses in Mark and the rest of that Gospel suggest?

3 Does evidence for later additions to Mark suggest that those verses should be attributed less authority?

1.1.3 OBJECTIVE
Identify the various verb forms in the Great Commission in Mark and Matthew.

The Great Commission in Mark and Matthew

For many centuries, the Gospel authors were called the four evangelists. A simple, yet careful, study of the four Gospels recorded by these evangelists clearly reveals the task before us.

The Gospels were written by different authors and, to a certain degree, for different purposes. Each concludes with an emphasis on the mission to which Jesus committed His disciples at the end of His earthly ministry. After devoting more than three years of His life to training His disciples, Jesus impressed on them the task before them—to carry on His mission to the world.

The Scripture passages that communicate our Lord's charge to His disciples concerning their mission are most often quoted only in part. The first three chapters of this course will examine the most commonly known excerpts of the **Great Commission** passages as well as the portions that often are omitted.

The Matthew and Mark accounts concerning the disciples' mission are the best known. This is probably because they are stated as commands in the imperative mood.

The Great Commission in Mark

Although Mark is almost certainly the earliest of the four Gospels, its Great Commission account was probably written after the Gospels of Matthew, Luke, and John were already being circulated in the Early Church. The most reliable early manuscripts, notably the **Codex Vaticanus** and **Codex Sinaiticus**, do not contain Mark 16:9–20. The following three factors contribute to the general belief that Mark 16:9–20 was not written by Mark:

1. About one-third of the significant Greek words in these verses do not appear elsewhere in Mark or are used differently from Mark's usage prior to Mark 16:9.

2. The Greek literary style is different from the rest of Mark.

3. Matthew and Luke parallel Mark until Mark 16:8. The pattern then changes notably, suggesting that the copy of Mark available to Matthew and Luke did not contain verses 9–20 (Walvoord, Zuck 1983, 194).

Although likely written after the other three Gospels, this additional material was included in Mark early enough in the transmission process to have gained recognition and acceptance by the Early Church. It was probably known through oral tradition to have been approved by the apostle John who lived until nearly the end of the first century (Walvoord, Zuck 1983, 194).

Though the Gospel of Mark was authored by John Mark, the original source of the material is probably Peter. **Irenaeus** wrote in AD 175, "Mark, the disciple and interpreter of Peter, also transmitted to us in writing the things preached by Peter." The closing portion in Mark might have been part of the oral tradition attributed to Peter. This would explain why the Early Church accepted it as historically authentic and inspired Scripture.

In most English translations of the Mark passage, "go" appears to be a command, but the only imperative in the sentence is "proclaim." The passage could be translated literally, "Going into all the world, proclaim the good news to all creation." The results of the proclamation are found in Mark 16:16–18. While these results are not given in the **imperative mood**, they are connected to the imperative of gospel proclamation.

Because the imperative in the Matthew account is "make disciples," some have suggested that Mark focuses on evangelism and Matthew on discipleship. This is an overly simplistic analysis, especially after examining all of Jesus' teaching in these passages.

The Great Commission in Matthew

4 What was the setting in which Matthew likely wrote his Gospel, and how did that environment shape his message?

After the ministry of Barnabas and Paul in **Antioch**, Matthew eventually was called there to provide pastoral leadership to the church at Antioch, which assumed primary responsibility for the Early Church's mission to the Gentiles (Lane 1978, 17).

Matthew probably wrote his Gospel while in Antioch. His work could be regarded as a teaching manual for church leaders who were committed to the task of evangelizing Gentiles in order to fulfill the ancient promise to Abraham (Genesis 12:3; 18:18; 22:18). In the first verse, Matthew identifies Jesus as "the son of David, the son of Abraham." This reflects the messianic promises to David and to Abraham that are fulfilled through Jesus (2 Samuel 7:12–16; Genesis 12:2–3). The promise to Abraham is an important key to Matthew's presentation of Jesus. The final promise of the Great Commission account states, "I am with you always, even to the end of the age" (Matthew 28:20). This reflects God's promise to Jacob when He renewed the covenant made earlier with Abraham: "I am with you and will keep you wherever you go" (Genesis 28:15).

The Great Commission passage quoted most often in Matthew is part of verse 19 of chapter 28: "Go therefore and make disciples of all the nations." Some add the rest of verse 19 and the first part of verse 20: "Baptizing them in the name of the Father and the Son, and the Holy Spirit, and teaching them to observe all that I commanded you."

As in Mark, the statement contains one primary imperative verb. In Matthew it is "make disciples" (or, simply, "**disciple**"). Three participles modify the verb and explain what is involved in making disciples. The participles are "go," "baptize," and "teach." The statement could be literally translated, "Going, disciple [people] in all nations, baptizing and teaching them."

1.1.4
OBJECTIVE

Describe three common elements in the Mark and Matthew passages.

An analysis of both the Mark and Matthew passages reveals three common elements:

1. Going is essential. The spiritually lost of this world are not obligated to come to the church to be rescued. We are obligated to go to them. The church cannot rest while any group of people waits for the redemptive message of Jesus.

5 What three key ideas connect the Great Commission in Mark and Matthew?

2. The message must be orally communicated. In Mark, the verb is "proclaiming." In Matthew the verb is "teaching." The Great Commission calls us to tasks of proclamation and discipling.

3. Both accounts include baptizing. The baptism of converts is an essential ingredient in fulfilling the Great Commission. Water baptism is not an optional ritual. Along with Communion, it represents one of two primary ordinances of the Church. Baptism is a confirmation to the believer that he has passed from death to life and an outward testimony of God's inward work. It demonstrates that the old spiritual life is buried and the believer is a new person in Christ.

I spent my childhood years in Tanzania, East Africa. Assemblies of God believers in that particular area maintain a custom established many years ago by Moravian missionaries. Before new believers are baptized in water, they choose new names for themselves as a testimony to their new life. When they are baptized, they announce their new names and are known by them from that point. Initially, they chose Bible names such as Mose (Moses), Davidi (David), or Petros (Peter). Eventually, they created names that were expressions of testimony. Examples of such names are Isakwisa (He is coming), Afwilile (He died for me), or Asagiwe (He has blessed me). My favorite is Asangalwisye (He has made me delightfully happy).

This wonderful custom provides more than an opportunity to give a Christian testimony merely by speaking one's name. It also exemplifies the essence of what water baptism represents—being born again and beginning a totally new life.

Water baptism is not an option for the believer. It is a command of the Lord and an integral part of the Great Commission.

The well-known commands of Jesus at the conclusion of Matthew and Mark convey a comprehensive mission not only to His disciples but also to the church of Jesus Christ today. These commands are a universal charge to all believers to proclaim Christ's message and disciple believers as followers of Christ.

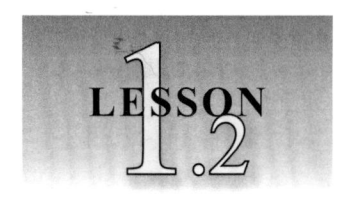

LESSON 1.2

The Great Commission in Luke/Acts and John

The Great Commission passages in Luke, Acts, and John are distinct from those in Matthew and Mark in two significant ways:

1. They are not in the form of a command as in Matthew and Mark. Instead, the writers report Jesus' instructions to His disciples concerning their mission.

2. Both Luke and John recorded Jesus' instruction in the context of the Holy Spirit's empowerment.

The Great Commission in Luke/Acts

1.2.1 OBJECTIVE
Describe the relationship between Luke and Acts

6 How does the Great Commission embrace Old Testament truth?

As with Matthew and Mark, Luke's Gospel concludes by focusing on the mission to which Jesus committed His disciples:

"These are My words which I spoke to you while I was still with you, that all things which are written about Me in the Law of Moses and the Prophets and the Psalms must be fulfilled." Then He opened their minds to understand the Scriptures, and He said to them, "Thus it is written, that the Christ would suffer and rise again from the dead the third day, and that repentance for forgiveness of sins would be proclaimed in His name to all the nations, beginning from Jerusalem. You are witnesses of these things. And behold, I am sending forth the promise of My Father upon you; but you are to stay in the city until you are clothed with power from on high." (Luke 24:44–49)

In the beginning of Acts, Luke recaps Jesus' instruction to His disciples:

Gathering them together, He commanded them not to leave Jerusalem, but to wait for what the Father had promised, "Which," He said, "you heard of from Me; for John baptized with water, but you will be baptized with the Holy Spirit not many days from now" and "you will receive power when the Holy Spirit has come upon you; and you shall be My witnesses both in Jerusalem, and in all Judea and Samaria, and even to the remotest part of the earth." (Acts 1:4–5, 8)

These accounts are especially instructive because they demonstrate that Luke and Acts are not separate works but two volumes of the same work. The two books were written on two rolls of nearly equal length, about thirty feet, the maximum practical length of a scroll in that day.

Jesus' words in Luke 24 and Acts 1 point back to Luke 3:3 when John the Baptist was "preaching a baptism of *repentance for the forgiveness of sins*" (emphasis added). These passages also recall Luke 3:16, "I baptize you with water; but One is coming who is mightier than I, and I am not fit to untie the thong of His sandals; He will baptize you with the Holy Spirit and fire." John the Baptist emphasizes Jesus' saving work in verse 17. Quoting from Isaiah's prophecy, he said, "His winnowing fork is in His hand to thoroughly clear His threshing floor, and to gather the wheat into His barn; but He will burn up the chaff with unquenchable fire" (Isaiah 30:24; Matthew 3:12; Luke 3:17).

The Salvation Message

1.2.2 OBJECTIVE
Summarize the content of the gospel message.

When Jesus revealed His disciples' mission, He used the context of Old Testament prophecies concerning Him: "Then he opened their minds to understand the Scriptures, and He said to them, 'Thus it is written, that the Christ would suffer and rise again from the dead the third day . . .'" (Luke 24:45–46). This bears a striking resemblance to Luke's account in Acts 17. There Luke described Paul's work in Thessalonica when Paul reasoned for three days in the synagogue from the Scriptures, "explaining and giving evidence that the Christ had to suffer and rise again from the dead, and saying 'this Jesus whom I am proclaiming to you is the Christ'" (Acts 17:3).

7 What is the simplest way to express the content of the gospel?

Luke's account provides the most complete description of the content of Christ's message. Christ's redemptive work is clearly the focus of the missionary message, which is "repentance for *forgiveness of sins* should be proclaimed in His name" (Luke 24:47, emphasis added). John the Baptist stated this succinctly at Jesus' water baptism, "Behold, the Lamb of God who *takes away the sin* of the world!" (John 1:29, emphasis added).

The content of the message to be proclaimed to all nations is simply the life, death and resurrection of Christ and the reason He gave His life for lost humanity. The end result of the Great Commission is that Christ is building His Church through His obedient servants. However, the Great Commission does not focus on recruiting people for a social movement but does focus on proclaiming that *each* person's sins can be forgiven.

When the apostle Paul stood before King Agrippa, he quoted Jesus' personal commission to him, "I am sending you, to open their eyes so that they may turn from darkness to light and from the dominion of Satan to God, that they may receive forgiveness of sins and an inheritance among those who have been sanctified by faith in Me" (Acts 26:17–18). Jesus' command to Paul is echoed in Paul's epistle to the Colossians, "For He rescued us from the domain of darkness, and transferred us to the kingdom of His beloved Son, in whom we have redemption, the forgiveness of sins" (Colossians 1:13–14).

The Great Commission in John

1.2.3 OBJECTIVE
Distinguish the unique nature of the Gospel of John.

The nature of John's Gospel is supplementary. It is not grouped with the **Synoptic Gospels** and was almost certainly the last Gospel written. More than 90 percent of John's content is not found in the other three Gospels.

Defining the Great Commission

8 What distinguishes the Gospel of John as unique?

The declaration of the disciples' mission quoted most often in John is, "As the Father has sent Me, I also send you" (John 20:21). But the complete statement gives a fuller description:

> When it was evening on that day, the first day of the week, and when the doors were shut where the disciples were, for fear of the Jews, Jesus came and stood in their midst and said to them, "Peace be with you." And when He had said this, He showed them both His hands and His side. The disciples then rejoiced when they saw the Lord. So Jesus said to them again, "Peace be with you; as the Father has sent Me, I also send you." And when He had said this, He breathed on them and said to them, "Receive the Holy Spirit. If you forgive the sins of any, their sins have been forgiven them; if you retain the sins of any, they have been retained." (John 20:19–23)

Completing the Mission

9 What dividing line does the Great Commission create in the history of salvation?

When Jesus spoke these words, His mission from the Father had been accomplished. John recorded His statement from the cross as a single Greek word, *tetelestai,* which means, "It is finished." Archaeologists have recovered papyri receipts for taxes with the word *tetelestai* written across them. This meant the bill was paid in full. When Jesus said, "It is finished," He meant that His redemptive work was completed. He had been made sin for humankind and had suffered the penalty of God's justice that sin deserved (2 Corinthians 5:21).

After showing His disciples His hands and side as proof of His bodily resurrection, the disciples were overjoyed. Then Jesus immediately addressed His mission for them and the significance His resurrection had for all sinners. His mission was accomplished. Theirs was just beginning. In Luke's account, the primary emphasis is on the disciples' responsibility to take the message of forgiveness of sins to the world. Jesus was impressing on His disciples that, dependent on their obedience, their mission would result in people seeking forgiveness for their sins or continuing to live in darkness.

The Centrality of Preaching

1.2.4 OBJECTIVE
Explain the central role of preaching in fulfilling the Great Commission.

10 Why is it essential that believers personally communicate the gospel?

The imperative word in Matthew focuses on the objective of making disciples. Both Mark and Luke emphasize the means of attaining that objective—**preaching**—as central to the Great Commission. The New Testament clearly shows the centrality and power that preaching the Word has in the church's mission.

Paul instructed Timothy, his young disciple, to "preach the Word." (2 Timothy 4:2). He wrote to the church at Thessalonica, "We also constantly thank God that when you received the word of God which you heard from us, you accepted it not as the word of men, but for what it really is, the word of God, which also performs its work in you who believe" (1 Thessalonians 2:13). Paul emphasized that the Word of God "performs its work" in those who believe. The Word is not merely a resource for sermons but is "living and active and sharper than any two-edged sword, and piercing as far as the division of soul and spirit, of both joints and marrow, and able to judge the thoughts and intentions of the heart" (Hebrews 4:12).

After teaching His parable concerning the sower and soils, Jesus told His disciples that the seed in the spiritual harvest is "the word of God"—the message (Luke 8:11). The Holy Spirit prepares the soil (people's hearts) to receive the message. The messenger's role is to enter into the Holy Spirit's work. As Jesus said, "The saying is true, 'One sows and another reaps.' I sent you to reap that for which you have not labored; others have labored and you have entered into their labor" (John 4:37–38).

Great miracles occurred on the Day of Pentecost. The response of the crowd that resulted in salvation was not because of the sound from heaven like a rushing mighty wind, the tongues like fire resting on the believers, or the variety of languages spoken by locals. Rather, it was in response to the Spirit-empowered Word that was preached.

The heart of the Great Commission is the message of Jesus Christ—His birth, sinless life, death, resurrection, ascension, and return for His Church.

The late missionary Bernhard Johnson saw more than 1.8 million people respond to salvation invitations in evangelistic crusades in Brazil. I once asked him, "What do you believe accounts for the great numbers who make decisions in your crusades?"

He replied, "I always exalt Jesus Christ."

Preaching Jesus is not merely documenting the life of a historical figure. It is proclaiming a living Christ who can be personally known, present within us and active in our lives. Being born again opens the way not only to salvation, but also to a relationship—even a friendship—with Christ.

Test Yourself

100%

Circle the letter of the *best* answer.

1. Each of the four Gospels concludes with
a) the final words of Christ and His ascension to the Father.
b) a summary of the divine nature of Christ and an exhortation to reject false messiahs.
c) a command or teaching concerning the mission to which Jesus committed His followers.
d) Jesus' final moments with His disciples.

2. Mark is probably the earliest of the four Gospels. The Great Commission in Mark was
a) a foundational pattern on which the Commissions in the other Gospels are modeled.
b) written after the Gospels of Matthew, Luke, and John.
c) amended by the other Gospel writers when they composed their books.
d) rejected by Early Church readers as an immature expression of Christ's command.

3. The Gospel of Mark was authored by John Mark, but his original source is probably
a) Peter.
b) Luke.
c) Mary, the mother of Jesus.
d) Josephus.

4. Matthew probably wrote his Gospel while
a) living as a recluse in the deserts of Arabia.
b) leading the church in Antioch.
c) traveling with Paul on his missionary journeys.
d) supporting himself as a tax collector in Jerusalem.

5. Matthew's identification of Jesus as "the son of David, the son of Abraham"
a) reflects Christ's fulfillment of the messianic promises to David and to Abraham.
b) demonstrates an exclusionist attitude on Matthew's part toward the Gentiles.
c) proves Matthew's inability to correctly identify genealogical sequence.
d) calls into question whether Matthew believed Jesus to be God's Son.

6. An analysis of the Great Commission in Mark and Matthew reveals
a) unfortunate contradictions between them.
b) strong agreement in the areas of going, proclaiming, and baptizing.
c) that they are written concurrently.
d) evidence of multiple authors in each Gospel.

7. Luke and Acts are
a) two parts of one whole, divided into components dictated by the limits of scroll length.
b) theoretically connected by liberal theologians to undermine the texts' validity.
c) contrasted as examples of theology (Luke) and history (Acts).
d) the only two books in the Bible that are components of a larger whole.

8. The salvation message can best be summarized as
a) an historical summary of Old Testament apocalyptic literature.
b) the embodiment of Christ's teaching in the Sermon on the Mount.
c) the life, death, and resurrection of Jesus Christ to accomplish the forgiveness of sins.
d) a divine enabling to obey the Ten Commandments.

9. John's Gospel, in relation to the other Gospels, is best described as
a) indistinguishable from the others.
b) a reordering of the principal events mentioned in the others.
c) supplemental to the others, with much unique material.
d) the Pentecostal Gospel.

10. The central role of preaching in fulfilling the Great Commission
a) proves that Christ has entrusted His mandate only to the clergy.
b) reflects the needs of an illiterate society and no longer applies in the Information Age.
c) is no longer in effect, since the death of the apostles.
d) is a call for all believers to personally share the gospel with the lost.

Responses to Interactive Questions
Chapter 1

Some of these responses may include information that is supplemental to the IST. These questions are intended to produce reflective thinking beyond the course content and your responses may vary from these examples.

1 Does the familiar command in Mark 16:15 fully express the Great Commission?

Jesus' commands and instructions to His followers in all four Gospels must be studied in order to grasp the Great Commission.

2 What do textual differences between the final verses in Mark and the rest of that Gospel suggest?

Mark is not the author of those verses, and they were added later to the text.

3 Does evidence for later additions to Mark suggest that those verses should be attributed less authority?

The full text of Mark gained recognition and acceptance by the early church as authoritative and inspired.

4 What was the setting in which Matthew likely wrote his Gospel, and how did that environment shape his message?

As a pastor in the Antioch church, Matthew wrote his Gospel with a likely focus on evangelizing Gentiles in the city's cosmopolitan environment and, by extension, the Gentile world.

5 What three key ideas connect the Great Commission in Mark and Matthew?

Both Gospels communicate the need for believers to take the gospel to the lost (*go*), to proclaim the gospel, and to baptize converts.

6 How does the Great Commission embrace Old Testament truth?

Jesus said that the Law and the Prophets and the Psalms speak of Him and are fulfilled in Him. The Great Commission calls for the proclamation of the fulfillment of Old Testament truth through Christ.

7 What is the simplest way to express the content of the gospel?

The gospel points to the life, death, and resurrection of Jesus Christ and His purpose in giving His life—to take away sin.

8 What distinguishes the Gospel of John as unique?

Its material is supplemental to the three Synoptic Gospels; more than ninety percent of its content is found only in John.

9 What dividing line does the Great Commission create in the history of salvation?

It forms the completion of Christ's redemptive mission and the beginning of the church's evangelistic mission.

10 Why is it essential that believers personally communicate the gospel?

Publicly preaching and personally proclaiming the gospel are the primary means God has chosen to offer His gift of salvation to the lost.

Analyzing the Great Commission

Missionary-evangelists John and Lois Bueno moved to El Salvador in 1961. After preaching tent crusades in Chile, they had been asked to accept a temporary assignment pastoring an evangelistic center in El Salvador's capital, San Salvador. Because of previous church problems, only one hundred believers filed into the two thousand seat sanctuary for services.

The temporary assignment lasted twenty-eight years. The church grew to more than 22,000 in Sunday attendance and planted more than 120 churches. The Buenos eventually established thirty-seven schools, each connected with a local church. In forty years' time, the school system educated more than 600,000 children.

The Buenos' ministry of evangelism and discipleship led the evangelistic center to make significant strides in a culture that clung to a rigidly divisive two-class system. Upper-class El Salvadorans worshiped alongside people from the lower class—previously unprecedented. Through the educational ministry of the Christian schools, multitudes of children from lower classes received an education and became prominent in the country's growing middle class.

John and Lois Bueno's work in El Salvador exemplifies both the comprehensive and inclusive nature of the Great Commission. Their passion for evangelism and discipleship compelled them to reach out inclusively to all people in the community. As a result, the church grew both numerically and spiritually.

Lesson 2.1   The Comprehensive Nature of the Mission

Objectives
2.1.1   *Identify the two constant components of the Great Commission.*
2.1.2   *Describe the concept of* pre-discipleship evangelism.
2.1.3   *Distinguish and describe* pre-evangelism discipleship.
2.1.4   *Summarize the ultimate goal of evangelism and discipleship.*

Lesson 2.2   The Inclusive Nature of the Mission

Objectives
2.2.1   *Describe the inclusive nature of the Great Commission in terms of regions.*
2.2.2   *Distinguish the homogeneous principle and the heterogeneous gospel.*
2.2.3   *Describe the social character of a biblical church.*
2.2.4   *Identify the need for both targeted and general evangelism.*

LESSON 2.1

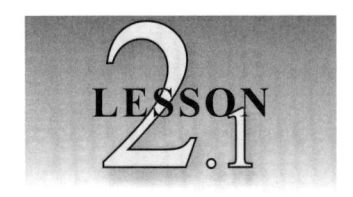

2.1.1 OBJECTIVE
Identify the two constant components of the Great Commission.

1 What are the two constant components of the Great Commission?

2.1.2 OBJECTIVE
Describe the concept of pre-discipleship evangelism.

2 What is the objective of evangelism?

The Comprehensive Nature of the Mission

The Great Commission passages in the Synoptic Gospels, as well as John, clearly present a comprehensive mission that includes both **evangelism** and **discipleship**. If viewed from a biblical perspective, evangelism goes beyond proclaiming the message and even leading people to a decision to receive God's forgiveness through Christ. The word *evangelism* is derived from the Greek word *euaggelion* that is translated "gospel" or "good news." An accurate and comprehensive definition of evangelism was given by William Temple who served as the ninety-eighth archbishop of Canterbury from 1881 until 1902: "Evangelism is to so present Jesus Christ in the power of the Holy Spirit that men might come to trust Him as Savior and serve Him as Lord in the fellowship of His church."

Treating evangelism and discipleship separately is an artificial distinction. The mission of reaching the lost includes proclaiming the gospel, leading people to a decision to follow Christ, and discipling them to become evangelists—messengers to the spiritually lost people of this world.

A study of the Great Commission passages in the Gospels and Acts reveals the comprehensive nature of the task. It also provides scriptural evidence that evangelism and discipleship are inseparable. To isolate one weakens the other. Evangelism and discipleship are not two parts of a progression that begins with evangelism and culminates in discipleship. Instead, they compose the **Great Commission cycle**. Evangelism should always be undertaken with the objective of discipleship, and discipleship should always prepare believers for evangelism.

Pre-Discipleship Evangelism

One of Jesus' best known teachings is usually called the Parable of the Sower. In it, He reveals a critical truth about the nature of spiritual harvest:

> "Behold, the sower went out to sow; as he was sowing, some seed fell beside the road, and the birds came and ate it up. Other seed fell on the rocky ground where it did not have much soil; and immediately it sprang up because it had no depth of soil. And after the sun had risen, it was scorched; and because it had no root, it withered away. Other seed fell among the thorns, and the thorns came up and choked it, and it yielded no crop. Other seeds fell into the good soil, and as they grew up and increased, they yielded a crop and produced thirty, sixty, and a hundredfold." (Mark 4:3–8)

In this parable, Jesus taught that the seed—the Word of God, or the message—will fall on different kinds of ground. Not all people who receive the message will respond, and not all who respond will remain. The person who "endures to the end" will be saved (Mark 13:13; Matthew 24:13). The end result of evangelism is about the good ground—those in whom life not only begins but also grows and multiplies.

Some people think the primary objective of evangelism is seeing a nonbeliever pray a sinner's prayer. The goal of evangelism is more than a salvation decision. It is a change in lifestyle, a life following Christ in obedience to His teaching and commands. The end objective is a *disciple*—a committed and faithful follower of Christ. Unfortunately, if a person arrives at a salvation decision without understanding the cost of following Christ, he can begin well but fail to continue following and serving Him. This situation is illustrated by the first three kinds of soil mentioned in the Parable of the Sower. People receive the message, but birds take the seed away, the sun scorches it, or thorns choke it.

Jesus explained that the birds, the sun and the thorns represented hindrances in people's spiritual lives, such as persecution or the desire for riches. These prevent the message from having a long-term effect.

Many years ago I conducted a funeral together with a Baptist pastor who was committed to the **Calvinistic** doctrine of eternal security. My custom in my early years of ministry was to seek the counsel of older, more experienced ministers concerning the life lessons they had learned. As we rode to the graveside service, I asked this older pastor for advice, and he said just one thing, "If I could start over in my ministry, I wouldn't pick people green." He explained that in his zeal to see people come to Christ, he had sometimes pushed people to decisions before they were ready. This came as a surprise to me. A rigid interpretation of the Calvinistic view of election requires every person to be either predestined for salvation or for eternal punishment. A person who is predestined for salvation will inevitably come to Christ. Yet, even from that theological perspective, this minister realized that God's work in the lives of the lost can be compromised when believers do not rely on the Holy Spirit's timing in sharing the good news.

As passionately as we want to see people make decisions for Christ, it is possible to push them to premature decisions rather than cooperating with the Holy Spirit as He leads them, first to a decision and then into discipleship.

Understanding that discipleship should be the objective of evangelism will affect how we share the message. Jesus taught that His followers should understand the cost of being His disciple: "Whoever does not carry his own cross and come after Me cannot be My disciple. For which one of you, when he wants to build a tower, does not first sit down and calculate the cost to see if he has enough to complete it?" (Luke 14:27–28).

3   What vital concept must be in mind before someone is ready to receive Christ as Savior?

A nonbeliever must understand the significance of the decision to receive Christ's forgiveness and follow Him. Believers must be careful not to emotionally manipulate people into decisions they neither understand nor are ready to make. When praying with a person to receive Christ, we must ensure that he understands what he is doing. This requires wisdom and sometimes restraint.

4   Why is it inaccurate to describe *evangelism* as "persuasion intended to convince the lost of the gospel's truth"?

We are not responsible for convincing people to commit their lives to Christ. Evangelism involves more than human persuasion. It is a work of the Holy Spirit. Jesus promised that the Holy Spirit would convince the world concerning "sin and righteousness and judgment" (John 16:8). We are responsible to share the message clearly; the Holy Spirit convinces and persuades the heart of the listener. When we understand that God takes the initiative and remains active in the evangelism process, it enables us to be bold, depending on His persuasive work. We can also be patient, trusting His timing rather than trying to push people to a premature decision. This allows us to be neither hesitant nor hasty in our witness.

Pre-Evangelism Discipleship

2.1.3
OBJECTIVE
Distinguish and *describe* pre-evangelism discipleship.

The cycle of evangelism and discipleship is completed when disciples become evangelists who make more disciples.

The church in America and other places of the West can learn greatly from the Third World church in this respect. In the last fifty years, church growth in Assemblies of God fellowships in many countries of the world has far surpassed that in the West. This is especially true in Latin America, Africa, and parts of Asia. One reason for this explosive, **exponential** growth is that in most developing countries, all believers are taught and expected to be evangelists.

Many believers in America expect a paid, professional church staff to do evangelism. In countries that do not have significant numbers of paid church staff, congregations are much more active in evangelism.

Being an effective witness does not necessarily depend on how long a person has followed Christ or even how spiritually mature he or she is. Extensive research in thousands of churches shows that most of the personal evangelism in any congregation is done by those who have been Christians less than a year.

Personal evangelism is an essential part of following Christ. It should be part of every believer's lifestyle to make an impact on the nonbelievers around him.

The Ultimate Objective

2.1.4 OBJECTIVE
Summarize the ultimate goal of evangelism and discipleship.

The mission of the Church is to enter into Christ's mission of "bringing many sons to glory" (Hebrews 2:10).

The objective of evangelism and discipleship is clearly described in Paul's letter to the Colossians: "He has now reconciled you in his fleshly body through death, in order to present you before Him holy and blameless and beyond reproach—if indeed you continue in the faith firmly established and steadfast, and not moved away from the hope of the gospel" (Colossians 1:22–23). Paul goes on to describe the objective of proclaiming the gospel, "We proclaim him, admonishing every man and teaching every man with all wisdom, that we may present every man *complete in Christ*" (Colossians 1:28, emphasis added). Notice that the ultimate goal is that each disciple is presented before the Lord holy, blameless, and beyond reproach—complete in Christ—at the end of life on this earth.

As they lead local churches in evangelism, pastors will often have to make decisions concerning how time and resources will be spent. We should, like Paul, be committed to evangelizing "by all means" (1 Corinthians 9:22). We should prioritize those means that result in the end objective defined by God's Word—disciples who are "complete in Christ." Sometimes this will mean opting for methods that might not produce as many initial decisions but which ultimately result in more disciples.

LESSON 2.2

The Inclusive Nature of the Mission

"All" is conspicuously prominent in the Great Commission passages in the Synoptic Gospels. It is the "all" that makes the Great Commission *great*. The Great Commission is an expression of God's love, and the love of God is totally inclusive.

As Luke begins the book of Acts, he picks up the same thought with which he ended his Gospel. In Acts 1:4, he reiterates Jesus' command in Luke 24:49 for His followers to stay in Jerusalem to wait for the baptism of the Holy Spirit the Father had promised. As in the Luke passage, he reinforces and even amplifies the inclusiveness of the Great Commission in Acts 1:8: "'You will receive power when the Holy Spirit has come upon you; and you shall be My witnesses both in Jerusalem, and in all Judea and Samaria, and even to the remotest part of the earth.'"

2.2.1 OBJECTIVE
Describe the inclusive nature of the Great Commission in terms of regions.

Not Only, But Also

Interestingly, the Authorized and New American Standard versions use the word *both* in Acts 1:8. Many modern translations exclude it. "Both" is a translation of a Greek particle *te*. *Te* is often used with other conjunctions, particularly *kai*, the most common Greek word for *and*. Translators probably used *both* here because the word is frequently used to connect two items, words, or concepts. Romans 1:14 is one example: "I am under obligation *both* (te) to Greeks *and* (kai) to barbarians, *both* (te) to the wise *and* (kai) to the foolish" (emphasis added).

When used with other conjunctions, this particle may have an emphatic function to strengthen the meaning or purpose of the word grouping. It can be translated "not only—but also" or "just as—so also." While the NIV and other Bible versions omit this distinction in Acts 1:8, it is significant. It indicates that each geographic area listed is an equally important part of the inclusive nature of the Great Commission. The geographic locations listed are grouped as one responsibility.

Both, in this usage, does not mean "two" as it does in modern English. In fact, Jesus lists four places: Jerusalem, Judea, Samaria, and the uttermost part of the earth. To consider the list by comparing and contrasting the various components will help us understand how inclusive the Great Commission is:

- Consider the disciples' responsibility to Jerusalem (where they were) and to Judea, Samaria, and the uttermost parts of the earth (where they were not).
- Consider their responsibility to Jerusalem and Judea (where Jews were) contrasted with Samaria and the uttermost part of earth (where non-Jews were).
- Consider their responsibility to Jerusalem, Judea, and Samaria (people within their nation) contrasted with the rest of the world (all people who were foreigners).

The emphasis of the enclitic particle *te* applies to all four listed areas, which means that the disciples should be witnesses in all of those areas—not prioritizing one over the other.

Applying this principle today means that both the individual believer and the local congregation as a whole have a responsibility to do all they can to proclaim the gospel in their communities and nation as well as send messengers to proclaim it in all the world.

5 Why is the concept of *both* in Acts 1:8 important to the full application of the Great Commission?

The Homogeneous Principle

In the last couple of decades, studies of church growth have increasingly emphasized what is often called the ***homogeneous principle***. Sociological research indicates that homogeneous groups generally function more smoothly and grow more rapidly than heterogeneous ones. People within homogeneous groups tend to have more common interests and fewer internal conflicts. Advocates of this principle teach that a church will usually grow more quickly and easily if its members share a common bond.

This lesson does not allow space to discuss the homogeneous principle in depth. An important valid application of this principle will be explored in a later chapter concerning small groups. In the context of evangelism and the Great Commission, the teaching of our Lord and of the apostles clearly indicates that we are obligated to present the gospel to every kind of person.

2.2.2 OBJECTIVE
Distinguish the homogeneous principle and the heterogeneous gospel.

6 Why is the homogeneous principle connected to some church growth models?

The Heterogeneous Gospel

Paul wrote to the Corinthians, "Though I am free and belong to no man, I make myself a slave to everyone, to win as many as possible. To the Jews I became like a Jew, to win the Jews . . . To the weak I became weak, to win the

2.2.3 OBJECTIVE
Describe the social character of a biblical church.

weak. I have become all things to all men so that by all possible means I might save some" (1 Corinthians 9:19–20, 22, NIV).

The heart of this great missionary apostle reached out to people to such an extent that he considered himself their slave. Paul gave his best to each to win as many as possible.

7 How does the gospel differ from the homogeneous principle?

Early in his epistle to the Colossians, Paul says, "We proclaim Him, admonishing every man and teaching every man with all wisdom, so that we may present every man complete in Christ" (Colossians 1:28). The Greek word (*pas*) translated "every" means "some of every kind" of person. This speaks of the wide variety of individuals to whom we must relate. We are called to reach people who are different from us. Christian witness should not only be to "our kind of people." The Holy Spirit will enable us to effectively communicate with many kinds of people.

Ron McManus became pastor of First Assembly of God in Winston-Salem, North Carolina, in 1988. At the time, the congregation of about 260 included only five African-Americans, but about half the population of the city is African-American. Pastor McManus felt directed by the Word and led of the Spirit to focus on all the spiritually lost of the community. He led the congregation to prayer for the lost with a view of intentionally reaching the African-American community. Pastor McManus believes that if they had not passed that test of welcoming people of different races, the church would have never experienced great growth. In sixteen years, the congregation grew to more than 2,500. A significant breakthrough took place when the church called its first African-American to the pastoral staff and elected an African-American on the deacon board. The church's transformation to a heterogeneous congregation that more truly reflected its surrounding community began only after more than two years of prayer and focused effort. The congregation eventually became more than 20 percent African-American.

A church that understands the Great Commission and ministers in the Spirit of Christ will focus on reaching all spiritually lost people within its sphere of influence. Of course, local congregations will vary in the degree to which they are heterogeneous, depending on the social makeup of the surrounding community. In principle, a church should be heterogeneous, if it is to be a Great Commission church.

Clubs or Families?

If a church's purpose is only to be a social institution—a gathering of people whose objective is to see how quickly that group can grow for its own sake—the homogeneous principle can go unquestioned. A church should be in the rescue business, like a hospital. For a hospital to turn away people who need help because they are not of a particular class is considered criminal. A Great Commission church should be inclusive, like a hospital, not exclusive, like a private club.

In small towns and villages of England in the nineteenth century, clubs became places where townspeople could come together to be sociable. As populations of larger towns and cities grew, these clubs became specialized so that members who shared a common interest or were from the same economic class could socialize. Consequently, clubs eventually became specialized groups where people could gather with "their kind of people" and get away from those who were not. They evolved from being places to be sociable into places to be *unsociable*.

A club is basically homogenous—one kind of people, whether they are like each other economically, educationally, racially, or because of a common interest such as golf, tennis, or coin collecting.

A church is not supposed to be a club. It is a family—God's family. God did not design the church to keep certain kinds of people out—but to bring all kinds of people in.

Recognizing Neighbors

Jesus addressed the human tendency to be exclusive in His parable of the Good Samaritan (Luke 10:25–37). When a lawyer tested Jesus about what he should do to inherit eternal life, Jesus asked him what was written in the Law. The man replied that the great commandment is to love God with all our heart, soul, strength, and mind and to love our **neighbor** as ourselves. Luke records that "wishing to justify himself" the lawyer asked Jesus, "And who is my neighbor?"

The man was really asking, "Who is *not* my neighbor?" He really wanted to know whom he did *not* have to love.

Jesus replied with a story in which a Samaritan (who was not the lawyer's "kind of people") was a neighbor to the wounded man in the ditch. The Greek word translated "neighbor" is *plesion*. The root word, *pelas*, simply means "near." This word is used seventeen times in the New Testament and almost always is translated "neighbor" or "near." Our neighbor is simply whoever is there—near enough that we have a responsibility to interact with him or her. Social status, race, or educational levels are not criteria. Our neighbor is simply someone within reach.

In the parable, the wounded man in the ditch is obviously a Jew, yet the priest and Levite—also Jews and, therefore, "his kind of people"—passed by and ignored his need. The Samaritan, who was not his kind of person, felt compassion and met his need. The Samaritan obviously did not help the man in the ditch because he was a Jew, but simply because he was there and in need.

Hooks and Nets

Harvesting was the most prevalent analogy Jesus used concerning reaching the lost. He also used fishing as an example.

Where I served as a missionary in the Samoan Islands, fishing is an essential part of life and survival. Samoans fish by two methods: hooks and nets. Fishing with hooks specifically targets certain species of fish. Nets, on the other hand, basically gather all kinds of fish in a fishing area, as long as they fit in the net.

Principles derived from both the hook and the net analogies apply in local church evangelism.

Pastor Mark Rose, his associate pastor, Bernie Bannin, and their intern, Eric Boulier, were burdened because Victory Assembly of God in Norfolk, Nebraska, was not effectively reaching the youth segment of the community. Eric was the first to begin regularly driving up and down the street where the youth hung out, praying for a breakthrough. Much like the Samaritan woman at the well became a catalyst for the breakthrough in the town of Sychar in John 4, a teenager named Dewey became the person through whom more than forty young people ultimately came to Christ in one year. When I visited the church, a large group of young new believers were present. They were not isolated in one

---

8 How does the Parable of the Good Samaritan apply to the Great Commission?

2.2.4 OBJECTIVE
Identify the need for both targeted and general evangelism.

9 How can a homogeneous approach to evangelism contribute to fulfilling the Great Commission?

section together; instead, they were scattered throughout the sanctuary among the obviously conservative and reserved middle-aged and elderly church members.

Targeting a homogeneous group, the pastors reached out to the teenagers, who became a means of helping the church become more heterogeneous.

A local congregation that is committed to obeying the Great Commission will be inclusive and diverse. It will cast its evangelistic net for all kinds of people in its community. But the hook method (homogeneous principle) is also valid in evangelism. As Pastors Ron McManus and Mark Rose illustrate, targeting unrepresented segments of a church's community ultimately diversifies and brings life and health to the church.

A Great Commission church will be committed to reaching every kind of person in its community as well as contributing to the cause of reaching the lost in all the world through prayer, financial support, and sending its own people in missions.

Test Yourself

Circle the letter of the *best* answer.

1. The Great Commission always includes the dual components of
   a) evangelism and discipleship.
   b) homiletics and exegesis.
   c) identifying sin and calling for repentance.
   d) the Golden Rule and turning the other cheek.

2. Jesus used the Parable of the Sower to
   a) illustrate four schools of thought in interpreting the Law.
   b) promote productive farming practices in His agricultural society.
   c) prove that God has preordained the eternal destiny of the elect and the lost.
   d) identify spiritual hindrances in people's spiritual lives.

3. The believer's role in personal evangelism is to
   a) offer irrefutable logical arguments for the existence of God and the deity of Jesus.
   b) confront the lost with their sin.
   c) clearly explain the gospel, allowing the Holy Spirit to convince the lost.
   d) assure the lost that God is love.

4. Studies have shown that most personal evangelism is carried out by
   a) seminary graduates.
   b) believers who have been Christians for less than a year.
   c) Christians who are 55 and older.
   d) nondenominational charismatics.

5. The ultimate goal of fulfilling the Great Commission is to
   a) eliminate poverty and illness and usher in the Millennium.
   b) present every kind of person to God complete in Christ.
   c) prove beyond doubt the inerrancy of Scripture.
   d) prove the continuing validity of the Ten Commandments.

6. Jesus' purpose in identifying geographical regions in the Great Commission was to
   a) distinguish specific callings to local pastors, evangelists, and missionaries.
   b) parallel the spread of the gospel with the Old Testament Diaspora.
   c) describe the equal importance of sharing the gospel in every part of the world.
   d) assign specific regions to specific disciples.

7. The homogeneous principle is
   a) an application of secular sociological research to church growth principles.
   b) a subtle endorsement of same-sex marriage.
   c) a tool for interpreting similar genres of literature identified in the Bible.
   d) proof that oil and water do not mix.

8. The hospital analogy of the church is used to
   a) promote the central role of divine healing in applying the gospel.
   b) prove that all sickness is a result of personal sin.
   c) contrast the church with the pleasures of the world.
   d) illustrate the church's role in reaching out to all spiritually lost people.

9. The lawyer's intent in asking Jesus to identify his neighbor was to
   a) identify those people the lawyer was not obligated to love.
   b) more carefully define the respective classes of Jews and Gentiles.
   c) prove that Jesus was breaking the Law.
   d) see if Jesus was the Messiah.

10. When considering the homogeneous principle in the light of personal evangelism, the believer is to
    a) recognize that it never applies to the Great Commission.
    b) view it as a spurious theory by liberal theologians.
    c) apply it as the first step in church planting.
    d) see it as a tool for connecting the gospel with specific types of people.

Responses to Interactive Questions
Chapter 2

Some of these responses may include information that is supplemental to the IST. These questions are intended to produce reflective thinking beyond the course content and your responses may vary from these examples.

1 What are the two constant components of the Great Commission?

The Great Commission always includes both evangelism and discipleship.

2 What is the objective of evangelism?

Evangelism seeks to lead a person to become born again—a new person in Christ—resulting in a life that obeys His teachings and commands.

3 What vital concept must be in mind before someone is ready to receive Christ as Savior?

That person should be aware of the cost of following Christ.

4 Why is it inaccurate to describe *evangelism* as "persuasion intended to convince the lost of the gospel's truth"?

Evangelists are to share the gospel message clearly, but the Holy Spirit convinces the nonbeliever of its truth.

5 Why is the concept of *both* in Acts 1:8 important to the full application of the Great Commission?

The both emphasis reveals that each regional designation in the Great Commission is equally important.

6 Why is the homogeneous principle connected to some church growth models?

Some church growth theorists advocate that a church will grow more quickly and smoothly if the congregation is composed of the same kind of people.

7 How does the gospel differ from the homogeneous principle?

The gospel is directed to the lost in every part of the world and does not make distinctions between people. It always seeks to draw every kind of person into fellowship with Christ and His church.

8 How does the Parable of the Good Samaritan apply to the Great Commission?

Believers should recognize all who are around them as neighbors and determine to reach them with the gospel.

9 How can a homogeneous approach to evangelism contribute to fulfilling the Great Commission?

Strategically targeting specific neglected groups of people diversifies the body of Christ.

CHAPTER 3

The Great Omissions

When the Holy Spirit led our founders to form the Assemblies of God during the Pentecostal revival early in the last century, the Fellowship's missionary character and priority were clearly defined. In the first General Council held in 1914 in Hot Springs, Arkansas, our leaders gave eloquent and passionate expression to the missionary purpose for forming the Fellowship. Later that year, during the second General Council held at Stone Church in Chicago, our early leaders made an amazing declaration, "We commit ourselves and the Movement to Him for the greatest evangelism that the world has ever seen."

World evangelization was stated as "the chief concern of the church." Even in the resolution concerning tithes, the Council resolved that after providing support for the local ministry, any surplus funds should be spent for "the spread of the gospel throughout the world."

This Spirit-imparted vision caused our mission to be extensive in geographic scope. Unlike many church bodies that focused missions efforts on certain parts of the world, our early leaders were compelled by the Spirit to obey our Lord's command to "go into all the world and preach the gospel" (Mark 16:15, NKJV).

The boldness of our forefathers' response to our Lord's command is astounding. How could such a small group of Christians even consider attempting to preach the gospel in all the world? Because they understood the eternal destiny of the spiritually lost and took seriously Jesus' command to reach the whole world. They also were convinced of His promise in Acts 1:8 that they would receive the Holy Spirit's power to do it.

Lesson 3.1   Why?—Divine Authority and Human Condition

Objectives
3.1.1   Identify the "why" of the Great Commission.
3.1.2   Cite the Gospels' identification of believers' divine empowerment.
3.1.3   List three parameters describing the human condition.
3.1.4   Describe Jesus Christ's unique role.

Lesson 3.2   How?—The Promised Empowerment

Objectives
3.2.1   Describe the Holy Spirit's "how" connection to the Great Commission.
3.2.2   Distinguish the relationship of the Spirit to believers in the Old and New Testaments.
3.2.3   Describe the imperative nature of the believer's need for the Holy Spirit.
3.2.4   Define the nature and duration of the power the Holy Spirit brings into the believer's life.

LESSON 3.1

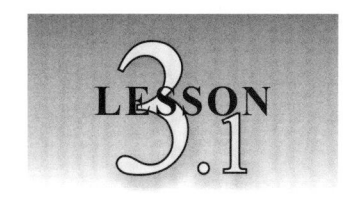

3.1.1 OBJECTIVE
Identify the "why" of the Great Commission.

Why?—Divine Authority and Human Condition

The "Why" Omissions

Any mission so big as to include all the world must be understood in light of two important points: (1) the destiny of the spiritually lost, and (2) the available means to accomplish the task.

In the Great Commission accounts in all four Gospels, Jesus' instruction to His disciples clearly told them what their mission was. But, in each case, the complete quotation also reveals why the disciples were commanded to proclaim Christ's message and make disciples in all the world. Jesus also instructed them concerning how it would be accomplished—in the empowerment of the Holy Spirit.

Unfortunately, most who quote the Great Commission passages from memory focus only on what the mission is. To adequately understand the Great Commission, it is essential that we examine the portions of Scripture that are almost always omitted when people quote Jesus' teaching and commands concerning His followers' mission. These common omissions provide vital instruction concerning both the why and the how of the Great Commission. They are so important that we could consider them the great omissions.

Divine Authority

3.1.2 OBJECTIVE
Cite the Gospels' identification of believers' divine empowerment.

A key conjunction contained within the most commonly quoted portion of the Great Commission in Matthew is "therefore." Jesus said, "Go therefore and make disciples of all the nations" (Matthew 28:19). But why is the word therefore used? It implies that what follows is based upon the information preceding it. What preceded is Jesus' statement, "All authority has been given to Me in heaven and on earth" (Matthew 28:18). The reason Jesus' disciples could undertake such a monumental task of making disciples in all nations was that the task was not merely their own. They were His representatives, extensions of our Lord's mission to this world based upon His divine authority. So are we.

1 What key conjunction points to the fuller context of the Great Commission, and what is that context?

The practical implications of that authority are not spelled out, with good reason. The spiritual authority to which Jesus referred is sweeping and universal. Jesus' statement was that all authority both in heaven and on earth had been given to Him. The details of what that implied did not need to be provided. The implication is clear that whatever spiritual authority was essential to fulfill the mission was provided in the authority of the risen Christ and His command to carry on the mission of God on earth.

This divine authority is also invoked in John 20:21: "As the Father has sent me, I also send you." The Greek word *kathos* translated "as" is significant here. It is often translated "even as" and means "just as," "in proportion to," or "in the degree that." It does not mean simply that Jesus was sending His disciples because the Father sent Jesus. It means He sent them with the same authority and in the empowerment of the same Spirit. When these passages in Matthew and John are examined together, the connection is clear between Jesus' authority and power and the authority and power of those He was commissioning.

In the Great Commission in Mark, Jesus stated that "in His name." His disciples would drive out demons, speak in tongues, and perform other supernatural signs (Mark 16:17). In Luke, the statement that "repentance for forgiveness of sins would be proclaimed *in His name* to all the nations" (Luke 24:47, emphasis added) follows the declaration that Christ suffered and rose from the dead on the third day. Christ's divine authority—proven by His resurrection—is foundational to the mission.

3.1.3
OBJECTIVE
List three parameters describing the human condition.

2 What three truths outline the spiritual state of humanity?

3 How does society's view of sin contrast with a biblical understanding of sin?

4 What is the nature of the eternal consequences of being lost?

The Human Spiritual Condition

The second aspect of why the Great Commission must be fulfilled is the spiritual condition of humanity. This is clearly presented in Mark and John. Mark records in 16:16 that immediately following Jesus' command to preach the good news to all creation, He said, "He who has believed and has been baptized shall be saved; but he who has disbelieved shall be condemned." The consequences to those who do not believe the gospel is reinforced in Jesus' statement in John 20:23: "If you forgive the sins of any, their sins have been forgiven them; if you retain the sins of any, they have been retained."

Three facts are inescapable: the lostness of humanity, the certainty of eternity and the exclusiveness of Christ.

1. Humanity Is Lost

Secular culture tries to explain away human sin. The plagues of immorality and violence are attributed to poverty, social injustice, and even genetics. The blame is placed everywhere except where it belongs—the sinful human heart. From the time of the Early Church, many have wishfully speculated that all people will eventually, somehow, reach heaven. God's Word clearly shows that all humankind is lost.

In one of Asia's modern cities, in the midst of gleaming skyscrapers, I visited a heathen temple. Thousands of onlookers stood in an outer courtyard. Unintentionally, in the press of the moving crowd, I found myself just three or four feet away from a priest who was chanting as worshipers submitted to a demonic trance. Rows of steel hooks pierced the flesh of their backs, yet not a drop of blood flowed. Each hook was connected to a chain that stretched back to a cart of rocks. The worshiper pulled the cart through the streets in an attempt to obtain forgiveness, healing, or prosperity. Each torturous yoke bore silent, graphic witness of the antithesis to God's grace.

As disturbing as these images are, it is important to remember that even in America some people claim to be Christians but do not personally know Christ. They are as lost as any who fit the description of *heathen*, one who does not acknowledge the God of the Bible.

God's will for the lost is plain in the Scriptures. Jesus revealed the priority of heaven in the parables of the Lost Sheep and the Lost Son. Whether they are wandering lost or willfully lost, the heart of the Father extends to each. (See Luke 15.) Heaven rejoices more over one lost sinner who repents than over the ninety nine who are already safe (Matthew 18:13). Peter said that the Lord wants no one to perish, but all to come to repentance (2 Peter 3:9).

2. Eternity Is Certain

Our culture is increasingly oriented to the present. Passions demanding instant gratification dominate. Our perspective on life is naturally framed in time, but God's perspective is eternal.

Perish in John 3:16 and 2 Peter 3:9 does not mean physical death or even the end of existence, but rather torment that lasts forever.

God is eternal, without beginning or end. Deuteronomy 33:27 says, "The *eternal* God is a dwelling place, and underneath are the *everlasting* arms" (emphasis added). While all created beings have a beginning, God's Word indicates that once life begins, existence never ends.

Many people—including some evangelical Christians—believe that unredeemed humanity will be judged and then, like animals, annihilated. Jesus taught otherwise: "Then he will also say to those on His left, 'Depart from Me, accursed ones, into the *eternal* fire . . . These will go away into *eternal* punishment, but the righteous into *eternal* life'" (Matthew 25:41, 46, emphasis added).

Jesus contrasted suffering in this life with eternal suffering. "If your hand causes you to sin, cut it off. It is better for you to enter life maimed than with two hands to go into hell, where the fire never goes out" (Mark 9:43, NIV).

Each person will face a final, lasting judgment. Whatever a person's destiny, it is eternal. Everlasting reward or punishment waits for every person on earth.

3. Jesus Christ Is the Only Way of Salvation

Jesus existed before His incarnation, is equal with God, has the power to forgive sins, has provided the ransom for the sins of all humankind, and grants eternal life to all who believe. After living a sinless life, Jesus offered up His life as the penalty for our sin, experienced death and conquered it. (See John 17:5; Philippians 2:6; Luke 7:48; 1 Timothy 2:6; John 11:25–26; Hebrews 2:9–10.)

Contemporary culture seems to have designated tolerance as the primary moral virtue. It promotes the idea that anything a person believes can be a pathway to eternal life and ultimate peace. According to God's revealed truth, only one way exists to peace with our holy Creator and everlasting life. Jesus is both the Door and the Way. He said, "I am the way and the truth and the life. No one comes to the Father except through me" (John 14:6, NIV). "Enter through the narrow gate. For wide is the gate and broad is the road that leads to destruction, and many enter through it. But small is the gate and narrow the road that leads to life, and only a few find it" (Matthew 7:13–14, NIV).

The issue is not religion—but relationship. "He who has the Son has the life; he who does not have the Son of God does not have the life" (1 John 5:12). Forgiveness of sin and eternal life are not granted merely for believing in God's existence and distinguishing right from wrong. Peace with God is obtained only through faith in Jesus, who broke down the wall of separation between our holy, loving Creator and sinful humankind. We who were enemies and far away from God, because of our sin, have been brought near by the blood of Jesus Christ (Ephesians 2:13). In Christ's birth, God came near to us. In His death, He brought us near to Him (1 Peter 3:18).

Peter said, "Salvation is found in no one else, for there is no other name under heaven given to men by which we must be saved" (Acts 4:12, NIV).

In East Africa, a pastor preached the gospel in a village where it had never been heard. No one responded.

On his way out of the village, he witnessed a horrible sight—a naked man covered with dirt was chained between two logs. The pastor asked the villagers why the man was bound between the logs. They explained that he had an evil spirit and had committed an unspeakable act of murder and cannibalism. The pastor knelt near the man and simply prayed repeatedly, "In the name of Jesus" The wild-eyed, raving man grew silent. The pastor left and journeyed back home.

The next day, a man came to the pastor's door. He simply asked, "Who is Jesus Christ?"

"Why do you ask?" the pastor replied.

"That name set me free!" was the reply.

The man standing at the pastor's door was the one who had been chained between the logs the day before.

Only through Jesus Christ can anyone be set free from the consequences of sin and Satan's power.

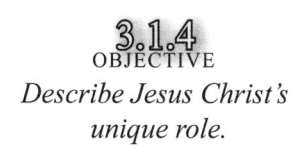

3.1.4 OBJECTIVE
Describe Jesus Christ's unique role.

5   How does the contemporary call for tolerance contradict the gospel?

LESSON 3.2

3.2.1 OBJECTIVE
Describe the Holy Spirit's "how" connection to the Great Commission.

How?—The Promised Empowerment

Because most references to the Great Commission are limited to the imperative passages in Matthew and Mark, the passages concerning the Great Commission in Luke, Acts and John are largely ignored. This is particularly unfortunate because Luke and John's records establish a direct connection between the Holy Spirit's empowerment and the mission of the disciples.

Jesus' last words recorded in Luke are these: "And that repentance for forgiveness of sins would be proclaimed in His name to all the nations . . . but you are to stay in the city until you are *clothed with power from on high*" (Luke 24:47, 49, emphasis added).

It would seem that the task of proclaiming Christ's message to all the nations should begin immediately. But Jesus told the disciples to wait for the Spirit's empowerment.

Luke begins Acts by reiterating Jesus' command. Then, before He ascended to heaven, Jesus spoke one last time to His disciples, "But *you will receive power when the Holy Spirit has come upon you*; and you shall be My witnesses both in Jerusalem, and in all Judea and Samaria, and even to the remotest part of the earth" (Acts 1:8, emphasis added).

John, who almost certainly had read all three Synoptic Gospels, supplements these accounts with another incident and records Jesus' words, "'As the Father has sent Me, I also send you.' And when He had said this, He breathed on them and said to them, '*Receive the Holy Spirit*'" (John 20:21–22, emphasis added). We don't know definitely what happened to the disciples in this circumstance. We do know that it could not have been the same as what happened later at Pentecost. It is significant that, as with the passage in Luke, Jesus connects the disciples' reception of the Spirit with their missionary task.

The Promise of Power

6 What fears preoccupied the disciples' minds during Jesus' final days before His crucifixion?

In the last days before Jesus was crucified, He gathered His followers to give them His final instructions. They had been with Him for three years during His public ministry. He knew they were troubled and afraid when they learned that He would be leaving them soon. He said, "All things that I have heard from My Father I have made known to you" (John 15:15). He had instructed them concerning how to live as His witnesses in the world. They were overwhelmed. How could they possibly obey all the commandments He had given them? It was one thing to understand what Jesus required of them. It was another to accomplish the purpose for which He had called them.

Jesus knew that fear would overcome their best intentions. But He had chosen them. He had prayed for them. He knew that in spite of their human weaknesses, they loved Him. After three years of teaching, He shared a wonderful promise with them. He said, "'I tell you the truth, it is to your advantage that I go away; for if I do not go away, the Helper will not come to you; but if I go, I will send Him to you'" (John 16:7). They would be more effective with the Spirit's presence in their lives than when Jesus was physically present with them.

While giving His last instructions to His disciples, Jesus taught them extensively about the Holy Spirit, whom He would send from the Father to be their Helper. He said, "'If you love Me, you will keep My commandments. I will ask the Father, and He will give you another Helper, that He may be with you forever; that is the Spirit of truth, whom the world cannot receive, because it does

The Great Omissions

not see Him or know Him, but you know Him because He abides with you and will be in you'" (John 14:15–17).

Jesus revealed a great mystery about God in this passage. The disciples knew Jesus and His power to help them. Now Jesus promised them another Helper. He was introducing them to the third Person of the Trinity, the Holy Spirit. The Old Testament writers taught about the Spirit of God, but the people could not understand the Holy Spirit until Jesus came. They understood even more after Jesus returned to heaven and sent the Holy Spirit as the Father promised.

In this setting, Jesus promised two things about what the Holy Spirit's relationship with them would be.

1. His permanence—the Spirit would be with them forever and abide, or remain, with them.
2. His presence—the Holy Spirit would be in them. The Old Testament spoke often about the Holy Spirit coming *on* prophets, priests, judges and kings. Jesus revealed that the Holy Spirit would come to be *in* His people.

God was with Adam and Eve in the Garden of Eden. In the Old Testament, God was with His people as they wandered in the wilderness. He showed His presence in the cloud by day and fire by night.

When Jesus, God the Son, became flesh and took on human form, God entered another relationship with humankind. John wrote, "The Word became flesh, and dwelt among us, and we saw His glory, glory as of the only begotten from the Father, full of grace and truth" (John 1:14). Jesus was God not only with His people but also among them. Now Jesus was teaching His disciples that God the Holy Spirit would come and be in them.

Jesus talked to His disciples about the Holy Spirit to prepare them for life without His physical presence. The Holy Spirit—the Helper—would be God's empowering presence to help them accomplish the mission He had given them.

The Empowerment Imperative

The promised empowerment of the Spirit was not given in the form of a suggestion. It was a command. In Luke's record of Jesus' instructions, the only imperative verb was that the disciples should "remain" in the city until they were "clothed with power" for their mission. When Luke reiterates this in the beginning of Acts, he clearly states that Jesus had "commanded" the disciples not to leave Jerusalem but to wait for the promise of the Father. He also recalls John the Baptist's words at Jesus' baptism when the Spirit descended upon Him, stating that the promised empowerment would be the baptism in the Spirit, which John the Baptist prophesied Jesus would give. Peter, who had heard Jesus' commands to His disciples firsthand, remembered and referred to the promise of the Father (Acts 2:33). He even quoted Joel's prophecy in his sermon on the Day of Pentecost (Acts 2:16).

John's recounting of Jesus' command is consistent with the imperative nature of the Spirit's empowerment in Luke and Acts. The only imperative verb used in John 20:22 was "receive."

Both Luke and John's accounts of Jesus' instructions to His disciples show that the promised empowerment of the Spirit is an integral part of the mission. They also reveal that our Lord's instruction concerning the Spirit's empowerment is not an option but a command, just as He commanded His followers to proclaim the gospel and make disciples in all the world.

3.2.2 OBJECTIVE
Distinguish the relationship of the Spirit to believers in the Old and New Testaments.

7 What two things did Jesus emphasize about the Holy Spirit's relationship to believers?

3.2.3 OBJECTIVE
Describe the imperative nature of the believer's need for the Holy Spirit.

8 If Jesus' final statements to the disciples are correctly understood, why is the Spirit's empowerment not merely an option for believers?

The promise of the Holy Spirit's power is for every believer. Peter said, "'For the promise is for you and your children and for all who are far off, as many as the Lord our God will call to Himself'" (Acts 2:39). The Spirit's empowerment isn't just a helpful option in evangelism. It is a vital necessity.

What *Power* Means

3.2.4 OBJECTIVE
Define the nature and duration of the power the Holy Spirit brings into the believer's life.

People often think of the Holy Spirit's empowerment in terms of signs, wonders and spiritual gifts. But the word translated "power" in Acts 1:8 (*dunamis*) is wonderfully comprehensive. It simply means "ability" and applies in practical ways to everyday life. The power Jesus promised His followers is for every aspect of Christian living, enabling us to do and be whatever He purposes in our lives.

9 What is the nature of the power the Holy Spirit brings into the believer's life?

Each individual is unique. We struggle with different personal weaknesses. The Holy Spirit knows our hearts, our motives, and our personal flaws. When we depend on Him, He helps us in our uniqueness to live in obedience to Christ. The help—the power—that we need will be different for each person. The shy, inhibited person may need courage to speak up. The outgoing, impulsive person may need restraint. The Holy Spirit's power will provide whatever help each believer needs.

God's people need the Holy Spirit's working, not just in church on Sunday, but every day—in our homes, at school, in our neighborhoods, and in the workplace.

A Continuing Need for Empowerment

When the Israelites were fleeing Egypt for the Promised Land, God gave them bread from heaven, called manna, to feed them during their wilderness journey. It was not a supply to be stored and carried with them. It was given to them as they needed it.

10 Why are believers called to be continually filled with the Spirit?

A life overflowing with the fullness of the Spirit is much the same. When Paul exhorted the Ephesian Christians to be filled with the Spirit, the verb tense he used means to "keep on being filled" (Ephesians 5:18). The infilling of the Spirit should be ongoing. We must keep praying in the Spirit, loving in the Spirit, and living in the Spirit. The Holy Spirit baptism—as wonderful as it is—is not just a one-time experience. We need to keep being filled. We need a continuing inpouring of the Spirit daily in our lives.

We don't need signs, wonders, and miracles every day. We do need the Holy Spirit's help in everyday living. We need the power of the Holy Spirit in our spiritual lives, in our emotions, and in our relationships. We are not naturally capable of being all God wants us to be without His divine help.

Together, the Great Commission passages in the four Gospels and Acts present a comprehensive mission of evangelism and discipleship to an inclusive audience of all spiritually lost people. Our Lord did not simply declare what the mission of the Church is in the world. He also taught why the mission must be fulfilled and how it can be accomplished in the power of the Holy Spirit.

The Great Omissions

Test Yourself

100%

CHAPTER 3

Circle the letter of the *best* answer.

1. When quoting the Great Commission, most believers emphasize the
   a) need to identify the elect.
   b) **mission component of going into the world and preaching the gospel.**
   c) original languages and the modern translation.
   d) second coming of Jesus Christ.

2. A key conjunction in the Great Commission in Matthew is *"All authority has been given to me. Go therefore + make disciples"*
   a) *nevertheless.*
   b) *however.*
   c) **therefore.**
   d) *because.*

3. Believers are empowered to fulfill the Great Commission
   a) **in the same manner Jesus Christ was empowered to fulfill His mission.**
   b) to the extent that they are living sinless lives.
   c) only while they are speaking in tongues.
   d) during times of prayer and fasting.

4. Which three truths outline the spiritual state of humanity?
   a) **All humanity is lost, facing eternal consequences, with Jesus Christ as the only hope.**
   b) All people are created equal, invited to live good lives, and promised eventual salvation.
   c) Humans are comprised of spirit, soul, and body.
   d) The elect are born to be saved, and the lost are born to be damned; only God knows who is who.

5. Spiritual tolerance, as called for by secular society, is
   a) a contemporary and valuable application of the Golden Rule.
   b) vital in a pluralistic society to avoid anarchy and terrorism.
   c) **a denial of the exclusive nature of Christ's salvation.**
   d) demonstrating an attitude of grace to unbelievers.

6. When Jesus spoke of going away, the disciples were most concerned about
   a) whether His claims to divinity were believable.
   b) **how they could fulfill the Great Commission and His other commands.**
   c) whether they would be able to find new jobs.
   d) who would be the next Roman governor.

7. When describing the Holy Spirit, Jesus emphasized the
   a) Spirit's convicting activity and the danger of offending Him.
   b) **permanence and intimate nature of the Spirit's presence in the believer's life.**
   c) Old Testament symbols of fire and wind.
   d) need to pray in tongues.

8. Jesus' instructions to the disciples concerning the Holy Spirit were to
   a) **wait in Jerusalem to be filled with the Spirit before embarking on the Great Commission.**
   b) continue making Mosaic sacrifices until they were filled with the Spirit.
   c) take communion daily while waiting for the Spirit's anointing.
   d) begin preaching the gospel since He had already breathed the Spirit into them.

9. The power the believer experiences through the Spirit is intended
   a) primarily as a means of identifying satanic forces at work.
   b) to facilitate the orderly exercise of spiritual gifts in church services.
   c) to provide uninterrupted health and wealth.
   d) **to empower the believer to live consistently for God and fulfill His purpose.**

10. The call to be filled with the Spirit is expressed in such a way as to imply that
    a) the Spirit fills the believer with a lifetime reservoir of His power.
    b) the Pentecostal Baptism is a component of gaining salvation.
    c) tongues and interpretation are the greatest spiritual gift.
    d) **continually being filled with the Holy Spirit is essential to spiritual effectiveness.**

43

Responses to Interactive Questions
Chapter 3

Some of these responses may include information that is supplemental to the IST. These questions are intended to produce reflective thinking beyond the course content and your responses may vary from these examples.

1 What key conjunction points to the fuller context of the Great Commission, and what is that context?

The conjunction *therefore* implies that information contained within the most commonly quoted portion of the Great Commission is based on preceding information, namely, that all authority in heaven and on earth has been given to Jesus Christ.

2 What three truths outline the spiritual state of humanity?

All humanity is lost, the consequence of that lost condition is eternal, and Jesus Christ provides the only way of salvation.

3 How does society's view of sin contrast with a biblical understanding of sin?

Rather than defining *sin* as a personal violation of a divinely established universal code of conduct, secularists remove God from the picture and translate all acts of immorality and violence as responses to external stimuli or genetic predisposition.

4 What is the nature of the eternal consequences of being lost?

The lost will perish (or, suffer the torments of divine judgment forever). Perish does not mean "an end to existence."

5 How does the contemporary call for tolerance contradict the gospel?

Contemporary tolerance is not a call to treat others with respect as much as it is a call to treat all claims to truth as equally valid. The Bible, God's inspired Word, clearly presents Jesus Christ as the only way of salvation.

6 What fears preoccupied the disciples' minds during Jesus' final days before His crucifixion?

They did not yet understand that His physical parting from them would become the means for God's Spirit to be with them always, empowering them to do those things Jesus had commanded them during His lifetime on earth.

7 What two things did Jesus emphasize about the Holy Spirit's relationship to believers?

He stressed both the permanence of the Spirit's presence and the intimate nature of His presence living in believers.

8 If Jesus' final statements to the disciples are correctly understood, why is the Spirit's empowerment not merely an option for believers?

Jesus did not ask, but commanded, His disciples to wait for the Spirit's empowerment. The call for Holy Spirit empowerment is stated as clearly as every other imperative of the Great Commission.

9 What is the nature of the power the Holy Spirit brings into the believer's life?

Where many believers tend to think of divine empowerment as an enablement to perform the miraculous, it also is empowerment to live consistently in all areas of Christian life.

10 Why are believers called to be continually filled with the Spirit?

The Spirit's empowerment is limitless, but it is steadily invested in the believer's life in response to a continual seeking on the believer's part.

UNIT PROGRESS EVALUATION 1

Now that you have finished Unit 1, review the lessons in preparation for Unit Progress Evaluation 1. You will find it in Essential Course Materials at the back of this IST. Answer all of the questions without referring to your course materials, Bible, or notes. When you have completed the UPE, check your answers with the answer key provided in Essential Course Materials. Review any items you may have answered incorrectly. Then you may proceed with your study of Unit 2. (Although UPE scores do not count as part of your final course grade, they indicate how well you learned the material and how well you may perform on the closed-book final examination.)

UNIT 2

Jesus and Personal Evangelism

When Jesus gave the Great Commission in its various forms to His disciples, it was not a new idea to them. Both through His teaching and example, Jesus had been preparing His disciples for their task of proclaiming His name and making disciples in all the world.

Jesus had revealed to His disciples the secrets of the Kingdom. The task before them was not merely to assemble another religious social movement. It was to participate in the divine activity of God in the world, redeeming lost humanity to himself. Just as the disciples had seen the loaves and fishes multiply, they would now participate in perpetuating and multiplying the message that Jesus had committed to them.

In His teaching, Jesus prepared them for the challenges they would face, and the hard realities before them. He also revealed to them what would be the triumph of their mission in the world.

In His parables and sermons, Jesus opened the understanding of His disciples to the principles of spiritual harvest and to the certain success of the gospel when sown in good ground.

He also modeled, in His relationships and encounters with people, how the disciples should communicate the message of the Kingdom to those for whom He came to give His life. Jesus' example in interpersonal relationships and conversations is as relevant today as when He walked the earth. Jesus is not only our Teacher but our greatest example in personal evangelism.

In addition to Jesus' instruction and example was His incredible promise of the Holy Spirit's presence and power for His followers. It couldn't have been stated more clearly than in His final words when He promised that, in the Spirit's power, His followers would be His witnesses "in Jerusalem, and in all Judea and Samaria, and even to the remotest part of the earth" (Acts 1:8).

Chapter 4   Jesus' Teaching

Lessons
4.1   The Parables
4.2   The Soils
4.3   The Sower
4.4   The Character of the Believer

Chapter 5   Jesus' Example

Lessons
5.1   The Opportunity
5.2   The Focus
5.3   The Message

Chapter 6   Jesus' Promise

Lessons
6.1   The Promise of Power
6.2   The Nature and Purpose of the Spirit's Power
6.3   Seeking the Spirit

CHAPTER 4

Jesus' Teaching

William Simpson, a young, single Assemblies of God missionary, carried the gospel message into the barren land of Tibet. It was a hard field. For fourteen years he led a lonely life, riding on horseback through rugged, forbidding mountains to share the gospel of Jesus. Through all his years of toil, he saw only a few Tibetans come to Christ. At age thirty-one he was ambushed and murdered in a mountain pass. Nearby villagers buried him in a shallow grave.

William's father, missionary W.W. Simpson, journeyed from China to the Tibetan mountainside to claim his son's body. As he stood over the shallow grave of his son, he lifted up his voice to sing William's favorite song:

The seed I have scattered in springtime with weeping,
And watered with tears and with dews from on high;
Another may shout when the harvester's reaping,
Shall gather my grain in the "sweet by and by."

Another may reap what in springtime I've planted,
Another rejoice in the fruit of my pain,
Not knowing my tears when in summer I fainted
While toiling sad-hearted in the sunshine and rain.

The thorns will have choked and the summers suns blasted
The most of the seed which in springtime I've sown;
But the Lord Who has watched while my weary toil lasted
Will give me a harvest for what I have done. (Spencer 1886)

Countless faithful servants of Jesus Christ have taken His message into all the world, depending on Jesus' promises concerning the certainty of the spiritual harvest.

Lesson 4.1 The Parables

Objectives

4.1.1 Define parable, *and explain the parable's function in Jesus' ministry.*
4.1.2 Recognize the limited and appropriate use of allegory in the parables.
4.1.3 Correlate the attitude of the listener to the purpose of the parable.
4.1.4 Explain the use of contrasting pairs in Jesus' parables.

Lesson 4.2 The Soils

Objectives

4.2.1 Identify the dichotomy in the Parable of the Sower.
4.2.2 Describe the challenges to the gospel illustrated by the unproductive soil.
4.2.3 Identify factors affecting the varying harvests within the productive soil.
4.2.4 Give evidence of Jesus' focus on personal choice.

Lesson 4.3 The Sower

Objectives

4.3.1 List the key reasons to identify the sower as the central focus in Jesus' parable.
4.3.2 Explain the commissioning function of the Parable of the Sower.
4.3.3 Explain the Old Testament imagery contributing to the parable's meaning.
4.3.4 Describe the implications of the Parable of the Sower for ministry.

Jesus' Teaching   47

Lesson 4.4   The Character of the Believer

Objectives

4.4.1   Identify the three metaphors Jesus used to describe His followers.
4.4.2   Describe the characteristics of each metaphor that illustrate the believer's life.
4.4.3   Utilize the warnings included in the metaphors to pursue spiritual maturity.
4.4.4   Apply the common denominator of the three metaphors in daily life.

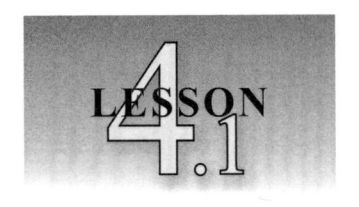

LESSON 4.1

4.1.1 OBJECTIVE
Define parable, and explain the parable's function in Jesus' ministry.

1   What theme is expressed in those parables common to all three Synoptic Gospels?

2   How did the interpretation of biblical parables evolve?

4.1.2 OBJECTIVE
Recognize the limited and appropriate use of allegory in the parables.

The Parables

Evangelism cannot be understood apart from Jesus' teachings. Jesus taught His first disciples the nature of His kingdom and the secrets of how that eternal Kingdom is established. For three years He instructed His disciples concerning their mission through both His words and actions. His purpose in coming to this world and taking on human form was clearly stated. It was to seek and save the lost (Luke 19:10). Our mission today to carry on that same work remains unchanged.

The only parables found in all three Synoptic Gospels are harvest analogies. Harvesting is probably the single most prominent activity used by Jesus to convey truths concerning the nature of His mission. Harvesting also is prominent in the teachings of Peter and Paul, who obviously followed Jesus' example. References to harvesting are evident in the Old Testament, as well.

The harvest analogy is especially revealing in Jesus' parables. The word *parable* comes from two Greek words (*para* and *ballo*), which together mean "to throw alongside." A parable makes a comparison between a known truth and an unknown truth by throwing them alongside each other.

A parable is a simple story taken from daily life to illustrate an ethical or spiritual truth. The parable should be understood in the context of its Hebrew counterpart, *masal*, which had a greater range of meaning than the Greek term *parabole*. *Masal* represents a wide variety of figures of speech, including proverbs, **metaphors**, allegories, riddles, fables, similes, as well as parables in the strict sense. All the forms of *masal* are found in the New Testament except for the riddle (Mounce 2002, 125).

In its biblical usage, *parabole* gradually widened its sphere of meaning (Cole 1961, 89). For centuries, teachings from the parables were largely allegorized, supporting particular theological positions even to the extent of ignoring obvious meanings. In the late nineteenth century Adolf Julicher advocated abandoning the allegorical approach and accepting parables as didactic stories that make one central point (Mounce 2002, 125). At that time, Julicher's point was especially significant. An **allegory** introduces several points, but an interpreter of Scripture runs the risk of adding an unintended meaning to the text by trying to attribute significance to every aspect of the story.

While a parable may be complex, it usually stresses just one main point. However, its secondary features affect the understanding of the parable as a whole (Lane 1974, 150). Many details of the parables that some scholars might view as merely incidental or window dressing have intended meanings. All God's creation reflects His glory, His purposes in creation, and the truth of His Word.

The harvest analogy should be seen not only as central to the teaching of Jesus and the apostles but also as part of God's great creative design.

Basic to Jesus' parables is the correlation of the natural realm and the redemptive. Through parables Jesus called attention to what previously had been hidden in the redemptive order. The realism of His parables comes from the fact that the relationship between nature and the redemptive order is not merely analogy, because both originate in the purpose of God. A contemplation of the one order can reveal or illuminate truths of the other, because both reflect God's intention (Lane 1974, 151).

Revealing and Concealing

Parables are designed both to reveal and conceal truth at the same time. Parables are not always understood without an explanation. One example is in the Old Testament passage where David did not understand Nathan's parable concerning the ewe lamb (2 Samuel 12:1–7).

Jesus taught that the condition and attitude of the heart predisposes a person's understanding of truth. He said, "If anyone is *willing to do His will*, he will know of the teaching, whether it is of God or whether I speak from Myself" (John 7:17, emphasis added).

The Parable of the Sower

Many parables are applicable to evangelism. Especially significant and instructive concerning the evangelism process is a series of parables found in the Synoptic Gospels. To adequately benefit from this lesson, read these parables in Matthew 13:1–52, Mark 4:1–34, and Luke 8:4–18.

In each series, the Parable of the Sower is the foundation of the other parables. Of the thirty-five parables in the Synoptic Gospels, only seven are found in more than one Gospel, and only three are in all three Synoptic Gospels.

Both before and after the parable, Jesus urged the crowd to listen carefully.

Contrasting Pairs

An important characteristic of Jesus' parables is that His examples are usually found in contrasting pairs. Jesus used this format in much of His preaching and teaching. In His parables He referred to two houses, the new cloth and the wineskins, the productive and unproductive soil, the wheat and weeds, two sons, two servants, two debtors, the Good Samaritan and those who passed by, the Prodigal Son and elder brother, and the Pharisee and the tax collector, to list a few pairs. In almost every context and frame of reference, Jesus contrasted two groups and challenged His hearers to choose to belong to one of them.

Jesus' concern is always focused on the eternal consequences of sin and the eternal destiny of each person. The focus of the gospel in the New Testament is on the salvation of individuals who will comprise the bride of Christ. The gospel calls each hearer to decide and respond to the proclamation of God's Word.

Matthew's record of the parables includes a particularly distinctive feature. He makes it clear that Jesus taught in parables at this stage of His ministry for the specific purpose of concealing the truth about himself and the kingdom of heaven from the crowds (Tasker 1961, 134). Early on, He had used parables as illustrations with meanings that were obvious. Later, He spoke in parables and interpreted them privately to His disciples. Of the Synoptic Gospel writers, only Matthew records that the disciples were surprised at this change.

---

3 What is the fundamental characteristic of the biblical parables?

4.1.3 OBJECTIVE
Correlate the attitude of the listener to the purpose of the parable.

4.1.4 OBJECTIVE
Explain the use of contrasting pairs in Jesus' parables.

4 How many key elements are typically found in a parable?

5 What shift did Matthew observe in Jesus' use of parables?

The parables that follow the Parable of the Sower serve to amplify its truths. In the Parable of the Mustard Seed, what starts with a very small beginning produces a result much greater in proportion to the size of the seed. Jesus was revealing that His kingdom would begin with a small group of people but grow to be the largest of all. In the Parable of the Tares, recorded in Matthew 12:24–30, 36–43, He reveals that the powers of evil will not be ultimately destroyed until the final judgment. Until then they will work against the Kingdom, but they will not succeed. In the parable of the Net (Matthew 13:47–50), He said there will be false members of the Kingdom until its final consummation. The Parables of the Costly Pearl and the Hidden Treasure conclude this series (Matthew 13:44–46). They emphasize the truth that the kingdom of heaven is the only eternal reality. It is precious beyond all earthly things and should be joyfully purchased at any sacrifice, including the loss of possessions, friends, or life itself.

Immediately following the series of parables recorded by Mark are three miracles that reveal Jesus' authority over the natural elements (wind and sea), demon possession (the spirit world), and death (Mark 4:35–41; Matthew 8:23–27; Luke 8:22–25; Mark 5:1–20; Matthew 8:28–34; Luke 8:26–39; Mark 5:21–43; Matthew 9:18–26; Luke 8:40–56). In each event, the presence of Jesus produces life and defeats death. The parables point to the ultimate victory and glory of God's kingdom. The three miracles demonstrate the sovereignty of the Son of God and show that nothing can ultimately defeat His eternal purposes.

LESSON 4.2

The Soils

Some approach the Parable of the Sower from a negative perspective because three of the four types of soil failed to produce lasting life. The parable looks beyond those hindrances to the ultimate triumph of God's Word in producing the kingdom of God. Even though much space in the parable is devoted to listing the three kinds of ground that are unproductive, only a small part of the seed would land on those places in an actual field. The parable does not imply that most of the sower's work is wasted (Hurtado 2001, 71).

Four Kinds of Soil, Or Two?

Most expositions of this passage treat the parable as having four kinds of soil: hard ground, shallow ground, thorny ground, and good ground. Because Jesus often presented truth in contrasting pairs, the parable also can be viewed as presenting two kinds of soil: productive and unproductive. Three examples are given for each of the two kinds of soil. Remember that these are parables concerning the kingdom of God, in which there are only two end results. Every person on earth faces one of only two ultimate destinies.

Unproductive Soil

The Hard Ground

The first kind of soil is preconditioned to failure. Because the hard ground is unprepared to receive the seed, the birds come and take the seed away before it has the chance to sprout. The seeds sown along the path represent the message that is not understood and is quickly snatched away by the evil one.

4.2.1 OBJECTIVE
Identify the dichotomy in the Parable of the Sower.

6 What evidence is there for Jesus' use of a contrasting pair in the Parable of the Sower?

4.2.2 OBJECTIVE
Describe the challenges to the gospel illustrated by the unproductive soil.

Jesus clearly attributes the hard ground to the action of Satan, adding that resistance to the message comes from a lack of understanding (Matthew 13:18–19). When the ground is well-trodden, packed down, and walked upon, it doesn't provide an adequate surface to receive the seed and give it an opportunity to sprout.

The Shallow Ground

Unless truth takes root in the human heart, it will be rejected again as soon as it faces opposition. Shallow soil produces only superficial commitment.

Jesus explains that the shallow ground immediately receives the message with joy. This is not a casual response. The problem is that the hearers have no firm root in themselves (Matthew 13:20–21). The temporary nature of the young plants is due to the lack of spiritual strength people have when affliction or persecution arises because of the message. They fall away as quickly as the life began. It was genuine life; it just didn't last. The very nature of the shallow soil causes the seed to sprout quickly, yet it also is the reason that it quickly dies—because of heat. This could be likened to people who make premature emotional decisions to follow Christ without understanding the cost of being a disciple. If this is the case, shallow soil can be nurtured and prepared to receive the message so that it can take root.

The Thorny Ground

Of the three kinds of unproductive soil, the thorny ground is especially tragic. The message genuinely takes root and grows, but the weeds grow faster than the wheat and choke the genuine life that was growing.

Anyone who has been in pastoral ministry can testify to the tragic examples of people whose lives are changed, but they eventually fall away. Even after years of following Christ and living in the fellowship of His church, their spiritual lives wither and die. In keeping with the harvest analogy, this tragedy underscores the importance of watering and cultivating, which could be equated with the discipling process. Even careful cultivation does not always result in lasting fruit. Some crop failure is in the nature of the person's choices. The emphasis in the parable doesn't seem to be on how the soil is tended but on the condition of the soil.

This example serves as a sobering reminder. It is sad when spiritual life that survived affliction and persecution ultimately can be defeated by what Jesus described as thorns—the worries of the world, the deceitfulness of riches, and the desires for other things. Materialism and the cares of life can destroy spiritual life when suffering and persecution could not!

A few years ago, I was approached after a service by a young woman from a former communist country. She asked me to pray with her concerning her father's spiritual condition. Under communism he was tortured for his faith in Christ and would not renounce his Lord. But after immigrating to America, he started a business and became very prosperous. With tears coming down her cheeks, his daughter told me sadly that her father no longer attended church and was not serving Christ. His faith had withstood physical torture but not prosperity.

The three kinds of unproductive soil could be summarized this way:

1. The hard ground produced no response.
2. The shallow ground provided no root.
3. The thorny ground allowed no room.

Enemies of the seed in the spiritual harvest of the Kingdom are referred to in Paul's letter to the Ephesians.

---

7 What spiritual tragedy does the thorny ground illustrate?

And you were dead in your trespasses and sins, in which you formerly walked according to the course of this world, according to the prince of the power of the air, of the spirit that is now working in the sons of disobedience. Among them we too all formerly lived in the lusts of our flesh, indulging the desires of the flesh and of the mind, and were by nature children of wrath, even as the rest. (2:1–3)

> 8 What three enemies seek to destroy the soul?

In these three verses, Paul clearly reveals three enemies of the soul: Satan, the flesh, and the world. In the Parable of the Sower, all three are at work against the spiritual life planted in the soul. Jesus clearly states that in the *hard* ground, Satan takes away the message. In the case of the *shallow* ground, the problem appears to be weaknesses of the *flesh*. The hearer of the message does not have the personal strength to withstand affliction and persecution. In the example of the *thorny* ground, the *world*—its cares, worries, and desires for material wealth—chokes the life of the message in the human heart.

Productive Soil

OBJECTIVE 4.2.3
Identify factors affecting the varying harvests within the productive soil.

> 9 What distinguishes the types of productive soil?

The Parable of the Sower offers three examples of why the unproductive soil ultimately failed. Jesus also gives three examples of productive soil. The soils only differences? The amount of multiplication. In studies of Palestinian fields and ancient agriculture methods, farmers considered a good yield to be a tenfold harvest (Hurtado 2001, 72). Certainly a thirtyfold harvest would be great, so a sixtyfold harvest was greater, and a hundredfold harvest was incredible! All three yields of the harvest in this parable are intended to depict a result above the ordinary. These were not normal harvests but miraculously abundant ones. "The emphasis is not on how much seed is lost but on the abundant result of the sowing" (Hurtado 2001, 72).

William Lane (1974) says, "The climax of the parable strongly emphasizes the glorious character of the harvest, the thirtyfold, sixtyfold and hundredfold yield . . . since this is seen against the background of many obstacles, it is clear that the emphasis does not fall on the enormity of the waste, but on the enormity and splendor of the harvest" (154).

In the Parable of the Sower, Jesus was preparing His disciples for their ultimate mission. In His teaching on the unproductive soil, He conveyed the hard realities concerning hearers who would be resistant and unresponsive. The climax of the parable was on the exceptionally bountiful harvest from the seed that landed on the good ground.

OBJECTIVE 4.2.4
Give evidence of Jesus' focus on personal choice.

Why doesn't the message produce the same result in every heart? The answer is that the operation of God's Word in the human heart is not automatic. While the truth of the message does not vary, the nature of the response is determined by the nature of the heart that receives it (Cole 1961, 89). The hard heart, the shallow heart, the crowded heart, and the good heart are all present when the Word of God is preached. This does not merely refer to the preaching of the gospel in its initial response of repentance or conversion. All Christian life is a continual and developing response to God's revelation and message (Cole 1961, 90).

How are people to blame for the condition of their hearts? Have they, by prior choices, determined the nature of their hearts? Jesus does not deal with that issue. The point of the parable is that the nature of people's hearts varies, and that variation affects their responses.

The meaning of Jesus' parables is hidden to those on the "outside." His teaching does not harden people's hearts. Instead, their hearts were already hardened. Since knowledge of truth carries with it the responsibility of an appropriate acceptance and appropriate response, the withholding of truth to those who are hardened against it could possibly be interpreted as a desire on Jesus' part not to increase judgment.

10 What is Jesus' motivation for calling on His audiences to carefully listen?

In both Matthew and Mark's accounts, Jesus began and ended the parables with the admonition to carefully listen. If we compare the parable to a picture, Jesus' exhortations to listen at the beginning and the end serve as a frame. This frame could be as significant as the picture itself.

By exhorting the whole audience to listen carefully, Jesus was implying that each person could choose how he or she listens. Otherwise, why would He exhort the entire crowd to listen carefully to a parable that He would later explain only to His disciples? His admonition that "he who has ears, let him hear" clearly implies that each person has the potential of being any kind of soil, resulting in being productive or unproductive.

LESSON 4.3

4.3.1 OBJECTIVE
List the key reasons to identify the sower as the central focus in Jesus' parable.

11 Why is it a mistake to prioritize the role of the soils in the Parable of the Sower?

12 How did Jesus' view of ministry as expressed in the Parable of the Sower contrast with the disciples' understanding of their mission?

4.3.2 OBJECTIVE
Explain the commissioning function of the Parable of the Sower.

The Sower

In recent years, some Bible scholars have suggested that the Parable of the Sower should be titled, "The Parable of the *Soils*." That idea comes from the understanding that the majority of the parable's content focuses on four kinds of soil. If the premise is that parables have only one point, a person would conclude that, since the majority of the parable's content relates to soils, they must be the primary focus. While the nature of the soils is of great importance in the parable, we will continue to refer to it as The Parable of the Sower for these reasons:

- Jesus titled it "The Parable of the Sower." In Matthew's record, Jesus said, "Hear then the parable of the sower" (Matthew 13:18).
- The large proportion of content devoted to unproductive soil doesn't necessarily indicate that the soils are the major focus of Jesus' lesson.
- Jesus clearly directed this teaching to His disciples as the future sowers of His message—the ones to whom He would entrust His mission on earth.
- The parable should be viewed as part of the fabric composed of a group of parables, all of which focus on the ultimate spiritual harvest. Together, they realistically assess challenges and hardships, but they do so in the context of the abundant ultimate harvest God will produce through the obedience of the sowers.

Part of the disciples' preparation for ministry was that they understand the hard realities facing them. Not all of their sowing would be productive. Jesus wanted them to understand why.

Remember that the disciples' perspective was limited when they heard this parable. They seemed to have been looking for Jesus to dramatically establish His messianic kingdom in their lifetime, as shown by their question in Acts 1:6: "Lord, is it at this time You are restoring the kingdom to Israel?"

This was one of the temptations the Lord decisively resisted in the desert: "The devil took Him to a very high mountain and showed Him all the kingdoms of the world and their glory; and he said to Him, 'All these things I will give You, if You fall down and worship me'" (Matthew 4:8–9).

What the disciples did not realize was that the kingdom, as they perceived it, was at the mustard seed stage. If Jesus had established His kingdom at that time, the majority of its future citizens to come in the next two thousand years would have been excluded. How small His kingdom would have been! (Cole 1961, 94).

The Parable of the Sower confronts the disciples with the difficult challenges the sowers of the message would face. The final conclusion describes an incredible harvest due to God's sovereign working in the hearts of people through the message.

Each of the Synoptic Gospel writers recorded different parables following the Parable of the Sower. But each series bring us toward two primary conclusions:

1. At the time of harvest, which Jesus explains is the end of the age, every person on earth will face one of two final judgments.
2. Ultimately, the kingdom of God will be triumphant, and the good harvest will be bountiful.

At the beginning of each explanation recorded in all three Gospels, Jesus makes it clear that the seed is the "word." Of course, the Bible as we know it did not exist in its present form when Jesus taught this. He was speaking of the proclaimed message of the Kingdom when He spoke of the word.

In these parables the implication is clear that all believers are called to be sowers. A bountiful harvest will take place only if the seed is sown. An Old Testament passage provides a similar call to the act of sowing in faith:

> He who watches the wind will not sow and he who looks at the clouds will not reap. Just as you do not know the path of the wind and how bones are formed in the womb of the pregnant woman, so you do not know the activity of God who makes all things. Sow your seed in the morning and do not be idle in the evening, for you do not know whether morning or evening sowing will succeed, or whether both of them alike will be good. (Ecclesiastes 11:4–6)

With great practicality the author of Ecclesiastes says that a person who looks at weather conditions and hesitates will not see harvest. There are few convenient times, safe places, or perfect opportunities to sow and reap. The sower must be committed to his work, regardless of the circumstances.

The prophet then rightly points out that we are essentially ignorant of many things, and gives two obvious examples: We don't know the path of the wind or what is happening in the womb of a mother as a child is forming. We also do not know "the activity of God who makes all things."

What, then, is the conclusion? The sower is to be faithful to sow in the morning as well as in the evening, not knowing which time of sowing will succeed or whether both will. It is significant that He did not provide a fourth alternative—that neither would succeed!

God's Word promises that when sowing is done in obedience to God's command, harvest is certain. Another relevant Old Testament commentary is Psalm 126:6: "He that goeth forth and weepeth, bearing precious seed, shall doubtless come again with rejoicing, bringing his sheaves with him" (KJV).

Notice that the harvest is not merely possible or even probable, but "doubtless"—it is certain.

The follower of Christ is called to sow the message. Both Jesus' teaching in the Parable of the Sower and the writer's musings in Ecclesiastes reveal that not all sowing will result in a lasting harvest. If the seed is faithfully sown, some will land on good ground and produce a great harvest.

In the Parable of the Sower, the attention of how the kingdom of God is built focuses on the individual. God's kingdom is built one person at a time. The primary focus of the parable is on the abundant harvest that results from effectiveness of the seed sown in obedience by the sower. That abundant harvest

---

4.3.3 OBJECTIVE
Explain the Old Testament imagery contributing to the parable's meaning.

13 How does Ecclesiastes expand the picture of the sower in Jesus' parable?

4.3.4 OBJECTIVE
Describe the implications of the Parable of the Sower for ministry

is comprised of individuals in whose hearts the message not only began life but also grew and matured until harvesttime.

From a number of perspectives, Jesus' parables concerning growth in the life of the believer and the Kingdom makes the objective of evangelism clear. The transmission of the good news is not merely proclaiming the message or even seeing people come to what often is called a salvation decision. The Parable of the Sower, as well as the parables that follow in the Synoptics, all point toward the ultimate harvest. Spiritual life must not only begin but also grow, endure, and reach maturity.

Why sowing in certain soils does not produce a harvest is, to a great extent, a mystery. Christians have struggled for centuries trying to understand why some people respond and others do not. Some of these questions cannot be answered in this life. One thing is clear—we are called to sow the message!

In the Parable of the Tares in Matthew, Jesus states that the field is the world. In the overall scheme of the harvest analogy in these parables, this account emphasizes the inclusiveness of Jesus' mission for His disciples and the Church. In the Great Commission, Jesus states that the whole world is to receive His message through the Church. No one is excluded from Christ's offer of salvation and everlasting life. As long as people are waiting for the message of Christ, the mission of the Church must go on until the Lord declares that its mission is accomplished.

14 What elements in the parable point to the value of discipleship?

15 What indication does the Parable of the Sower give of the universal appeal of the gospel?

LESSON 4.4

4.4.1 OBJECTIVE
Identify the three metaphors Jesus used to describe His followers.

The Character of the Believer

Jesus only used three metaphors—salt, light, and branches—to reveal the nature of what His followers were to be.

In what is possibly Jesus' best known body of teaching, the Sermon on the Mount, He likens His followers to two things: salt and light. In the Beatitudes, Jesus describes the character of the blessed life. He then goes on to say:

> You are the salt of the earth; but if the salt has become tasteless, how can it be made salty again? It is no longer good for anything, except to be thrown out and trampled under foot by men. You are the light of the world. A city set on a hill cannot be hidden; nor does anyone light a lamp and put it under a basket, but on the lampstand, and it gives light to all who are in the house. Let your light shine before men in such a way that they may see your good works, and glorify your Father who is in heaven. (Matthew 5:13–16)

4.4.2 OBJECTIVE
Describe the characteristics of each metaphor that illustrate the believer's life.

The Salt of the Earth

To fully understand why Jesus used salt as an example of what his followers should be, we must consider salt's purpose during New Testament times.

The major emphasis of Jesus' brief description focuses on the property of salt called "savor" or, as the NIV puts it, "saltiness." Savor is essentially salt's capacity to act on or affect something else.

16 What three characteristics of salt connect with the believer's responsibilities?

In New Testament times, salt was not merely something added to food to improve the taste. It had three other essential uses:

1. Salt is a preservative. People in those times had no refrigeration and almost all food was perishable. Salt was used to preserve food.

2. Salt stimulates thirst.

3. Salt enhances what it serves.

As salt affects whatever it serves, Christians are to affect the world around us.

During the eighteenth century, England had deteriorated socially and become morally decadent. Crime had reached its highest level, as had the birthrate of illegitimate children. Violence and drunkenness were rampant.

Then came the greatest spiritual revival in England's history. God raised up bold and passionate messengers of the gospel, such as John Wesley and George Whitefield, who preached God's Word in open fields, because the established church did not willingly receive them. Often they were publicly ridiculed in newspapers. Churches could not have contained the crowd anyway, so Whitefield and Wesley took to preaching in open areas, including marketplaces and fields.

As spiritual revival swept England and even extended to other European countries and the United States, the effect of the revival not only spiritually renewed the church, but it also had a powerful social impact on the culture. Crime, violence, and illegitimate births declined drastically. British society, for the most part, was radically transformed.

Throughout the reign of Queen Victoria, British society was marked by clarity of moral virtue. Historians have rightly given credit to Queen Victoria for her positive influence on the moral character of England that developed in the Victorian era. It is also likely that this positive surge in morality and the improvement of an entire society is as attributable to the Wesleyan revival as to Queen Victoria's influence. This positive impact on England lasted for many decades. The church can have a pervasive effect on an entire nation, when Christians live as our Lord intended.

God's people should be a moral preservative in their culture. As salt affects that with which it comes in contact, Christians should have an effect on nonbelievers in our neighborhoods or workplaces. Our presence should stimulate a spiritual desire for God and a hunger for truth and righteousness.

While Christians are not of the world, we are to be actively in the world, making a difference in the lives of those around us.

The Light of the World

Jesus said, "You are the light of the world." Consider the qualities of light:
- A light reveals things as they are.
- Light gives guidance and direction.

Sin blinds people to reality, but the Truth sets people free. As God's messengers in the world, we are to communicate that liberating truth.

When Jesus described the last days, He repeatedly warned His followers not to be deceived (Matthew 24, 25; Luke 21). In current culture, deception abounds. Conventional wisdom distorts.

Jesus said that a lamp on a stand gives light to all who are in the house, and a city set on a hill cannot be hidden. The church should be visible in the community as a testimony of truth and right living.

The lost of this world are searching. They are blind because of sin and do not really know what they are searching for, but they are searching. Followers of Christ have the answer—Jesus Christ, the Redeemer of mankind and Savior of the world. To a world that is lost and wandering in sin, we are to show them the way to forgiveness, reconciliation with God, and everlasting life.

Many years ago, I met an Evangelical Free missionary. He told about a man in a village in Pakistan who had received Christ. As it happened, this new Christian

17 How are Christians to be like light?

was the first person to receive electricity in his village. He was allocated 1,000 watts of power. He could have put several 100-watt lightbulbs in his house, illuminated several rooms and still had enough power to operate a few small appliances. Instead, this new Christian used his entire 1,000-watt allocation to power a 1,000-watt lightbulb on a pole in the corner of his yard. The streetlight illuminated the entire corner of the village. In the evening, older people gathered near the light to talk, and children played.

When the missionary talked to this Pakistani man, he learned that this new believer had not yet read Matthew 5:16: "Let your light shine before men in such a way that they may see your good works, and glorify your Father who is in heaven." Still, the Spirit of God had given him the desire to bless others rather than serve himself. He was a testimony of what a Christian should be—a giver of light to those who are in spiritual darkness.

The Vine and the Branches

4.4.3 OBJECTIVE
Utilize the warnings included in the metaphors to pursue spiritual maturity.

Among His final teachings to His disciples, Jesus revealed another picture of what His followers should be:

"I am the true vine, and My Father is the vinedresser. Every branch in Me that does not bear fruit, He takes away; and every branch that bears fruit, He prunes it so that it may bear more fruit. You are already clean because of the word which I have spoken to you. Abide in Me, and I in you. As the branch cannot bear fruit of itself unless it abides in the vine, so neither can you unless you abide in Me. I am the vine, you are the branches; he who abides in Me and I in him, he bears much fruit, for apart from Me you can do nothing." (John 15:1–5)

18 How does the metaphor of the vine uniquely connect to both the believer and to Christ?

Jesus is the Vine—the source of our spiritual life. We are to be branches through which the life of Christ flows and bears fruit. Jesus said, "'You did not choose Me but I chose you, and appointed you that you would go and bear fruit, and that your fruit would remain'" (John 15:16).

Being a Christian is not merely choosing a religion or way of life. A Christian is connected to our Lord by a living faith—a personal relationship. The presence of God's Holy Spirit within us brings spiritual life.

19 What warnings are implicit in the metaphors Jesus used?

Just being branches of the vine is not sufficient. Jesus warned of the uselessness of salt that has lost its savor and of branches that do not bear fruit. Lifeless branches have lost their intended purpose and become fit only for a much lesser and short-lived purpose—to become firewood.

Jesus warned that salt is not useful merely because it exists, but because it has the capacity of affecting what it serves. If salt has lost its savor or saltiness, it becomes useless—good for nothing.

4.4.4 OBJECTIVE
Apply the common denominator of the three metaphors in daily life.

A church that makes no impact on its environment may be a church in name, but it is not what God designed it to be. God did not design any believer not to bring forth fruit! He destined us to be productive in cooperation with His activity in people's lives. If we will be what He has destined and called us to be (salt, light, branches) and do our part, we will bear fruit.

20 What common denominator runs through the three metaphors?

Notice that the only three metaphors Jesus used to reveal the character of His followers share one primary quality. All have an effect beyond themselves. Salt affects whatever it touches. Light shines upon everything within its reach. Branches extend the life in the vine to the fruit that is produced. The lives of all followers of Christ should make an impact on those within their sphere of influence.

Test Yourself

Circle the letter of the *best* answer.

1. A shared theme of the parables found in the Synoptic Gospels is their
   a) focus on harvest analogies.
   b) emphasis on the cost of discipleship.
   c) use of Aramaic.
   d) reliance on symbolic numbers.

2. Jesus' common use of two contrasting elements in His parables was intended to
   a) illustrate the dual nature of all reality in the universe.
   b) challenge His hearers to apply one element.
   c) dumb down spiritual truth for people who could not visualize additional concepts.
   d) avoid a blasphemous use of the Trinitarian number *three*.

3. The contrasting pair in the Parable of the Sower is found in the
   a) implied reference to the sheep and the goats of the Last Judgment.
   b) dead and living seed.
   c) unproductive and productive soils.
   d) people who live by the Law and those who accept God's grace.

4. Both the shallow and thorny ground point to the possibility of
   a) being transformed by the gospel, then later rejecting it.
   b) only pretending to accept the truth of the gospel.
   c) falling into pseudo-Christian heresies.
   d) the elect being the only ones who can understand the gospel.

5. Jesus' concluding description of the abundant harvest
   a) depicts results far above the ordinary, and points to the miraculous result of the sowing.
   b) has a practical application in modern farming technology and the use of fertilizers.
   c) heralded His later miracle of feeding the 5,000.
   d) made the crowd angry and ready to stone Him for sowing on the Sabbath.

6. Jesus' private explanation of His parables to the disciples was intended to
   a) ensure the damnation of all who could not understand Him.
   b) keep the Pharisees and Sadducees from arresting Him before His time.
   c) avoid a premature declaration of His kingdom on earth.
   d) make sure that their receptive hearts received the right interpretation.

7. God's Word promises that when sowing is done in obedience to God's command,
   a) the obedient sower has preserved his own life by rescuing the lost.
   b) harvest is certain.
   c) the gifts of the Spirit come into evidence.
   d) gleaners will be blessed with the leftovers.

8. The various harvesting parables call for discipleship as well as evangelism,
   a) as evidenced by the crops Jesus referenced and their metaphorical meanings.
   b) because the true harvest is one that lasts until the end, despite opposing forces.
   c) because all parables have multiple applications.
   d) since Jesus began His ministry by calling fishers of men.

9. Jesus used which three metaphors to describe His followers?
   a) Body, soul, and spirit
   b) Water, bread, and new wine
   c) Salt, light, and branches on a vine
   d) Passover, Pentecost, and the Feast of Trumpets

10. The key difference in the analogy of the branches and vine from the salt and light metaphor is
    a) its use of a living substance.
    b) its connection to the new wine of the Spirit.
    c) the warning of possible ineffectiveness and being cut off.
    d) its focus on Christ's empowering role in believers' activities.

Responses to Interactive Questions
Chapter 4

Some of these responses may include information that is supplemental to the IST. These questions are intended to produce reflective thinking beyond the course content and your responses may vary from these examples.

1   What theme is expressed in those parables common to all three Synoptic Gospels?

The parables found in the Synoptic Gospels focus on harvest analogies.

2   How did the interpretation of biblical parables evolve?

Over time, people began to expand the meaning of symbols in parables to give support to their own theological positions.

3   What is the fundamental characteristic of the biblical parables?

Jesus used parables to correlate physical elements of the natural realm with unseen spiritual elements.

4   How many key elements are typically found in a parable?

Jesus usually presented two contrasting elements in order to challenge His hearers to choose to stand in alignment with one of them.

5   What shift did Matthew observe in Jesus' use of parables?

Jesus shifted from parables whose meanings were obvious to the crowds to more obscure parables that He explained privately to the disciples.

6   What evidence is there for Jesus' use of a contrasting pair in the Parable of the Sower?

The three unproductive soil varieties contrast with the three productive soils.

7   What spiritual tragedy does the thorny ground illustrate?

The thorny ground shows the real danger of the gospel being rejected even after a person has experienced its transforming power.

8   What three enemies seek to destroy the soul?

Satan, fleshly desires inherent in the sinful nature, and the unredeemed culture surrounding the believer.

9   What distinguishes the types of productive soil?

Jesus gave three examples of productive soil based on their amount of multiplication.

10   What is Jesus' motivation for calling on His audiences to carefully listen?

Jesus was emphasizing each person's responsibility to apply the truth of the parable.

11   Why is it a mistake to prioritize the role of the soils in the Parable of the Sower?

Doing so ignores Jesus' focus on the sower, gives unwarranted weight to the descriptive content of the parable, and fails to consider the parable's commissioning purpose.

12   How did Jesus' view of ministry as expressed in the Parable of the Sower contrast with the disciples' understanding of their mission?

Jesus understood the hardships the disciples would face in spreading the gospel. The disciples still believed that the kingdom of God would immediately be established.

13   How does Ecclesiastes expand the picture of the sower in Jesus' parable?

Ecclesiastes identifies the sower's need for diligence, God's role in bringing about the harvest, and the guarantee of that harvest.

14 What elements in the parable point to the value of discipleship?

The true harvest was the one that lasted. The failed harvests all pointed to factors compromising the continued effectiveness of the gospel. Implicit in the parable's teaching, then, is the need for the sower to take steps to preserve the harvest.

15 What indication does the Parable of the Sower give of the universal appeal of the gospel?

The field, in representing the world, shows that the gospel is intended to be shared with all people.

16 What three characteristics of salt connect with the believer's responsibilities?

Like salt, believers are to be a force for preservation, are to engender spiritual thirst in those around them, and are to improve their environment.

17 How are Christians to be like light?

They are to reveal the true nature of things and offer guidance and direction.

18 How does the metaphor of the vine uniquely connect to both the believer and to Christ?

Where the other two metaphors focused on the believer's roles, the metaphor of the vine and branches clarifies that only through the life-giving power of Christ can believers carry out those roles.

19 What warnings are implicit in the metaphors Jesus used?

Whether it is salt losing its saltiness, light that is hidden, or a branch that separates from the vine, there is a common theme of personal loss and ineffective witness through lack of faithfulness.

20 What common denominator runs through the three metaphors?

Each illustration reminds the believer that he or she is to have a positive effect on others for the cause of Christ.

CHAPTER 5

Jesus' Example

Gustav Bergstrom was a missionary in Brazil for fifty-five years and one of the greatest personal witnesses I have ever known. A few years ago, I had the opportunity to preach in Rio de Janeiro and mentioned Gustav Bergstrom in my message. After the service, a Brazilian man approached me and told me his story.

"I am a believer because of Gustav," he began. The man had been a conductor on a train. Gustav rode many trains as he traveled throughout Brazil to witness and plant churches. He always had quantities of gospel tracts and usually carried Bibles to give to those who were responsive to his witness.

As the conductor was collecting tickets, Gustav witnessed to him. The porter was eager to learn more but didn't have a Bible. At the time Gustav had none, but he promised to bring one when the train passed through town again.

"When will you return?" Gustav asked.

"In three days," the porter replied. "But we arrive at three a.m. and will stop only to refuel."

"I will be here," Gustav said.

The conductor didn't believe him and quickly forgot about the promise.

Three days later, in the middle of the night, the train lumbered into the town and stopped at the station. In the dim light the porter saw a lone, shadowy figure standing on the platform. It was Gustav Bergstrom. Without a word, Gustav bowed his head toward the porter, handed him a Portuguese Bible, and walked away.

"Because of that meeting, I found Christ," he said. "Today I am an Assemblies of God pastor."

Most believers have not been reached in a church service or stadium crusade but through a personal encounter.

Lesson 5.1   The Opportunity

Objectives

5.1.1   Recognize that opportunities for sharing the gospel exist every day.
5.1.2   Identify natural circumstances that lend themselves to a gospel witness.
5.1.3   Recognize and propose counteraction to social barriers to communicating the gospel.
5.1.4   Describe people's spiritual hunger and redemptive potential.

Lesson 5.2   The Focus

Objectives

5.2.1   Explain that personal evangelism is not the pursuit of victorious argument.
5.2.2   Structure evangelism efforts around the interests of another person.
5.2.3   Translate the gospel into language that is easily understood.
5.2.4   Recognize the inseparable nature of the subjects of sin and salvation.

Lesson 5.3   The Message

Objectives

5.3.1   Explain the pitfalls of religious questions and differences.
5.3.2   Defend relationship as the central theme in any evangelistic presentation.
5.3.3   Explain God's proactive promotion of the evangelism relationship.
5.3.4   Identify Jesus Christ as the central message in all evangelism.

LESSON 5.1

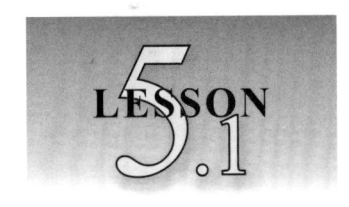

5.1.1
OBJECTIVE
Recognize that opportunities for sharing the gospel exist every day.

The Opportunity

Early in his Gospel, the apostle John records in chapters 3 and 4 two of Jesus' encounters with individuals—Nicodemus and the Samaritan woman. These accounts provide clear examples concerning how we should interact with nonbelievers. The contrasts and similarities of these two encounters are striking.

First, consider the differences between Nicodemus and the Samaritan woman. Nicodemus was a man; the Samaritan was a woman. His encounter with Jesus was intentional; hers was not. He was likely a respected Jewish religious leader; she was an immoral woman. He was respectful toward Jesus; she was initially indifferent and a little defensive. He was educated; she was unlearned. He was serious about the conversation; she was much more casual, at least in the beginning.

Both of these people needed what only Jesus could give them. As great as the differences were between Nicodemus and the Samaritan woman, their spiritual needs were essentially the same. They both needed a relationship with God rather than a mere form of religion. In both encounters, Jesus not only focused on that relationship, but He also revealed himself as the answer to their spiritual need.

John's account of Jesus' conversation with Nicodemus ends rather abruptly, and we are not told if Nicodemus makes a definite decision. The story of the Samaritan woman, on the other hand, ends with a clear result of her decision. Her response to Jesus changed not only her own life but also the rest of her community.

John's account of Jesus' conversation with the woman at the well is the most complete account of an encounter He had with a nonbeliever. From it, we can learn the process through which Jesus brought truth and spiritual understanding in everyday circumstances.

The story of Jesus' encounter with the woman at the well provides a wonderful example of how clearly and sensitively Jesus talked with people on their level. He was conscious of their respective cultures and their personal understanding and needs. His conversation with the Samaritan woman is an example of effective interpersonal communication.

While every personal encounter with a nonbeliever is unique, an examination of this account offers inspiring and instructive help to anyone engaged in personal evangelism. Reading through John 4 reveals how Jesus dealt with the woman step-by-step, providing us with examples of potential issues we face when communicating spiritual truth with nonbelievers.

Everyday Occasions

He left Judea and went away again into Galilee. And He had to pass through Samaria. So He came to a city of Samaria called Sychar, near the parcel of ground that Jacob gave to his son Joseph; and Jacob's well was there. So Jesus, being wearied from His journey, was sitting thus by the well. It was about the sixth hour. (John 4:3–6)

When John recorded that Jesus "had to pass through Samaria," the Greek word he used was *dei*, which states that something is a necessity.

Some have interpreted that Jesus needed to go through **Samaria** because He knew in advance of His divine appointment with the woman. Although the Holy Spirit later revealed to Him her marital status, the text gives no indication that Jesus had any prior conscious leading of the Spirit concerning the woman.

---

1 Does the Greek verb usage in this passage indicate that Jesus was acting on divine foreknowledge when He passed through Samaria?

In that day, Jews commonly took a longer route when journeying between Judea and Galilee, intentionally bypassing Samaria. Time was a factor. The route through Samaria was the quickest and most direct way. Even considering the common Jewish custom of bypassing Samaria, the wording of the text implies that Jesus was not conscious of the impending encounter with the Samaritan woman. John records that Jesus sat down by the well because He was tired from His journey. This resulting surprise encounter is a reminder to all believers to be ready to seize the moment when God ordains it.

Although Jesus probably took the Samaria route because it was the quickest, the divine interruption of His journey resulted in His staying in Samaria two days. During that time the Samaritan woman and many others came to believe in Him.

Most opportune moments for personal evangelism don't happen when Christians go door-to-door on Saturdays. Instead, they come in everyday circumstances. While we're doing the ordinary activities of life, God opens the door of opportunity for witness. The omniscient Holy Spirit, who "searches the hearts" (Romans 8:27), knows when nonbelievers are ready for the seed of God's message to be planted or watered.

2 When do most opportunities for personal evangelism occur?

Natural Opportunities

5.1.2 OBJECTIVE
Identify natural circumstances that lend themselves to a gospel witness.

"There came a woman of Samaria to draw water. Jesus said to her, 'Give Me a drink.' For His disciples had gone away into the city to buy food" (John 4:7–8).

Day-to-day life provides natural reasons why we must interact with people. These natural interchanges often can be opportunities for witness. Evangelism encounters don't need to be contrived. They just happen. The Holy Spirit uses them to prepare the way for us in the mission to which our Lord has called us. In His instruction to His disciples after this event, Jesus said, "Others have labored and you have entered into their labor" (John 4:38). The Holy Spirit goes before us and works in lives and circumstances, preparing good works for us, according to Ephesians 2:10. Our responsibility is to be alert for those opportunities and respond.

The one thing it will cost us most often is time.

3 Why can believers be confident in the effective nature of unplanned witnessing opportunities?

Social Barriers

5.1.3 OBJECTIVE
Recognize and propose counteraction to social barriers to communicating the gospel.

"Therefore the Samaritan woman said to Him, 'How is it that You, being a Jew, ask me for a drink since I am a Samaritan woman?' (For Jews have no dealings with Samaritans)" (John 4:9).

John's explanatory comment bears significance. It was not the Samaritan woman who said that Jews had no dealings with Samaritans. John included the information. Since he wrote his Gospel many years after this incident, he thought it necessary to explain the social segregation of Jews and Samaritans.

The normal custom of Jesus' day would have prohibited public conversations between men and women, especially Jews and Samaritans. A Jewish rabbi would go thirsty rather than violate these customs. By drinking from the Samaritan woman's vessel Jesus would be **ceremonially unclean** (Walvoord and Zuck 1983, 285).

4 What social barriers were represented at the meeting between Jesus and the Samaritan woman?

Even most Christians who are committed to being witnesses for Christ develop a mental profile of the kind of people they think God will use them to reach. Usually, they think they will reach people like themselves.

But God wants us to be ready, as Jesus was, to reach across social barriers to touch spiritually lost people who are culturally unlike ourselves.

Jesus' Example

As emphasized in Chapter 2, God has called us to reach all kinds of people. If we allow social or political barriers to hinder us, we will miss opportunities to share Christ with nonbelievers. We must do as the apostle Paul said, "No longer regarding one from a worldly point of view" (2 Corinthians 5:16).

During my adult ministry, I have traveled to many countries. In every culture I have been amazed to find that people's basic human needs are fundamentally similar. We must look past the surface cultural exteriors to see people as Jesus does. I have had the opportunity to witness to people of many races and nationalities, young and old, men and women. Their spiritual needs are the same. While traveling in airplanes I have talked with an Indian guru, several psychiatrists, doctors, lawyers, students, businessmen, housewives, musicians, actors, and professional athletes. Every person needs to discover his or her purpose for being, find peace with God through a relationship with Jesus Christ, and receive forgiveness of sins and the gift of everlasting life.

Believe in People

"Jesus answered and said to her, 'If you knew the gift of God, and who it is who says to you, "Give Me a drink," you would have asked Him, and He would have given you living water'" (John 4:10).

Jesus' attitude toward the Samaritan woman was amazing. His statement to her reveals that He perceived a spiritual hunger within her that would cause her to seek the "living water" He had, if she only knew who He was. She was living in sin, yet Jesus believed in her heart's desire for spiritual truth.

Much is said about *vision* in the Christian world. Some talk about a vision for great ministry or work. I believe we need the Holy Spirit to give us vision to see the spiritual potential in people in spite of their appearance.

The revelation of God's Word and personal experiences prove that only Jesus can satisfy the deepest need and longing of our hearts. That is true of everyone. The nonbeliever does not yet know that. We should not assume we will find resistance and hostility in people and then allow that perception to keep us from confidently sharing the good news.

No matter how people may appear on the outside or how negative we perceive their attitude to be toward spiritual things, underneath it all, they have a spiritual hunger that only Jesus can satisfy.

5.1.4 OBJECTIVE
Describe people's spiritual hunger and redemptive potential.

5   What did Jesus' offer of living water to the Samaritan woman reveal about His attitude toward her?

LESSON 5.2

The Focus

Potential Argument

"She said to Him, 'Sir, You have nothing to draw with and the well is deep; where then do You get that living water? You are not greater than our father Jacob, are You, who gave us the well, and drank of it himself and his sons and his cattle?'" (John 4:11–12).

When the woman asked Jesus this rhetorical question, she was really stating that Jesus was not greater than Jacob. Jesus could have responded defensively or with negative information concerning Jacob. Instead, He refused to allow himself to be drawn into such a discussion.

5.2.1
OBJECTIVE

Explain that personal evangelism is not the pursuit of victorious argument.

6   What is a common misconception about personal evangelism?

Our task is not to win arguments but to win people. When talking with people about spiritual matters, invariably subjects of controversy will arise concerning moral or social issues. We may even be challenged or confronted by nonbelievers. With someone's eternal soul at stake, we dare not allow personal pride or defensiveness to draw us into an argument.

Lessons following concerning *response evangelism* will emphasize that we cannot control what people will say and how they will treat us. The potential for argument when discussing spiritual issues is always present. We must be on our guard not to allow the conversation to deteriorate into personal conflict that will close the door for effective witness.

Focus of Interest

5.2.2
OBJECTIVE

Structure evangelism efforts around the interests of another person.

"Jesus answered and said to her, 'Everyone who drinks of this water will thirst again; but whoever drinks of the water that I will give him shall never thirst; but the water that I will give him will become in him a well of water springing up to eternal life.' The woman said to Him, 'Sir, give me this water, so I will not be thirsty nor come all the way here to draw'" (John 4:13–15).

To engage nonbelievers in meaningful conversation, the subject must be interesting to them. A fundamental factor in interpersonal communication is that to engage a person in a meaningful dialogue, even if we are leading someone to discussing subject matter in which they are not initially interested, we must begin with their desires and interests. This concept will be dealt with more extensively in Chapter 9.

A study of the Gospels reveals that Jesus both captured and maintained the interest of His hearers. He primarily used everyday things that were of interest to and relevant to His audience. His encounter with the Samaritan woman at the well is one compelling example. The focus of interest in that conversation was water.

7   What was the cultural context of Jesus' reference to water?

In a modern, technological context, water is taken for granted. It is accessible to drink in bottles available at every convenience store, supermarket, gas station, and airport. In Jesus' day, water had to be carried every day from a well. It was an essential task of life. Jesus took something that was a daily necessity for physical existence and built a bridge to the spiritual realm by talking to the woman about living water.

8   Where is the starting point for effective evangelism?

Effective communication, particularly persuasive communication, needs to start with something that is known and understood by people before leading them to comprehend something unknown such as spiritual truth. Determining an appropriate focus of interest in a conversation will depend upon several things:

- *The importance of effective listening*. Unfortunately, most Christians seem to think of witnessing as one-way communication—sort of like preaching a sermon—to one person. Effective communication involves listening even more than speaking. Sometimes more than half of effective witnessing is simply listening and being attentive to learn what a person's concerns and interests are. Jesus' conversation with the Samaritan woman exemplifies effective listening.

- *The nature of response evangelism*. Usually, the most effective means of witness is not a predetermined evangelistic routine, but rather a personalized message that responds to the interests and needs of a nonbeliever. To be capable of focusing on something that is of interest and

9 When responding to evangelism opportunities, how can the believer be prepared when the opportunities are unexpected?

relevant to an individual, our mind needs to be increasingly filled with truth from God's Word. This is a lifelong pursuit.

Jesus said that the Holy Spirit would remind His disciples of things that Jesus had taught. The same promise is true for His followers today. A lifestyle of studying God's Word will make truth available for the Holy Spirit to bring to our minds. In contrast, the Holy Spirit will not recall to our memory something that is not been put there already.

- *The need for creative connections.* Rely on the Holy Spirit to help you link people's interests and desires to their deepest needs, which are finding the purpose of existence, forgiveness of sin, and everlasting life. The Holy Spirit can guide conversations. He can even guide nonbelievers to pursue conversation that will open doors for witness. Again, listening is a key. If you will make a focused effort and prayerfully be still, asking the Holy Spirit to guide the conversation, He can and will help you to think and speak creatively as people talk about themselves.

- *The necessity of being understood.* When applying spiritual truth to subjects that interest a hearer, ensure that you do everything possible to use vocabulary with which he or she is familiar. Theological vocabulary or Christian jargon will only confuse those who are unfamiliar with such terms.

5.2.3 OBJECTIVE
Translate the gospel into language that is easily understood.

There is one subject in which everyone is interested—themselves. In most conversations with people I have just met, I ask what they do for a living and get them talking about themselves, beginning with their occupation. An excellent second question is to ask them about their family. Amazingly, the opportunities for spiritual application will open up, especially if you focus on people's desires. When they start talking about what they really want in life, bridges can easily be built to talk about their deepest needs and wants and how only Jesus Christ can satisfy those longings.

5.2.4 OBJECTIVE
Recognize the inseparable nature of the subjects of sin and salvation.

The Sin Issue

"He said to her, 'Go, call your husband and come here.' The woman answered and said, 'I have no husband.' Jesus said to her, 'You have correctly said, "I have no husband;" for you have had five husbands, and the one whom you now have is not your husband; this you have said truly'" (John 4:16–18).

Jesus intentionally raised the issue of the woman's sin.

10 Why is it vital to include the subject of *personal sin* within any presentation of the gospel?

The issue of sin cannot be avoided in evangelism. The good news can be understood only in the context of the bad news concerning our sin. Some people try to witness by removing the sin issue from the picture and dealing only with positive topics. Salvation is not possible without forgiveness. There is no forgiveness without confession of sin and no confession of sin without conviction of sin. John the Baptist summed up Jesus' mission when he said, "Behold the Lamb of God who takes away the sin of the world!" (John 1:29).

Most of my personal witnessing takes place on airplanes, where I have the most uninterrupted time with people. During all my experiences, only one person was unwilling to acknowledge his sin. He was a Harvard University professor. Through rationalization he had come to the intellectual conclusion that there are no moral absolutes.

Rarely are people unwilling to acknowledge the issue of sin. Instead, most make excuses for their sins. People are willing to admit they have sinned, yet many are unwilling to refer to themselves as "sinners." Instead of trying to convince a person that he or she is a sinner, I turn the situation around. I try to identify with the nonbeliever by talking about how I know I am a sinner. I do this also when praying with people at an altar. Although we must deal with the sin issue, it should not be in a self-righteous or judgmental manner. Remember, we are all sinners saved by grace. The subject of sin should be dealt with clearly, but it must be done graciously.

LESSON 5.3

5.3.1 OBJECTIVE
Explain the pitfalls of religious questions and differences.

11 Why isn't *religion* a beneficial topic in personal evangelism, in most cases?

12 Is it always a bad idea to discuss religion practices when witnessing?

5.3.2 OBJECTIVE
Defend relationship as the central theme in any evangelistic presentation.

The Message

The Great Diversion—Religion

"The woman said to Him, 'Sir, I perceive that You are a prophet. Our fathers worshiped in this mountain, and you people say that in Jerusalem is the place where men ought to worship'" (John 4:19–20).

In any witnessing encounter, a topic that can pull a conversation off track more than any other is *religion*. When a conversation turns to spiritual issues, people often gravitate to religious questions and differences. Often the religious issues aren't major but are minor points that have little or no bearing on a person's eternal destiny.

The issue upon which the Samaritan woman focused was the question of where people should worship—at mount Gerizim, where the Samaritans worshiped, or in Jerusalem, where the Jews worshiped. Jesus shifted the emphasis from where people should worship to how they should worship.

Consider just one example of how the religion issue can distract in contemporary times. A person might mention being raised in a church that baptizes by sprinkling rather than immersion. When people have questioned me about the different baptism rituals, my response is simple: "Whether you are sprinkled or immersed, you can start as a dry sinner and finish as a wet sinner. The physical water is not what cleanses you."

Baptism by immersion is important, but don't get sidetracked arguing such differences in church doctrine or practice with someone who does not personally know Christ. Until a person is born again, points about water baptism, communion, tithing, or church membership really don't matter.

The apostle Paul gives sound advice to Timothy about keeping the focus on the things that matter: "Keep reminding them of these things," Paul says, "Warn them before God against quarreling about words; it is of no value, and only ruins those who listen" (2 Timothy 2:14, NIV). Talking about religion issues requires alertness and sensitivity to discern when it is productive and when it is a diversion. Anything that takes away from the focus on a personal relationship with God through Jesus Christ will likely be counterproductive.

The Real Issue—Relationship

Jesus said to her, "Woman, believe Me, an hour is coming when neither in this mountain nor in Jerusalem will you worship the Father. You worship what you do not know; we worship what we know, for salvation is from the Jews. But an hour is coming, and now is, when the true worshipers will worship the Father in spirit and truth; for such people the Father seeks to be His worshipers. God is spirit, and those who worship Him must worship in spirit and truth." (John 4:21–24)

Jesus moved the woman away from discussion concerning religious form to the real issue—a personal relationship with God. Jesus said that worshiping Him involved "spirit and truth."

13 What does it mean to worship God in spirit and in truth?

To worship God in spirit is to commune with Him personally and directly through no other medium. To worship Him in truth is to validate the relationship we have in prayer and worship with our behavior. We worship Him not only with our lips but also with our lives. God doesn't want symbols of our relationship with Him but the relationship itself. The difference is whether someone knows about God or truly knows Him as Savior, Lord, and Friend.

One of Billy Graham's first books addresses the heart of this issue. Even the title, *Peace With God*, describes our ultimate longing. If someone is not personally at peace—in right relationship with God—church attendance, tithing, and good works are meaningless in the light of eternity.

Jesus said that God seeks true worshipers to worship Him. In the Parable of the Prodigal Son, the father did not wait for the son to come home. When the father saw the lost son still a long way off, the father ran to him and embraced him. Jesus told this parable to describe the loving heart of our heavenly Father, as He seeks a relationship with all of His children.

5.3.3 OBJECTIVE
Explain God's proactive promotion of the evangelism relationship.

14 Who takes the initiative in establishing a relationship between God and lost people?

When we are witnessing to spiritually lost people, we should always remember that God is seeking them. As the loving, forgiving father in the story of the Prodigal Son ran to his wayward child, God is pursuing each sinner to reconcile him or her to himself. He gives us the privilege of being involved in the process of communicating His love to the lost. The Holy Spirit will do the convincing as Jesus promised He would (John 16:8). Our responsibility is to clearly communicate the loving relationship God wants with each of His lost children.

The Central Message—Jesus

5.3.4 OBJECTIVE
Identify Jesus Christ as the central message in all evangelism.

"The woman said to Him, 'I know that Messiah is coming (He who is called Christ); when that One comes, He will declare all things to us.' Jesus said to her, 'I who speak to you am He'" (John 4:25–26).

Jesus' encounter with the Samaritan woman resulted in a revelation of who He was. Afterward, the woman ran into the town and said, "Come, see a *man*" (John 4:29, emphasis added). She stated the heart of the matter well. What mattered was not the theological issue of worshiping on Mount Gerizim or in Jerusalem, but a relationship with Jesus the Messiah.

15 What about the Samaritan woman's announcement to her village showed that Jesus had successfully prioritized relationship?

The introduction to Chapter 2 referred to missionary John Bueno, whose life made an incredible impact on the nation of El Salvador. John and his wife Lois went as missionaries to El Salvador in 1961. The church they pastored grew steadily from one hundred to three hundred in nine years. Then came a breakthrough. John felt led to preach a sermon on the lordship of Christ. He didn't receive the response from the congregation he felt was needed, so he preached the same sermon the next Sunday. He still didn't see the response he felt the Spirit wanted, so he preached the same message again and again, thirteen weeks in a row. Within six months the church was packed with two thousand people each Sunday. People were confronted with who Jesus truly is and His claim upon their lives. When they were called to decision and challenged to discipleship, they entered a new dimension—a greater level of commitment. In eleven years the church reached 22,000 in Sunday morning attendance. The breakthrough that started this incredible church growth was a bold, clear and repeated emphasis on the personal lordship of Jesus Christ.

Every Christian witness will face the challenge of learning to avoid merely a propositional approach to truth and focusing on a personal approach. Jesus said, "*I* am . . . the truth" (John 14:6, emphasis added). Systematic theology is helpful in organizing our thoughts and understanding. For the nonbeliever, we must often avoid the systematic in favor of the relational. The issue is not merely what someone believes, but in whom he or she believes. As the apostle Paul stated, "I know whom I have believed" (2 Timothy 1:12).

Following lessons will show that the central focus of the preaching and teaching of both Peter and Paul was Jesus Christ. The objective of evangelism is not to persuade people to become a part of our church—to join a group of nice people with higher-than-average moral standards. The objective is to introduce people to Jesus Christ.

A study of the four Gospels reveals that some of Jesus' disciples were much more prominent in the Gospel records than others. Of the twelve, the most prominent in the Gospel records is Peter. No other disciple is mentioned more, quoted more, or spoken to by Jesus more. He is also the most prominent of the twelve in the book of Acts.

But Peter was there because of another man, his brother, Andrew. In the Synoptic Gospels, Andrew is only mentioned as being present. Andrew's words or deeds are not recorded. In the Gospel of John, the last Gospel to be written, (to supplement the other three), the apostle John, as an old man, recalled three significant instances concerning Andrew. In John 1, Andrew brought his brother Simon (later Peter) to Jesus. In John 6, he brought the boy with the loaves and the fish to Jesus, when Jesus fed the five thousand. In John 12, he brought the Greeks who wanted to see Jesus to Him, when Phillip likely would have sent them away. Only three things are recorded about Andrew. In each case, he was always doing the same thing—he brought people to Jesus.

Evangelism is not merely verbal proclamation or persuasion. It is introducing people to the risen Christ, a living Lord. If, in whatever way we can, we simply get people in contact with Jesus, they will never be the same.

Evangelism is, in word and deed, bringing people to Jesus. He will save them.

Test Yourself

Circle the letter of the best answer.

1. Most opportunities for personal evangelism occur
   a) during ordinary activities of life. ✓
   b) as a result of preplanned outreaches.
   c) in the Sunday school classroom.
   d) on Christmas and Easter Sunday.

2. Believers can be confident in the effective nature of unplanned witnessing opportunities,
   a) as long as they are witnessing in a group environment.
   b) if they have memorized the Roman Road.
   c) because God has predestined certain people to be saved.
   d) when they recognize the work of the Holy Spirit in lives and circumstances. ✓

3. Jesus' offer of living water to the Samaritan woman revealed
   a) His perception of her spiritual hunger, despite her seeming indifference. ✓
   b) that He saw through her questions and was putting her in her place.
   c) Jesus' commitment to speak in symbols.
   d) the woman's identity as an adulterer.

4. It is common for people to misunderstand personal evangelism as a
   a) sacrament to be observed along with baptism and communion.
   b) task to be carried out in order to earn salvation.
   c) means of condemning the lost by exposing them to knowledge of the truth.
   d) series of arguments to be won. ✓

5. To engage a nonbeliever in meaningful conversation with evangelistic potential, one must
   a) be prepared to quote the relevant Scripture passages.
   b) fast at least a week.
   c) first find a subject that genuinely interests the other person. ✓
   d) wait until a relationship has been established.

6. The key to connecting spiritual truths to everyday subjects
   a) is to have several tracts to hand out.
   b) involves tongues and interpretation.
   c) depends on how clearly the witnesser reads the relevant biblical texts.
   d) is to use vocabulary familiar to the listener. ✓

7. It is important not to neglect the subject of sin, even in relational evangelism, because
   a) unflinching condemnation will draw people to Christ.
   b) the myth of sin needs to be exposed, and people need to be assured of God's love.
   c) an understanding of sin is needed in order to pursue forgiveness and salvation. ✓
   d) the example of the believer's victorious spiritual life will draw the lost to God.

8. The subject of religion during a personal witnessing presentation
   a) is the first step toward getting people to explore the gospel.
   b) works best just before a person prays the sinner's prayer.
   c) most often results in divisive questions that distract from the real message. ✓
   d) is a good idea, as long as the religion discussed is in contrast to Christianity.

9. When considering the relationship between God and lost people,
   a) God takes the initiative in making the relationship possible. ✓
   b) the lost person takes the initiative, because God gives free will.
   c) remember that God only reaches out to the lost who are the elect.
   d) one can be encouraged, because all the lost will eventually be saved.

10. The central message of the gospel is the
    a) lost condition of humankind.
    b) person of Jesus Christ. ✓
    c) special role of the Jews in salvation history.
    d) prophecies of Daniel.

Responses to Interactive Questions
Chapter 5

Some of these responses may include information that is supplemental to the IST. These questions are intended to produce reflective thinking beyond the course content and your responses may vary from these examples.

1 Does the Greek verb usage in this passage indicate that Jesus was acting on divine foreknowledge when He passed through Samaria?

The text gives no evidence of Jesus' foreknowledge and portrays Him as interacting spontaneously with the woman.

2 When do most opportunities for personal evangelism occur?

Personal evangelism opportunities most commonly occur during ordinary activities of life rather than during preplanned outreaches.

3 Why can believers be confident in the effective nature of unplanned witnessing opportunities?

The Holy Spirit works in lives and circumstances to create opportunities when people will be receptive to the gospel.

4 What social barriers were represented at the meeting between Jesus and the Samaritan woman?

Racial, gender, and religious barriers were present in this encounter.

5 What did Jesus' offer of living water to the Samaritan woman reveal about His attitude toward her?

Jesus perceived her spiritual hunger despite her seeming indifference and sinful public reputation.

6 What is a common misconception about personal evangelism?

People often mistake personal evangelism as a call to aggressively counter the challenges and arguments of an unsaved person.

7 What was the cultural context of Jesus' reference to water?

Jesus used the difficulty of obtaining vital water in His day to build a bridge to a spiritual application, living water.

8 Where is the starting point for effective evangelism?

The believer must learn about the person with whom he or she is sharing the gospel and begin with something relevant to that person.

9 When responding to evangelism opportunities, how can the believer be prepared when the opportunities are unexpected?

Lifelong study of God's Word and daily reliance on God's Spirit combine to offer the believer spiritually solid answers to unexpected questions.

10 Why is it vital to include the subject of *personal sin* within any presentation of the gospel?

It is only within the context of sin that the gospel is recognized as good news that counters personal failure, moral loss, and eternal damnation.

11 Why is not *religion* a beneficial topic in personal evangelism, in most cases?

Religious issues are usually tangential to the real issue of relating to God, and the subject of religion often creates a confrontational atmosphere.

12 Is it always a bad idea to discuss religion practices when witnessing?

In some cases it can be productive. Spiritual sensitivity is needed in order to identify those situations. It is important to avoid being unnecessarily sidetracked by fringe issues.

13 What does it mean to worship God in spirit and in truth?

To worship in spirit is to commune with God directly. To worship in truth is to live a lifestyle consistent with that communion.

14 Who takes the initiative in establishing a relationship between God and lost people?

God seeks for people to become true worshipers and enjoy a relationship with Him.

15 What about the Samaritan woman's announcement to her village showed that Jesus had successfully prioritized relationship?

By inviting her neighbors to "come see a man," the woman rightly focused on Jesus' person rather than theological issues.

CHAPTER 6

Jesus' Promise

Many years ago, an immigrant family from Europe was traveling on a ship to the United States to begin a new life. The family had limited means, and the parents had packed a large supply of crackers and cheese to sustain them on the journey. The family stayed together in one cabin, and at each mealtime ate crackers and cheese together.

Most of the journey was over. Only a few days remained. As the family was walking along the deck before lunch time, the wonderful aromas from the kitchen wafted onto the deck. Tired of eating crackers and cheese, the children savored the delicious smells and pleaded with their father for some of the food.

When his family returned to their cabin, the father approached the ship's captain privately and asked, "How much would it cost for my family to have one meal in the ship's dining room?"

The captain replied, "I don't know what you mean. Haven't you been eating in the dining room?"

"No," the father replied. "We have been eating food we brought with us."

The captain said, "Didn't you know that when you bought your tickets, the price included all of your meals in the dining room?"

The crackers and cheese sustained the family on their journey, but they did not enjoy the plentiful feast that was available to them and had already been purchased.

A person can live a Christian life without experiencing the Holy Spirit baptism. But why should anyone settle for less than what God has promised and wants for us?

Lesson 6.1   The Promise of Power

Objectives

6.1.1   Define the Holy Spirit baptism as essential empowerment to fulfilling the Great Commission.
6.1.2   Prioritize the Holy Spirit baptism over secondary theological questions.
6.1.3   Describe the distinct personality of the third Person of the Trinity.
6.1.4   Describe the nature of the Holy Spirit's relationship with believers.

Lesson 6.2   The Nature and Purpose of the Spirit's Power

Objectives

6.2.1   Describe the everyday ability the Holy Spirit brings in living for God.
6.2.2   Distinguish the works of the flesh from the fruit of the Spirit.
6.2.3   Compare the consistent supernatural empowerment of the Spirit to the spectacular and miraculous.
6.2.4   Explain the purpose of the Holy Spirit baptism—witnessing to the lost.

Lesson 6.3   Seeking the Spirit

Objectives

6.3.1   Describe the believer's need for God's power and the inability to earn merit for that power.
6.3.2   Identify speaking in tongues as the initial evidence of the Spirit's fullness.
6.3.3   Describe the four purposes of speaking in tongues.
6.3.4   Explain the need to seek the fullness of the Spirit and to continue being filled with the Spirit.

Lesson 6.1

The Promise of Power

In the last days before Jesus' crucifixion, He gave His followers final instructions. They had been with Him for three years during His public ministry. He knew they were troubled and afraid when He told them that He would be leaving them soon.

He had patiently taught them. He said, "'All things that I have heard from My Father I have made known to you'" (John 15:15). He had instructed them concerning how to live as His witnesses in the world. They were overwhelmed. How could they possibly obey all the commandments He had given them? It was one thing to understand what Jesus required of them. It was another to accomplish the purpose for which He had called them to follow Him.

The Essential Empowerment

Jesus knew that fear would overcome His disciples' best intentions. He had chosen them. He had prayed for them. He knew that in spite of their human weaknesses, they loved Him. After three years of teaching, He shared a wonderful promise with them. He said, "I tell you the truth, it is to your advantage that I go away; for if I do not go away, the Helper will not come to you; but if I go, I will send Him to you" (John 16:7).

Such a statement must have surprised the disciples. How could His leaving be an advantage to them? They didn't understand that they would be more effective with the Spirit's presence in their lives than when Jesus was physically present with them.

Jesus' last recorded words in Luke say, "'Repentance for forgiveness of sins would be proclaimed in His name to all the nations, beginning from Jerusalem. You are witnesses of these things. And behold, I am sending forth the promise of My Father upon you; but you are to stay in the city until you are clothed with power from on high'" (Luke 24:47–49).

It would seem that a task so great—proclaiming Christ's message to all the nations—should commence immediately. Jesus told the disciples to wait in the city to be "clothed with power from on high."

For several years the American Express company had an effective series of television commercials. A person on a trip away from home has just lost his or her wallet or purse. Confused and without the necessary financial resources, the person is advised, "Don't leave home without it!"—an American Express card.

In Luke 24, Jesus gave His disciples the same advice—they should not begin their mission without having the spiritual resources they needed. Only then would they be equipped to accomplish the task.

The Priority of Heaven

Before Jesus ascended to heaven, He spoke one last time to His disciples:

"He commanded them not to leave Jerusalem, but to wait for what the Father had promised, 'Which,' He said, 'you heard of from Me; for John baptized with water, but you will be baptized with the Holy Spirit not many days from now.' So when they had come together, they were asking Him, saying, 'Lord, is it at this time You are restoring the kingdom to Israel?'" (Acts 1:4–6).

Jesus' answer was clear and direct: "'It is not for you to know the times or dates the Father has set by his own authority. But you will receive power when the Holy Spirit comes on you; and you will be my witnesses in Jerusalem, and in all Judea and Samaria, and to the ends of the earth'" (Acts 1:7–8, NIV).

6.1.1 OBJECTIVE
Define the Holy Spirit baptism as essential empowerment to fulfilling the Great Commission.

1 How did Jesus describe the value of the Holy Spirit's presence in the disciples' lives?

6.1.2 OBJECTIVE
Prioritize the Holy Spirit baptism over secondary theological questions.

2 How did Jesus help the disciples recognize the priority of a relationship with the Holy Spirit?

Jesus directed His disciples' focus to the task before them, which was to be witnesses to a lost world by the power of the Spirit. He redirected their attention from the concerns of time to those of eternity. Understanding the future of political kingdoms was insignificant compared with experiencing the Holy Spirit's empowerment to fulfill their purpose be His witnesses in the world.

The Helper

The fulfillment of our Lord's promise of power for His followers happened on the Day of Pentecost. The promised power was and is granted through the Holy Spirit.

Because of the Bible's clarity in revealing the personalities of God the Father and God the Son, they are usually better understood than the Holy Spirit. We can vividly see the personality of God the Father revealed throughout the Old Testament and clarified even further through Jesus' teaching in the New Testament.

6.1.3 OBJECTIVE
Describe the distinct personality of the third Person of the Trinity.

God the Son is foretold in the Old Testament and revealed throughout the New Testament in the person of Jesus.

Jesus taught about the Holy Spirit, and we see the ministry of the Holy Spirit in the book of Acts and in the teaching letters of the New Testament writers, especially the apostle Paul. Because a significant part of the Holy Spirit's work is to glorify the Son, many have difficulty understanding the Holy Spirit as a person rather than merely a power or force.

3 What personality characteristics described in the Scriptures show that the Holy Spirit is not a force?

The Bible teaches that the Holy Spirit is a distinct person with attributes of personality. He corrects, helps, and intercedes. He inspired the prophets to speak.

The Holy Spirit is also divine. Characteristics only used of God are attributed to the Holy Spirit. He is present everywhere, knows all things, is all powerful, and is eternal—without beginning or end. He is described as working in creation and doing miracles. Jesus commanded that believers be baptized in the name of the Father, and the Son, and the Holy Spirit.

4 What action on Jesus' part indicated the value He placed on the Holy Spirit's ministry among believers?

In Jesus' final hours before His crucifixion, He taught the disciples extensively about the Holy Spirit, whom He would send from the Father to be their Helper:

> If you love Me, you will keep My commandments. I will ask the Father, and He will give you another Helper, that He may be with you forever; that is the Spirit of truth, whom the world cannot receive, because it does not see Him or know Him, but you know Him because He abides with you and will be in you. (John 14:15–17)

Jesus revealed a great mystery about God. Jesus had been with the disciples, and they knew how He helped them. Now He promised them "another Helper." He was introducing them to the third person of the Trinity, the Holy Spirit. The Old Testament writers taught concerning the Spirit of God, but the people could not understand the Holy Spirit until Jesus came and, even more, after Jesus returned to heaven and sent the Holy Spirit as the Father promised.

6.1.4 OBJECTIVE
Describe the nature of the Holy Spirit's relationship with believers.

A Two-fold Relationship

Jesus promised two things concerning what His followers' relationship with the Holy Spirit would be.

5 What two characteristics did Jesus emphasize about the Holy Spirit's relationship to believers?

1. His permanence—the Spirit would be with them forever and abide (or remain) with them.

2. His presence—the Holy Spirit would be in them.

This was certainly a mystery revealed. The Old Testament spoke often about the Holy Spirit coming on prophets, priests, judges, and kings. Jesus revealed that the Holy Spirit would come to be in His people.

God was with Adam and Eve in the Garden. In the Old Testament, God was with His people as they wandered in the wilderness, showing His presence in the cloud by day and fire by night.

When Jesus, God the Son, became flesh and took on human form, God entered another relationship with humankind. The apostle John wrote, "The Word became flesh, and dwelt among us, and we saw His glory, glory as of the only begotten from the Father, full of grace and truth" (John 1:14). Jesus was God with and among His people. Now Jesus was teaching His disciples that God the Holy Spirit would be in them.

God's relationship with His people progressed from being *with* them to being *among* them to finally being *in* them!

LESSON 6.2

The Nature and Purpose of the Spirit's Power

The Greek word used in the New Testament to describe Jesus' teaching concerning the Holy Spirit is *parakletos*. The title originally was used to describe a person who was called in to help someone, which is why some Bible versions translate the word as "Comforter," "Counselor," or "Advocate." The simplest translation is "Helper."

In the final hours before His death, Jesus taught His disciples concerning the Holy Spirit to prepare them for life without His physical presence with them. The Holy Spirit—the Helper—would provide God's empowering presence to equip them for their mission.

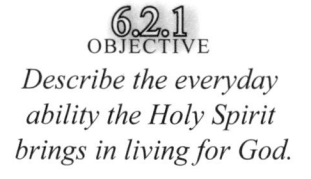

The Gift of Adequacy

People often think of the Holy Spirit's empowerment only in terms of signs and wonders and spiritual gifts. The word translated "power" in Acts 1:8 (*dunamis*) is broad and comprehensive. It simply means "ability" and applies in practical ways. It means the Spirit will supply whatever it takes for us to accomplish the work to which God has assigned us. The power Jesus promised His followers is His gift of adequacy for every aspect of Christian living, enabling us to do and be whatever our Lord has purposed in our lives.

Each individual is unique. We struggle with different personal weaknesses. The Holy Spirit knows our hearts, our motives, and our personal flaws. When we depend on Him, He will help us in our uniqueness to live in obedience to our Lord. The help needed varies with each individual. The shy, inhibited person may need courage to speak up. The outgoing, impulsive person may need restraint to stay silent. The Holy Spirit's power will provide whatever help we need. This means He enables us to win what is the most challenging battle for most people, that which takes place within our own hearts.

The power of the flesh—our physical desires—is strong. In the Garden of Gethsemane, when Peter was overcome by his body's desire for sleep, Jesus said, "The spirit is willing, but the flesh is weak" (Matthew 26:41; Mark 14:38).

Feeding desires only temporarily satisfies them. Anyone who has battled a physical habit knows this. The person bound by alcohol, drugs, or any other

---

6.2.1 OBJECTIVE
Describe the everyday ability the Holy Spirit brings in living for God.

6   Why is it important to recognize the broad meaning of the word translated "power" in Acts 1:8?

sinful indulgence knows that satisfying sinful desires brings only temporary gratification. Soon the desire comes back even stronger, like an animal that grows and requires more food the larger it becomes.

7 In regard to human desires, how do other world religions differ from Christianity?

This problem of sinful desire within the human heart is a focus of most world religions. Even people who have never read a Bible understand the problems our desires cause us. The objective of some religions is to gratify those desires. Other religions try to repress desire or eliminate it altogether.

The Bible teaches that our desires can be changed by God's power. Paul wrote to the church at Philippi: "It is God who is at work in you, both to will and to work for His good pleasure" (Philippians 2:13).

6.2.2
OBJECTIVE
Distinguish the works of the flesh from the fruit of the Spirit.

The only power that can defeat the desires of the flesh is the power of the Holy Spirit. Paul told the Galatians:

> So I say, live by the Spirit, and you will not gratify the desires of the sinful nature. For the sinful nature desires what is contrary to the Spirit, and the Spirit what is contrary to the sinful nature. They are in conflict with each other, so that you do not do what you want. But if you are led by the Spirit, you are not under law. The acts of the sinful nature are obvious: sexual immorality, impurity and debauchery; idolatry and witchcraft; hatred, discord, jealousy, fits of rage, selfish ambition, dissensions, factions and envy; drunkenness, orgies, and the like. I warn you, as I did before, that those who live like this will not inherit the kingdom of God. But the fruit of the Spirit is love, joy, peace, patience, kindness, goodness, faithfulness, gentleness and self-control. Against such things there is no law. Those who belong to Christ Jesus have crucified the sinful nature with its passions and desires. (Galatians 5:16–24, NIV)

8 Why is it critical to distinguish the works of the flesh from the fruit of the Spirit?

Notice that Paul does not talk about the works of the Spirit or the fruit of the flesh. We can naturally perform all of the works of the flesh he describes. Love, joy, peace, patience, and the other characteristics of the **fruit of the Spirit** cannot be performed by us, even if we have the right intentions. They can be produced only through the Spirit who lives within us. This is why the fullness of the Spirit must be maintained in each of our lives.

The fruit of the Spirit Paul describes is not a list of works we can perform naturally. They are spiritual attributes that are really a description of Jesus' character. The indwelling Holy Spirit produces that fruit in our lives.

We need the Holy Spirit's working, not just in church on Sunday, but every day in our homes, at school, in our neighborhoods, and in the workplace.

6.2.3
OBJECTIVE
Compare the consistent supernatural empowerment of the Spirit to the spectacular and miraculous.

Spectacular or Supernatural

When people think of the power of the Holy Spirit, visible, spectacular works usually come to mind. Most of the time, the kind of power we need in everyday life is neither spectacular nor sensational, but it is supernatural. Accomplishing God's purposes in the world requires divine help beyond our natural abilities. Supernatural living is not always outwardly dramatic.

After the outpouring of the Holy Spirit in the book of Acts, spectacular miracles took place. According to Acts 5:15, the sick were brought into the streets and laid on beds and couches so that the shadow of Peter might touch them. Likewise, Luke records, "God was performing extraordinary miracles by the hands of Paul, so that handkerchiefs or aprons were even carried from his body to the sick, and the diseases left them and the evil spirits went out" (Acts 19:11–12).

Notice that Luke describes these miracles as "extraordinary." Other translations use the words "special" or "unusual." Placing the sick where Peter's shadow would touch them or taking Paul's handkerchiefs or aprons to the ill were not regular practices of believers. Instead, the sick were instructed to call for the elders of the church and be anointed with oil (James 5:14).

In recent years, much has been taught concerning signs and wonders. Those two words are frequently used in the book of Acts (2:19; 2:22; 2:43; 4:30; 5:12; 6:8; 7:36; 14:3; 15:12). Jesus only spoke about signs and wonders in two ways. He warned His followers not to be deceived by false prophets in the last days who would show signs and wonders (Mark 13:22). When the Capernaum official whose son was sick came to Him, Jesus said, "Unless you people see signs and wonders, you simply will not believe" (John 4:48).

When Jesus taught His disciples about the characteristics that would be convincing marks of His followers, He did not talk about signs and wonders but about love. He said, "By this all men will know that you are My disciples, if you have love for one another" (John 13:35).

9 What did Jesus call for as the primary outward evidence of believers' relationship to Him?

The fruit of the Spirit in the believer's life—love, joy, peace, patience, and all the other characteristics Paul describes in Galatians 5—may not seem spectacular. They are supernatural, beyond our natural capacities. When people look at our lives and see love (especially for those who have wronged us), overflowing joy in the midst of sorrow, peace in the crises of life, patience in tribulation, and gentleness in response to hostility, these can be supernatural evidences that we are not mere subjects to our own fleshly emotions. We are empowered by the Holy Spirit to live the life to which our Lord has called us. The supernatural working of the Spirit will not always be spectacular or sensational, but it is convincing evidence of the presence and life of the Spirit within us.

Power for Purpose

6.2.4 OBJECTIVE
Explain the purpose of the Holy Spirit baptism—witnessing to the lost.

Jesus clearly stated that the essential purpose of the Spirit's empowerment is to be His witnesses. The Holy Spirit baptism is a promised gift to all believers. Receiving the gift is not a guarantee that the promised power will be used for its intended purpose.

10 What specific purpose did Jesus connect to the Spirit's empowerment in the believer's life?

I heard this intriguing report on the radio: ninety-five percent of all sport utility vehicles sold in the United States are never taken off the road. Of course, during Minnesota winters, four-wheel drive is a great help in winter weather. Why would someone need four-wheel drive on the freeways of southern California? These vehicles were equipped for a purpose for which most are rarely, if ever, used.

This reminds me of many people's experience concerning the Holy Spirit baptism. They receive this wonderful gift, yet they don't put it into action or may not even fully understand the purpose for which this equipping power was given.

Jesus' promise to His followers was that they would be His witnesses wherever they went. Unfortunately, many equate being a witness with only verbal witnessing. Effectiveness in reaching the spiritually lost requires a witness beyond words.

Paul wrote to the believers at Thessalonica, "Our gospel did not come to you in word only, but also in power and in the Holy Spirit and with full conviction; just as you know what kind of men we proved to be among you for your sake" (1 Thessalonians 1:5).

The effectiveness of the message is not limited to words. Paul's message was not "in word only." He connects both power and full conviction with the proclamation of his message "in the Holy Spirit." When Jesus' disciples received His promised power on the Day of Pentecost, these ordinary people became messengers of extraordinary effectiveness. That effectiveness was a direct result of the connection of the Spirit's power with the purpose for which the empowerment was given.

The Holy Spirit helps us in every part of our spiritual lives. For example, one of our greatest personal needs is motivation. The Spirit works in our desires. He moves us to do what we don't have the internal motivation to do. He inspires our passion.

God's Word is clear. Just knowing His Word is not enough. James 1:22 says we are to be doers of the Word, not merely hearers of it. The motivational power of the Holy Spirit encourages us to obey and takes our Christian living beyond thoughts and words to action.

The divine empowerment Jesus promised His disciples was for the specific purpose, that they would proclaim His message and be His witnesses in all the world.

LESSON 6.3

Seeking the Spirit

God's Empowering Presence

The promise of the Holy Spirit's power is for every believer. Even many who understand this promise are hesitant to seek. Some feel they don't deserve this blessing. The apostle Paul taught in Galatians 3:14 that we receive the promise of the Spirit by faith. It is not something we earn. It is a gift.

6.3.1 OBJECTIVE
Describe the believer's need for God's power and the inability to earn merit for that power.

11 What is the one qualification a person must have to receive the Holy Spirit baptism?

If a person has received Jesus Christ as Savior, he or she is already qualified to receive the Holy Spirit baptism. On the Day of Pentecost, Peter said, "Repent and be baptized, every one of you, in the name of Jesus Christ for the forgiveness of your sins. And you will receive the gift of the Holy Spirit. The promise is for you and your children and for all who are far off—for all whom the Lord our God will call" (Acts 2:38–39, NIV).

No one must become better than he or she is to deserve the gift of the Spirit God has promised. Paul compares our spiritual lives to clay jars. He says, "We have this treasure in jars of clay to show that this all-surpassing power is from God and not from us" (2 Corinthians 4:7, NIV). Clay has imperfections. So do we. God knows that. He receives us as we are and will fill us with the Holy Spirit, who will enable us to change.

Encourage people to recognize their need of His power. Many believers speak of needing more of God. The issue for most of us is really that God needs more of us. We make room for His fullness by surrendering every area of our lives to Jesus' lordship and inviting Him to fill us with the Spirit to empower us to live for Him.

Jesus' disciples had to wait for God to pour out of His Spirit as He had promised through the prophet Joel (Joel 2:28–29). We need to seek the Spirit baptism, but we do not have to wait in the same way the disciples did. The Spirit's outpouring took place on the Day of Pentecost once and for all. Now we seek His inpouring individually.

6.3.2 OBJECTIVE
Identify speaking in tongues as the initial evidence of the Spirit's fullness.

The Initial Evidence of the Spirit's Fullness

We cannot fully understand why God chose speaking in tongues as the **initial evidence** of the Spirit's empowerment. Some believe the reason is found in the teaching of James, who says in 3:8 that "no one can tame the tongue." That idea can actually be misleading to people who are seeking the Holy Spirit baptism, because they might expect the Holy Spirit to take control of their tongue. Acts 2:4 says, "All of them were filled with the Holy Spirit and began to speak in other tongues as the Spirit enabled them" (NIV). The Spirit enabled. He did not control. The Bible is very clear that we do the speaking, although the Holy Spirit enables us.

12 What distinction is important when considering the Holy Spirit's interaction with the believer during the expression of tongues?

Three dramatic signs accompanied the outpouring of the Holy Spirit on the Day of Pentecost:

1. A rushing mighty wind
2. Tongues of fire appearing on the believers' heads
3. Speaking with other tongues (languages)

The wind and fire were not repeated after Acts 2, but speaking with tongues continued to occur when people were filled with the Spirit. (See Acts 10:46 and 19:6.)

The book of Acts is a sequel to the Gospel of Luke. Luke and Acts are a two-volume work about the lives of Jesus and His followers. To understand the first part of Acts, we must go back to the last part of Luke and remember Jesus' final instructions and commands to His followers. He said to them, "Thus it is written, that the Christ would suffer and rise again from the dead the third day, and that repentance for forgiveness of sins would be proclaimed in His name to all the nations, beginning from Jerusalem. You are witnesses of these things. And behold, I am sending forth the promise of My Father upon you; but you are to stay in the city until you are clothed with power from on high" (Luke 24:46–49).

It is difficult to imagine a more convincing sign to assure the disciples that they had truly been "clothed with power from on high" than speaking in languages they had never learned.

Some sincere Christians have interpreted this to mean that missionaries who are filled with the Holy Spirit would not need to learn other languages. I know two missionaries who temporarily received the miracle of being able to speak in another language, but it happened only once in their lives under unusual circumstances and was never repeated.

We do not totally understand why God uses the manifestation of speaking in tongues, but it certainly is a sign that what God is doing is supernatural.

While my parents were missionaries in East Africa, a man and his wife came forward in a church service to receive Christ. When the pastor prayed for them, the woman was filled with the Holy Spirit. She began to worship and praise God eloquently in English. After her time of worship and prayer, the pastor, who was fluent in English, spoke to her in English and she did not understand a word.

6.3.3
OBJECTIVE
Describe the four purposes of speaking in tongues.

Four Purposes of Tongues

Praying in tongues has four purposes in the lives of Spirit-filled believers.

1. Confirmation. Speaking in tongues is the first outward sign of the Holy Spirit baptism. This is found in Acts 2:4 and also in Acts 10 and 19. Acts 10:46 is especially instructive, because Luke records that the Jewish believers were convinced that the Gentiles had received the gift of the Holy Spirit when they heard them "speaking with tongues and exalting God."

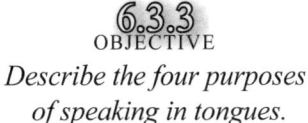

13 What are the four purposes of speaking in tongues?

2. Adoration. Our finite minds are incapable of comprehending, and our own language is inadequate to totally express, our hearts' worship to God. Speaking in tongues (what many refer to as a prayer language) frees us to communicate the worship of our hearts that is inexpressible in our limited vocabulary.

3. Edification. Praying in the Spirit edifies, or builds up, in two ways: (1) It edifies the individual who prays in the Spirit, and if interpreted, (2) it edifies the church. Paul said he spoke in tongues more than all of the Corinthians, yet he reminded them in 1 Corinthians 14:26 that in the church setting tongues should be interpreted so that all could be edified. This does not restrict the private use of tongues for personal edification, because praying in tongues spiritually builds up the believer.

With the stresses, pressures, and challenges of life, we have the blessing of praying in the Spirit beyond our own wisdom and understanding. The best way to begin every day is with prayer. The gift of praying in tongues enables us to pray beyond ourselves for each day when we do not know what we face. The Holy Spirit will pray through us to effectively seek God's divine help in everyday living.

4. Intercession. Romans 8:26 says, "The Spirit also helps our weakness; for we do not know how to pray as we should." When we pray in the Spirit, He enables us to pray beyond our understanding. Paul said, "With all prayer and petition pray at all times in the Spirit, and with this in view, be on the alert with all perseverance and petition for all the saints" (Ephesians 6:18, NASB). God uses us to work His purposes in the lives of others through the ministry of intercession.

Many years ago, my uncle was leading the regular Wednesday night Bible study and prayer meeting at his church in Wisconsin. During the prayer time, a godly deacon who worked for the railroad began praying quietly in tongues. The group fell silent and listened as he prayed in the Spirit for about ten minutes.

When he finished praying, a visiting woman stood and gave a testimony. Passing through town, she had seen a light in the church and entered the service. A missionary in Tibet for twenty years, she told the congregation that the deacon had been praying in the Tibetan dialect she knew. The deacon prayed for a Christian in China by name who was suffering under tremendous persecution. He eloquently interceded on the persecuted Christian's behalf.

Praying in the Spirit is a wonderful part of the Holy Spirit's empowerment. It confirms the experience of the Holy Spirit baptism, empowers us to effective worship, builds us up spiritually, and enables us to intercede for others beyond our own intelligence and wisdom.

Seeking Until

6.3.4 OBJECTIVE
Explain the need to seek the fullness of the Spirit and to continue being filled with the Spirit.

When people are seeking the Spirit baptism, encourage them not to worry that they will have a false experience. Jesus taught,

Ask, and it will be given to you; seek, and you will find; knock, and it will be opened to you. For everyone who asks, receives; and he who seeks, finds; and to him who knocks, it will be opened. Now suppose one of you fathers is asked by his son for a fish; he will not give him a snake instead of a fish, will he? Or if he is asked for an egg, he will not give him a scorpion, will he? If you then, being evil, know how to give good gifts to your children, how much more will your heavenly Father give the Holy Spirit to those who ask Him? (Luke 11:9–13)

14 What is a common concern of Christians who are seeking the baptism in the Holy Spirit?

If a person sincerely seeks the Lord for what He has promised, God will answer. Encourage seekers to shut the door on outside distractions and center their minds and hearts on Jesus. He is the Baptizer, and He will fill them.

If believers you know do not receive the infilling immediately, encourage them to continue seeking the Lord Jesus in faith until they receive the Spirit's fullness. God's promise and desire is to baptize every believer with the Holy Spirit.

Jesus told His followers to ask, seek, and knock. In the original Greek language, these words describe a continuous action. A more accurate translation is to keep asking. If we keep asking, keep seeking, and keep knocking, we will receive.

A Continuing Inpouring

When the Israelites fled Egypt for the Promised Land during the Exodus, God gave them bread from heaven, called manna. This heavenly food sustained them during their wilderness journey. The manna was not to be stored up and carried with them. It was given to them as they needed it.

15 Does the baptism in the Spirit guarantee a lifetime of the Spirit's full expression in the believer's life?

A life overflowing with the fullness of the Spirit is much the same. In Ephesians 5:18, when Paul exhorted the Ephesian Christians to be filled with the Spirit, the verb tense implies to "keep on being filled." The infilling of the Spirit should be ongoing. We must keep praying in the Spirit, loving in the Spirit, and living in the Spirit. The Holy Spirit baptism is not a one-time experience. We need to keep being filled. We need a continuous inpouring of the Spirit daily in our lives. His presence makes the difference between ordinary living and living with power.

Test Yourself

Circle the letter of the best answer.

1. Jesus described His imminent departure from the disciples as
   a) a blessing to them, because He would send the Holy Spirit to help them.
   b) the sign of the end of the old covenant and the beginning of the new.
   c) a parable involving five foolish and five wise bridesmaids.
   d) their ultimate test of faith in the face of persecution.

2. The Holy Spirit is best described as
   a) the third person in the Trinity whose actions are scripturally connected to personhood.
   b) an infinitely divisible flame that distributes tongues of fire among believers.
   c) a completely intangible force best described as the Holy Ghost.
   d) a dove.

3. The Holy Spirit's ministry among believers is characterized by
   a) a rushing mighty wind and tongues of fire.
   b) His permanence with them, and His presence within them.
   c) a still, small voice that directs the believer day to day.
   d) signs and wonders.

4. The word translated "power" in Acts 1:8 (*dunamis*) is best understood
   a) in the context of miracles and special revelations given to the apostles.
   b) broadly to include whatever level of ability the believer needs to obey God.
   c) as the overwhelming urge to preach the gospel.
   d) as the rushing mighty wind heard by the 120 in the Upper Room.

5. In contrast with other world religions, Christianity deals with human desires by
   a) making it clear that only the power of God can positively change those desires.
   b) recognizing that all human desire is under Satan's total control.
   c) contrasting human desire with animal desire.
   d) denying the reality of human desire.

6. When describing the evidence of a believer's walk of faith, Jesus referred to
   a) signs and wonders performed in that believer's ministry.
   b) the believer's love for others in the body of Christ.
   c) His parable of the Good Samaritan.
   d) the seven vials of judgment in Revelation.

7. The Holy Spirit baptism was given to believers for the specific purpose of
   a) encouraging them in their walk of faith.
   b) convincing them of Christ's resurrection.
   c) empowering them to share the gospel with the lost.
   d) empowering them to perform signs and wonders.

8. The one requirement in a person's life in order to receive the Holy Spirit baptism is to
   a) belong to a Pentecostal fellowship or denomination.
   b) live by the Ten Commandments and the Sermon on the Mount.
   c) accept Jesus Christ as personal Savior.
   d) renounce all attachment to the world and its wealth.

9. The four purposes of speaking in tongues are
   a) confirmation, adoration, edification, and intercession.
   b) prophecy, interpretation, word of wisdom, and word of knowledge.
   c) love, joy, peace, and longsuffering.
   d) foreign evangelism, ethnic outreach at home, confrontation with the lost, and sanctification.

10. When seeking the Holy Spirit baptism, believers can confidently receive it because
    a) it is automatically bestowed within a week of one's salvation experience.
    b) anything the believer claims in Jesus' name is guaranteed.
    c) Jesus promised it as a gift of His loving heavenly Father.
    d) all Christians will receive the Holy Spirit baptism before Jesus returns.

Responses to Interactive Questions
Chapter 6

Some of these responses may include information that is supplemental to the IST. These questions are intended to produce reflective thinking beyond the course content and your responses may vary from these examples.

1 How did Jesus describe the value of the Holy Spirit's presence in the disciples' lives?

He said the disciples would be more effective with the Spirit's presence than when Jesus was physically present.

2 How did Jesus' help the disciples recognize the priority of a relationship with the Holy Spirit?

Jesus redirected the disciples' focus from questions about the future of earthly kingdoms to the eternal impact the Holy Spirit would have in their lives as they fulfilled their immediate call to be Christ's witnesses.

3 What personality characteristics described in the Scriptures show that the Holy Spirit is not a force?

The Holy Spirit corrects, helps, and intercedes for the believer. He inspired the prophets to speak and the writers of the Scriptures to write. He clearly acts as a Person.

4 What action on Jesus part indicated the value He placed on the Holy Spirit's ministry among believers?

Jesus used much of His final hours before His crucifixion to teach the disciples extensively about the Holy Spirit.

5 What two characteristics did Jesus emphasize about the Holy Spirit's relationship to believers?

Jesus promised that the Holy Spirit would permanently remain with believers and that the Spirit would be present in believers.

6 Why is it important to recognize the broad meaning of the word translated "power" in Acts 1:8?

Believers are prone to equate Jesus' promise of power with spectacular demonstrations of divine activity, when Jesus' promise is an all-encompassing power for the day-to-day challenges of living the Christian life.

7 In regard to human desires, how do other world religions differ from Christianity?

Some religions offer to gratify human desire, others to repress or eliminate it. The Bible teaches that human desires can by changed by God's power.

8 Why is it critical to distinguish the works of the flesh from the fruit of the Spirit?

We can naturally perform the acts of the flesh. They are part and parcel of our works, done in our own power. Only the Spirit can bring about the characteristics connected to His ministry. They are His fruit.

9 What did Jesus call for as the primary outward evidence of believers' relationships to Him?

Jesus said that the believers' love for one another would prove their relationship with Him.

10 What specific purpose did Jesus connect to the Spirit's empowerment in the believer's life?

Jesus said the Spirit would empower believers to be His witnesses.

11 What is the one qualification a person must have to receive the Holy Spirit baptism?

That person must have faith in Jesus Christ as Savior. The Baptism is promised to all who are saved.

12 What distinction is important when considering the Holy Spirit's interaction with the believer during the expression of tongues?

The Holy Spirit enables the believer to speak in tongues, but He does not control the believer's act of speaking.

13 What are the four purposes of speaking in tongues?

When speaking in tongues, the believer confirms the experience of the Holy Spirit baptism, is enabled to adore and worship God beyond the limits of human language, offers encouragement to the local body of believers and experiences personal encouragement, and intercedes most effectively for the needs of others.

14 What is a common concern of Christians who are seeking the baptism in the Holy Spirit?

Believers are often concerned that they will allow their desire for the Holy Spirit's infilling to cloud their judgment and cause them to have a false experience.

15 Does the baptism in the Spirit guarantee a lifetime of the Spirit's full expression in the believer's life?

Believers are commanded to keep on being filled with the Spirit. It is an ongoing experience believers need to experience throughout life.

UNIT PROGRESS EVALUATION 2

Now that you have finished Unit 2, review the lessons in preparation for Unit Progress Evaluation 2. You will find it in the Essential Course Materials section at the back of this IST. Answer all of the questions without referring to your course materials, Bible, or notes. When you have completed the UPE, check your answers with the answer key provided in the Essential Course Materials section, and review any items you may have answered incorrectly. Then you may proceed with your study of Unit 3. (Although UPE scores do not count as part of your final course grade, they indicate how well you learned the material and how well you may perform on the closed-book final examination.)

UNIT 3

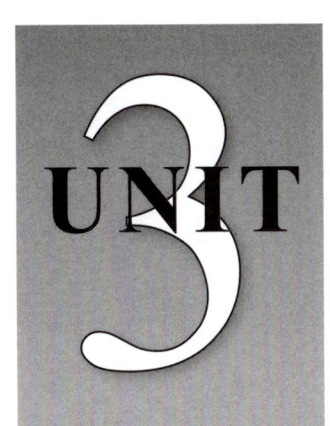

The Apostles in Evangelism

When Jesus commissioned His followers to proclaim the good news of salvation, they experienced the promised empowerment of Pentecost just ten days later.

The persecution Jesus had predicted soon followed. The response of these Spirit-filled believers was to pray not for God's protection but that they would speak the Word of God with boldness. God answered their prayer!

Peter and John, who were the only disciples who ran to the tomb with Mary after Jesus' resurrection, were filled with the Spirit and boldly declared Jesus. When the Jewish rulers, elders, and teachers of the Law "saw the courage of Peter and John and realized that they were unschooled, ordinary men, they were astonished and they took note that these men had been with Jesus" (Acts 4:13, NIV). The religious leaders decided that in order "to stop this thing from spreading any further among the people, we must warn these men to speak no longer to anyone in this name" (Acts 4:17, NIV). Then they commanded Peter and John not to speak or teach at all in the name of Jesus. Peter and John replied, "Judge for yourselves whether it is right in God's sight to obey you rather than God. For we cannot help speaking about what we have seen and heard" (Acts 4:19–20).

One of the persecutors of the Early Church, Saul of Tarsus, became an apostle and bold preacher of the gospel of Jesus. The fire of evangelism had begun to spread from Jerusalem to Antioch and out into the world.

Although almost two thousand years have passed, the message and methods of the apostles are as effective today as in the first century. The message of the apostles was focused on our Savior and Lord. They preached one message, as the apostle Paul wrote to the Corinthians: "Jesus Christ, and Him crucified" (1 Corinthians 2:2). Not only was their message clear, but their methods were practical and effective.

A study of Peter's preaching in the book of Acts and Paul's instructions in his epistles equips believers today to be effective witnesses for the Lord we serve.

Chapter 7   Evangelism in Peter's Preaching

Lessons
7.1   Peter's Message in Acts
7.2   Peter's Message in Mark

Chapter 8   Evangelism in Paul's Teaching

Lessons
8.1   Comprehensive Witness
8.2   The Spiritual Harvest Process
8.3   Paul's Principles

Chapter 9   Paul's Evangelism Practices

Lessons
9.1   Pray for Open Doors
9.2   Share Christ Clearly
9.3   Be Wise with Outsiders
9.4   Make the Most of Opportunities
9.5   Speak with Grace
9.6   Respond Individually

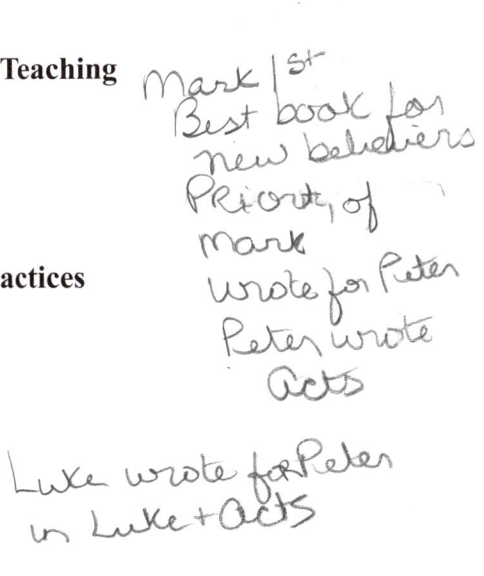

Chapter 10   Motivation for Evangelism

Lessons
10.1   Motivation Levels
10.2   Maintaining Motivation

CHAPTER 7

Evangelism in Peter's Preaching

Missionary Bernhard Johnson saw more than 1.8 million people come forward to receive Christ in evangelistic outreaches in Brazil. I once asked him, "What about your preaching do you believe accounts for the great numbers who respond in your services?"

I thought Bernhard would respond concerning "the confirmation of the word with signs following" (Mark 16:20, KJV). Many miracles had taken place in his crusades. Lame people walked, and blind people received sight. I thought it was the manifestation of the miraculous that produced so many salvation decisions.

Bernhard's response surprised me.

He replied, "I always exalt Jesus Christ."

From the earliest days of missions in our Fellowship, we have depended upon the powerful working of the Holy Spirit in signs and wonders. However, it is the clear preaching of the gospel of Jesus Christ that produces the results.

W.W. Simpson, one of the earliest Assemblies of God missionaries to China, said that the Pentecostal message "is the simple preaching of the real Jesus as revealed in the Gospels . . . showing how He really took our place on the cross and became our sin and thus put away our sins forever as proved by His rising from the dead."

Lesson 7.1   Peter's Message in Acts

Objectives

7.1.1   Identify the two primary themes of Peter's gospel proclamations in Acts.
7.1.2   Outline the outworking of Peter's themes in each of five messages.
7.1.3   Explain the priority of the identification of who Jesus is and the purpose of His mission when communicating the gospel.
7.1.4   Explain how to preserve an accurate understanding of Jesus' identity and mission in the face of false popular conceptions.

Lesson 7.2   Peter's Message in Mark

Objectives

7.2.1   Describe the value of the simple power of the Gospel of Mark as an evangelism tool.
7.2.2   Explain the rationale for crediting Peter as Mark's primary source.
7.2.3   Identify the two primary themes concerning Jesus in Mark's Gospel.
7.2.4   Cite the expressions of two primary themes throughout Mark.

LESSON 7.1

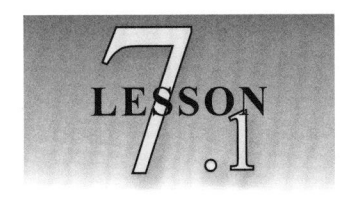

7.1.1 OBJECTIVE
Identify the two primary themes of Peter's gospel proclamations in Acts.

1   In Peter's five proclamations in the book of Acts, what are his two themes?

7.1.2 OBJECTIVE
Outline the outworking of Peter's themes in each of five messages.

Peter's Message in Acts

After Jesus' ascension, the apostle Peter became one of the most prominent voices in the New Testament church. In the power of the Holy Spirit, this uneducated fisherman became an eloquent and forceful preacher of the good news about Jesus.

As a testimony of God's redemptive mercy, Peter was chosen by God to preach the sermon on the Day of Pentecost, only fifty-three days after Peter denied his Lord. In the Spirit's power and anointing, Peter, who had been fearful of a woman's accusation that he was one of Jesus' followers, now boldly proclaimed the message of the Savior.

The appendices of this course present a variety of well-known approaches to presenting the plan of salvation, such as the ABCs of Salvation, the Roman Road, and the Four Spiritual Laws. I have found the simplest and most effective approach to sharing Christ with a nonbeliever is patterned after the apostle Peter's preaching in the book of Acts and the Gospel of Mark.

In the book of Acts, Luke records simple proclamations of the gospel by Peter in chapters 2, 3, 4, 5, and 10. When these presentations are analyzed, they show that in each presentation Peter addresses two basic truths: *who* Jesus is and *why* He gave His life. A similar presentation of these two points is found in the Gospel of Mark, which is probably Mark's record of Peter's apostolic preaching.

The Day of Pentecost

Peter preached his best-known sermon on the Day of Pentecost. The key components of the passage relating to who Jesus is and why He gave His life are in italics.

"Men of Israel, listen to these words: Jesus the Nazarene, *a man attested to you by God with miracles and wonders and signs which God performed through Him in your midst, just as you yourselves know*—this Man, delivered over by the *predetermined plan and foreknowledge of God*, you nailed to a cross by the hands of godless men and put Him to death. "But *God raised Him up again, putting an end to the agony of death, since it was impossible for Him to be held in its power.* "For David says of Him, 'I saw the Lord always in my presence; for He is at my right hand, so that I will not be shaken. Therefore my heart was glad and my tongue exulted; moreover my flesh also will live in hope; because you will not abandon my soul to Hades, nor allow your holy one to undergo decay. You have made known to me the ways of life; you will make me full of gladness with your presence.' "Brethren, I may confidently say to you regarding the patriarch David that he both died and was buried, and his tomb is with us to this day. "And so, because he was a prophet and knew that God had sworn to Him with an oath to seat one of His descendants on His throne, he looked ahead and spoke of the resurrection of the Christ, that He was neither abandoned to Hades, nor did His flesh suffer decay. *"This Jesus God raised up again, to which we are all witnesses. "Therefore having been exalted to the right hand of God, and having received from the Father the promise of the Holy Spirit, He has poured forth this which you both see and hear.* "For it was not David who ascended into heaven, but he himself says: 'The Lord said to my Lord, "Sit at my right hand, until I make your enemies a footstool for your feet." "Therefore let all the house of Israel know for certain that *God has made Him both Lord and Christ*—this Jesus whom you crucified." (Acts 2:22–36, emphasis added)

Through these statements, Peter proclaimed who Jesus is and why He gave His life. Following are the portions of his sermon that address each of those themes:

Who

- A man attested to you by God with miracles and wonders and signs which God performed through Him in your midst
- God has made Him both Lord and Christ

Why

- Predetermined plan and foreknowledge of God
- God raised Him up again, putting an end to the agony of death, since it was impossible for Him to be held in its power
- This Jesus God raised up again, to which we are all witnesses
- Having been exalted to the right hand of God, and having received from the Father the promise of the Holy Spirit, He has poured forth this which you both see and hear

Other Sermons in Acts

7.1.3 OBJECTIVE
Explain the priority of the identification of who Jesus is and the purpose of His mission when communicating the gospel.

The following key points are found in four additional Acts' passages. (The wording is from the NASB.)

Acts 3

Who

- His servant Jesus
- The Holy and Righteous One
- The Prince of life
- The Christ

Why

- His Christ would suffer
- That your sins may be wiped away, in order that times of refreshing may come from the presence of the Lord
- Heaven must receive
- Bless you by turning every one of you from your wicked ways

Acts 4

Who

- Jesus Christ the Nazarene
- The Stone that was rejected
- The chief cornerstone

Why

- Crucified, whom God raised from the dead
- Salvation in no one else; for there is no other name under heaven that has been given among men by which we must be saved

Acts 5

Who

- Prince
- Savior

Evangelism in Peter's Preaching

Why

- Put to death by hanging Him on a cross
- The one whom God exalted to His right hand
- Grant repentance to Israel
- Forgiveness of sins

Acts 10

Who

- Lord of All
- Jesus of Nazareth
- Anointed Him with the Holy Spirit and with power
- He went about doing good and healing all who were oppressed by the devil, for God was with Him
- One who has been appointed by God as Judge of the living and the dead

Why

- Put Him to death by hanging Him on the cross
- God raised Him up on the third day
- Through His name everyone who believes in Him receives forgiveness of sins

Who and Why

Peter's preaching in the book of Acts (2:22–36; 3:12–26; 4:8–12; 10:34–43) always answers two basic questions:

1. Who was Jesus?
2. Why did He give His life?

Being prepared to discuss these two questions will equip a person to effectively share Christ with nonbelievers.

1. Who was Jesus?

To nonbelievers with no Christian background, I suggest first looking at the question, "Who was Jesus?" in an historical context—speaking of Jesus incarnate in human form two thousand years ago—before progressing to "Who is Jesus?"—the living, resurrected Christ.

When sharing the message of Jesus with a nonbeliever, it is important not only to communicate who Jesus was but also who He was not.

In recent years, Jesus has received attention in the media. Cover stories about Jesus have appeared in many national news magazines. Television programs and miniseries have been made about Him.

Accounts of Christ's life by secular media almost always present Jesus as a fictional character. Even when He is shown as an historical person, He is depicted as a great teacher, or even a prophet, but only a man.

Jesus was much more than a teacher and prophet. He was God in human form. He was conceived by the Holy Spirit, born of a virgin, lived a sinless life, died for our sins, and conquered death by rising again to offer us forgiveness of sin and the gift of everlasting life.

If Jesus Christ was not who He claimed to be, if He is not the crucified and risen Son of God, then as the apostle Paul declared in 1 Corinthians 15:17, our

---

7.1.4 OBJECTIVE
Explain how to preserve an accurate understanding of Jesus' identity and mission in the face of false popular conceptions.

2 Why must a full presentation of Jesus' identity also explain who He is not?

3 What is Christianity if Jesus is not divine?

faith is useless. Paul wrote, "There is one God and one mediator also between God and men, the man Christ Jesus" (1 Timothy 2:5).

2. Why did He give His life?

The Jews nor the Romans can be blamed for Jesus' death. His life was not taken from Him. He gave it. Jesus said, "The Father loves Me, because I lay down My life so that I may take it again. No one has taken it away from Me, but I lay it down on My own initiative. I have authority to lay it down, and I have authority to take it up again" (John 10:17–18). The sins of all humankind are responsible for Jesus' death.

John the Baptist announced why Jesus came to earth when he said, "Behold, the Lamb of God who takes away the sin of the world!" (John 1:29). Why? The existence of the cross clearly establishes two facts:

1. We are sinners.

2. There is nothing we could do about it.

The reason Jesus gave His life is because each of us has sinned and is separated from God. The punishment for sin is death, according to Romans 6:23. This kind of death is not physical. It means our spirit, which lives forever, will be in everlasting punishment in hell. Jesus explained that hell is like a lake of fire and that everyone who goes there is separated from God forever and burns in fire that never ends. (See Mark 9:47–48 and Revelation 20:15.)

God sent His Son to pay the penalty for our sins. Jesus was born as a man, but He lived His life without sin. Men lied about Him and judged Him guilty of things He had never done. Then they hanged Him on a cross to die. Jesus never sinned, but He was punished for sin. So death had no power over Him, and He came back to life after three days (Mark 8:31; 9:31; 14:27–28). Now He offers everlasting life to anyone who receives Him.

It is significant that like Peter, Paul communicated the same two truths at Thessalonica. Luke summarizes Paul's teaching in the synagogues on Sabbath days. "According to Paul's custom, he went to them, and for three Sabbaths reasoned with them from the Scriptures, explaining and giving evidence that the *Christ had to suffer and rise again from the dead*, and saying, '*This Jesus whom I am proclaiming to you is the Christ*'" (Acts 17:2–3, emphasis added).

A simple presentation of the gospel should include these two facts about Jesus—who He is and why He gave His life. Both are essential to understanding God's grace that was manifest through Jesus' death on the cross, His resurrection, and His consequent purchase of the redemption of all mankind. He accomplished what John the Baptist prophesied He would do, take away the sin of the world (John 1:29).

4 Why is it inaccurate to blame the Romans or Jews for Jesus' death?

5 Why is it wrong to view God the Father as judge in contrast to God the Son as love?

LESSON 7.2

Peter's Message in Mark

The Character of the Gospels

The Gospel of John is the most distributed book of the Bible. No single Bible verse is better known than John 3:16. For many decades, John's Gospel has been widely distributed. Because of the Gospel's extensive distribution, many assume it to be the most appropriate book of the Bible for evangelism. Many involved in missions and evangelism prefer to use Mark's Gospel when witnessing to nonbelievers.

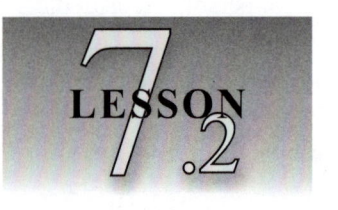

The Distinctive of Mark

7.2.1 OBJECTIVE
Describe the value of the simple power of the Gospel of Mark as an evangelism tool.

For centuries scholars believed that the Gospel of Mark was a condensed version of Matthew. This persuasion was scarcely challenged until the nineteenth century. After careful scholarship, scholars now accept that Mark's Gospel was the first of the four written records of Jesus' life.

7.2.2 OBJECTIVE
Explain the rationale for crediting Peter as Mark's primary source.

Mark traveled extensively with both the apostles Paul and Peter. He was influenced first by the lucid and powerful doctrinal teaching of Paul and then, after Paul's death, by Peter's firsthand accounts of Jesus' life and teaching. We know from church historians that Mark wrote what he learned from Peter's preaching about Jesus. Irenaeus wrote in AD 175, "Mark, the disciple and interpreter of Peter, also transmitted to us in writing the things preached by Peter."

6 What distinguishes the Gospel of Mark from the other three Gospels?

Of the four Gospels, Mark's record is the simplest, shortest, and most direct presentation of Jesus' life, written in the common language of the marketplace. None of the other Gospels devotes as great a portion of its content to Jesus' suffering, death, and resurrection. Mark does not mention Christ's genealogy or birth. He begins his Gospel by describing John the Baptist's preaching and baptism, followed by Jesus' baptism and temptation. He then records Jesus' public ministry in Galilee, giving special attention to His miraculous works that prove Him to be the Son of God.

7 What were the circumstances under which Mark wrote his Gospel?

Mark wrote his account of Christ's life during a time of great persecution under the Roman emperor, Nero. Many Christians in Rome were living in underground caves, hiding for their lives. Anyone who confessed Jesus Christ as the Son of God could be tortured and put to death by cruel methods.

Mark's Gospel was intended to comfort the early Christians during the hardest time the Church had experienced. Mark's words strengthened Christians and encouraged them to be faithful to Jesus at a time when the Christian life meant either the catacombs or the arena.

In a call to discipleship, Jesus demanded a radical surrender of life: "If anyone wishes to come after Me, he must deny himself, and take up his cross and follow Me. For whoever wishes to save his life will lose it, but whoever loses his life for My sake and the gospel's will save it. For what does it profit a man to gain the whole world, and forfeit his soul?" (Mark 8:34–36).

The Gospel of Mark has an unmistakable touch of reality. Because most of the information in Mark almost certainly came from Peter, it contains details that could be known only by an eyewitness to Jesus' life. Mark's Gospel contributes a special sense of historical accuracy to the written record of Jesus' life. For example, when speaking of Jesus and the children, only Mark tells that Jesus took the children in His arms (Mark 9:36). In the account of the demon-possessed man (5:5), only Mark tells that the man was always crying out and bruising himself with stones. Only Mark tells that during the storm at sea, Jesus was in the back of the boat, sleeping on a cushion (4:38).

Mark gives the actual words of Jesus in the Aramaic language more often than the other Gospel writers. Since Mark's Gospel is probably a written account of what Peter shared orally, it seems that Peter must have recalled the actual voice of Jesus speaking in Aramaic, Jesus' first language, rather than Greek.

Who and Why

7.2.3 OBJECTIVE
Identify the two primary themes concerning Jesus in Mark's Gospel.

The Gospel of Mark is really a sermon in written form and is especially helpful for presenting Christ to a nonbeliever.

As with all of Peter's sermons about Jesus recorded in the book of Acts, his presentation of Christ in the Gospel of Mark answers two simple but critical questions. The book is divided almost equally in half. The first half presents who Jesus is, and the second half presents why He gave His life.

The first half of Mark powerfully builds the case for who Jesus is in two ways:

1. By the succession of His miraculous works.
2. By continually confronting the reader to make a decision concerning who Jesus is.

From the earliest part of chapter 1 through the end of chapter 8, Mark records seventeen of Jesus' miracles and repeatedly draws attention to the significance of who Jesus is. In the first half of Mark's Gospel, the word *who* is often used.

In the first chapter, Mark declares that Jesus is the Son of God. Even demons gave this testimony: "I know who you are—the Holy One of God!" (Mark 1:24). Jesus did not permit the demons to speak "because they knew who he was" (Mark 1:34).

In Mark 2:7, the scribes said, "Who can forgive sins but God alone?" In chapter 4, after Jesus miraculously calmed the storm, the disciples said to one another, "Who then is this, that even the wind and the sea obey Him?" (4:41).

The climax of Mark's presentation of who Jesus is comes at the close of chapter 8: "Jesus went out, along with His disciples, to the villages of Caesarea Philippi; and on the way He questioned His disciples, saying to them, 'Who do people say that I am?' They told Him, saying, 'John the Baptist; and others say Elijah; but others, one of the prophets.' And He continued by questioning them, 'But who do you say that I am?' Peter answered and said to Him, 'You are the Christ'" (Mark 8:27–29).

The second half of Mark focuses on why Jesus gave His life. It describes the final week of Jesus' life on earth—His suffering, death, and resurrection. In a series of statements, Jesus reveals the purpose for which He was sent into the world: "He began to teach them that the Son of Man must suffer many things and be rejected by the elders and the chief priests and the scribes, and be killed, and after three days rise again" (Mark 8:31). He said to His disciples, 'The Son of Man is to be delivered into the hands of men, and they will kill Him; and when He has been killed, He will rise three days later'" (Mark 9:31). Later, He said, "'We are going up to Jerusalem, and the Son of Man will be delivered to the chief priests and the scribes; and they will condemn Him to death and will hand Him over to the Gentiles. They will mock Him and spit on Him, and scourge Him and kill Him, and three days later He will rise again'" (Mark 10:33–34).

The Confessions

Also contained in Mark are three dramatic confessions. In the first verse, Mark confesses Jesus as the Son of God. This is followed by Peter's confession in the middle of the book (8:29), "You are the Christ," and builds to the Roman centurion's confession, "Truly this man was the Son of God!" (15:39). These three confessions can be reiterated to encourage a person to make a decision to follow Christ.

The simple, yet powerful, witness of Mark's Gospel is appropriate for evangelism and new believers, because it presents the good news concerning who Jesus is and why He gave His life.

Mark's record of Peter's apostolic preaching concerning the life, death, and resurrection of Jesus is an extended version of the same two essential truths that characterize Peter's preaching in the book of Acts. Those two points are as essential today as when Peter and Paul preached them almost two thousand years ago.

---

8 What literary form does Mark take with his Gospel?

9 What theme pervades the first half of Mark's Gospel?

10 How does Mark focus the second half of his Gospel?

7.2.4 OBJECTIVE
Cite the expressions of two primary themes throughout Mark.

Evangelism in Peter's Preaching

Test Yourself

Circle the letter of the best answer.

1. In Peter's five proclamations in the book of Acts, the apostle focuses on the two themes of
   a) who Jesus is and why He gave His life.
   b) the promise of the Holy Spirit and its fulfillment in the lives of believers.
   c) the reward of the righteous and the punishment of the wicked.
   d) the gospel as expressed to the Jews and as expressed to the Gentiles.

2. A full proclamation of Jesus' identity often includes
   a) an explanation of who Jesus is not.
   b) messages of tongues and interpretation to endorse the message.
   c) quotations from the Sermon on the Mount.
   d) the connection of the New Testament name *Jesus* with the Old Testament name *Joshua*.

3. The Scriptures make it clear that the believer's faith is useless unless
   a) the believer also obeys the Ten Commandments.
   b) he or she speaks in tongues.
   c) he or she serves on the foreign mission field for at least a year.
   d) Jesus Christ died and rose again.

4. The Romans and the Jews, for their part in Jesus' crucifixion, are best understood as
   a) primarily responsible for Jesus' death but forgiven.
   b) primarily responsible for Jesus' death and guilty through the generations.
   c) obedient servants of God the Father in carrying out His plan for His Son.
   d) representative of all sinful people for whom Jesus gave His life.

5. John the Baptist said that Jesus came to "take away the sin of the world." Therefore,
   a) everyone will eventually be saved for eternity.
   b) no one is any longer guilty of sin.
   c) anyone, regardless of background or sins committed, can accept God's forgiveness.
   d) there has been an eternal, uncrossable line drawn between the elect and the lost.

6. The Gospel of Mark is distinguished from the other three in that it is
   a) the simplest, shortest, and most direct record of Jesus' life.
   b) written in Greek.
   c) dated last in composition.
   d) best understood by mature believers who have studied the other three Gospels.

7. Mark wrote his Gospel during a time when Christians
   a) had become prosperous and were compromising their faith.
   b) were following heretical teachings about Jesus.
   c) were being severely persecuted and needed encouragement.
   d) had split into two churches and elected two popes.

8. The structure of the Gospel of Mark is best described as
   a) a biography of Jesus' life used as a model by many secular historians.
   b) a sermon in written form ideally suited for presenting Christ to nonbelievers.
   c) a parable that connects Jesus' divine identity with the symbols He used in His teaching.
   d) iambic pentameter.

9. The early chapters of Mark portray who Jesus is by
   a) connecting Jesus' birth with Old Testament prophecy.
   b) recounting Jesus' miracles and confronting the reader to make a personal choice.
   c) examining Jesus' teaching from the Sermon on the Mount.
   d) relating Mark's life and interaction with Jesus as a disciple.

10. When Mark considers why Jesus gave His life, he uses
    a) allegory and extensive metaphor.
    b) cross-references from Paul's early writings.
    c) extensive details of Jesus' last week on earth and Jesus' own statements.
    d) Stephen's promise to Mary that a sword would pierce her heart.

Responses to Interactive Questions
Chapter 7

Some of these responses may include information that is supplemental to the IST. These questions are intended to produce reflective thinking beyond the course content and your responses may vary from these examples.

1   In Peter's five proclamations in the Book of Acts, what are his two themes?

Peter spoke of who Jesus is and why He gave His life.

2   Why must a full presentation of Jesus' identity also explain who He is not?

Popular presentations of Jesus in today's media distort His identity as God, presenting Him as fictional or only human.

3   What is Christianity if Jesus is not divine?

The Scriptures make it clear that our faith is useless if Jesus is not the crucified and risen Son of God.

4   Why is it inaccurate to blame the Romans or Jews for Jesus' death?

Jesus gave His life freely for the redemption of all humanity, according to John 10:17–18.

5   Why is it wrong to view God the Father as *judge* in contrast to God the Son as *love*?

The Trinity worked in cooperation to bring about redemption. God the Father sent His Son to save the world. The Son obediently came.

6   What distinguishes the Gospel of Mark from the other three gospels?

Mark is the simplest, shortest, and most direct presentation of Jesus' life.

7   What were the circumstances under which Mark wrote his Gospel?

Mark wrote his account of Christ's life during a time of great persecution in the Roman Empire. It was intended to comfort and encourage Christians.

8   What literary form does Mark take with his Gospel?

Mark wrote his Gospel as a sermon on the life of Christ. This renders his Gospel especially helpful for presenting Christ to the lost.

9   What theme pervades the first half of Mark's Gospel?

Mark powerfully builds the case for who Jesus is by recounting Christ's miracles and confronting the reader with a challenge to accept or reject that evidence.

10 How does Mark focus the second half of his Gospel?

Mark considers why Jesus gave His life as he describes Jesus' final week of life on earth and uses Jesus' statements to identify Jesus' purpose.

Evangelism in Paul's Teaching

In 1954, Assemblies of God evangelist Paul Cantelon conducted a crusade on the island of Guernsey, off the coast of England. In a rented hall, he preached evangelistic meetings for a week. Not one person responded to the salvation invitations. Paul Cantelon left the island discouraged, feeling that the ministry was a failure.

Unknown to Cantelon, John Blanchard, a twenty-two-year-old civil servant, was invited to the crusade by a young lady from one of the Elim churches. John attended several services with her. On the last night, although he did not respond openly to the invitation, he prayed and accepted Christ. Four days later he began witnessing and preaching to young people on the island. John Blanchard married the girl who invited him to Cantelon's evangelistic meetings. Within seven years, nearly eighty young people had come to Christ, and over twenty were called into full-time ministry.

In 1977, Blanchard was invited to become the minister of Westminster Chapel in London. He declined because of the conviction that God wanted him to continue his international ministry of evangelism and Bible teaching. He has preached around the world and written many books, including *Right With God*, which was Britain's best-selling evangelistic book for seven years; it has been translated into fifteen languages.

While speaking in Glendale, California, he shared his testimony. He mentioned that he had been converted under the ministry of Paul Cantelon but had never met him or had the opportunity to tell him. A member of the staff made some inquires, then handed John Blanchard Paul Cantelon's address.

John Blanchard wrote to Paul Cantelon:

My beloved father in Christ, no words of mine will ever be able to express adequately what, under God, I owe to you. Nearly 25 years ago your faithful ministry was the means of bringing me out of darkness "into His marvelous light." I still have the leaflet advertising those meetings, and I treasure it deeply, but no mere souvenir can take the place of the miracle of the new birth that happened to me then, nor of the glorious new life that has been mine ever since.

The very least I can do is to send you this letter of heartfelt thanks and to let you know of the esteem in which I shall forever hold you. I trust that it will be a means of encouragement to you, and yet another confirmation in your own heart that "the gospel is the power of God unto salvation."

I simply send you a gratitude that is beyond all words, and praise God that you responded to that call many years ago to preach on our little island.

It cannot be known how many people have come to Christ through the ministry of John Blanchard, the young man who gave his heart to Christ on the last night of that crusade on the island of Guernsey back in 1954.

Lesson 8.1   Comprehensive Witness

Objectives

8.1.1   Identify the three components of a comprehensive, effective witness.
8.1.2   Develop the content of personal witness around the subject of Jesus Christ.
8.1.3   Describe how to conform your manner of speech and lifestyle to your personal witness content.
8.1.4   Explain how to recognize and depend on the Holy Spirit's ability to empower all three components of your witness.

Evangelism in Paul's Teaching

Lesson 8.2   The Spiritual Harvest Process

Objectives

8.2.1   *Recognize the potential in any person to respond to the gospel.*

8.2.2   *Define one's responsibility and privilege to communicate God's Word to the lost.*

8.2.3   *Explain how to rely on God to continually be at work in unbelievers' lives.*

8.2.4   *Describe four ways in which God's Word impacts a life.*

Lesson 8.3   Paul's Principles

Objectives

8.3.1   *Identify Paul's evangelism message, method, and means.*

8.3.2   *Explain the relationship in evangelism between dependence and discipline.*

8.3.3   *Describe the role of personal will and action in relation to God's activity.*

8.3.4   *Describe the function of response evangelism.*

LESSON 8.1

8.1.1 OBJECTIVE
Identify the three components of a comprehensive, effective witness.

1. What three elements of a comprehensive gospel witness do both Paul and Peter identify?

Comprehensive Witness

Paul wrote to the believers at Thessalonica, "Our gospel did not come to you in word only, but also in power and in the Holy Spirit and with full conviction; just as you know what kind of men we proved to be among you for your sake" (1 Thessalonians 1:5).

Paul's witness was not merely *what* he said ("not … in word only"), but also how he said it ("in power and in the Holy Spirit and with full conviction") and who he was ("you know what kind of men we proved to be among you for your sake").

Peter presents the same three components of effective witness in his first epistle: "But in your hearts set apart Christ as Lord. Always be prepared to give an answer to everyone who asks you to give the reason for the hope that you have. But do this with gentleness and respect, keeping a clear conscience, so that those who speak maliciously against your good behavior in Christ may be ashamed of their slander" (1 Peter 3:15–16, NIV).

Notice that Peter indicates what witnesses should say: "the reason for the hope that you have." He also emphasizes how we should say it: "with gentleness and respect." He stresses the importance of who we are—our character, speaking of a "clear conscience" and "good behavior in Christ."

More than three hundred years before Paul and Peter wrote their epistles, Aristotle, the Greek philosopher, in his book *Rhetoric*, presented the following three components of public speech and communication:

1. *Logos*, translated "the word" in John 1:1: "In the beginning was the *word*," refers to the content of our message.

2. *Pathos*, from which we get the English words "passion" and "pathetic," has to do with feeling and emotion. Aristotle believed that the emotion with which content is communicated is an integral part of the message.

3. *Ethos*, from which we get the word ethnic, means what *kind* of person the speaker is. The speaker's reputation and character are also vital to the message.

Aristotle said almost the same thing as Peter and Paul. Our message is what we say, how we say it, and who we are.

Teaching these three principles of communication will help believers develop a comprehensive approach to personal witness.

Vocal Witness (What We Say)

8.1.2 OBJECTIVE
Develop the content of personal witness around the subject of Jesus Christ.

Our Lord's commands are clear. Evangelism involves speech. A term that has come into prominence is *lifestyle* evangelism. An excellent book by that title was written by Joseph Aldrich. It rightly emphasized a critical need for forming friendships with nonbelievers and living credible Christian lives in personal evangelism. Unfortunately, some have interpreted lifestyle evangelism as an excuse not to share their faith vocally.

2 How can the valuable concept of *lifestyle evangelism* be misused?

The gospel is a message that must be conveyed in words. The study of evangelism in the New Testament reveals that the focus of our message should be Jesus.

When the Early Church was born, the message of believers always focused on the person Jesus Christ. As they boldly and clearly proclaimed Jesus, great numbers believed.

Vital Witness (How We Say It)

8.1.3 OBJECTIVE
Describe how to conform your manner of speech and lifestyle to your personal witness content.

Our words must have vitality. How we say things communicates as much as what we say. Passion is contagious. It is not necessarily conveyed by volume but through evident sincerity and conviction. To be convincing, we must first be convinced. If we are not moved by our message, it is unlikely we will move anyone else.

3 What is a key component to giving our words vitality?

Our emotions, attitudes, and actions are as much a part of our message as our words. In his letter to the Colossians, Paul said, "Conduct yourselves with wisdom toward outsiders, making the most of the opportunity. Let your speech *always be with grace*, as though seasoned with salt, so that you will know how you should respond to each person" (Colossians 4:5–6).

Peter wrote, "Always be prepared to give an answer to everyone who asks you to give the reason for the hope that you have. But *do* this with gentleness and respect, keeping a clear conscience, so that those who speak maliciously against your good behavior in Christ may be ashamed of their slander" (1 Peter 3:15–16, NIV).

Notice that both Paul and Peter emphasize a witness that includes more than mere words. Paul says our speech should "always be with grace." Peter says we should speak "with gentleness and respect."

Valid Witness (Who We Are)

4 Why is Christian character vital to the communication of the gospel?

The validity of our witness is related to the credibility of our lives. Effective witness depends on character. This has always been true, but in a culture that is increasingly skeptical of Christianity, it is even more critical. The content of our message will be hindered if our manner and actions are inconsistent with our words. With many people, especially those we know personally, our testimony of the difference Christ has made in our lives and its consistent proof through our actions will be what most compels them to Christ.

In many countries, Christianity is not a prominent religion. The Christian population is small, and Christian media do not exist. This can offer a great advantage in evangelism, because the first witness unbelievers in those countries receive is from someone they know whose life has changed after receiving Christ.

Evangelism in Paul's Teaching

They do not have to overcome negative perceptions that come from knowing people who communicate a Christian message but whose lives do not affirm it.

In a society where people are losing faith in the integrity of government and business leaders, the personal credibility of Christians is not merely an added blessing in witness but an essential requirement.

Power for All Three Components of Witness

8.1.4 OBJECTIVE
Explain how to recognize and depend on the Holy Spirit's ability to empower all three components of your witness.

In Paul's testimony to the Thessalonians concerning his witness, he states that it was "in power and in the Holy Spirit." As Jesus promised, the Holy Spirit's power enables us in the three components of our message—what we say, how we say it, and who we are. The Spirit's power is wonderfully broad and applies in every way that is needed to be His witnesses.

The Holy Spirit empowers our witness in what we say. As He did for the New Testament Christians after the Day of Pentecost, the Spirit gives us the internal motivation to speak about Jesus, confident in His (the Spirit's) convincing work. The early Christians prayed for that kind of help: "Grant that Your bond-servants may speak Your word with all confidence" (Acts 4:29).

5 What role does the Holy Spirit play in our effective gospel witness?

The Holy Spirit also helps us in how we speak to communicate Christ as Paul did "in power and in the Holy Spirit and with full conviction" (1 Thessalonians 1:5). The Spirit moves us in our witness with a sincere, compelling passion.

The Holy Spirit enables our character to become what God has called us to be as the fruit of the Spirit—the nature of Jesus Christ—become evident in our lives.

The power Jesus promised His followers is for every aspect of Christian living. It enables us to do and be whatever our Lord has purposed in our lives. The Holy Spirit baptism opens the way to a life of effective witness for Christ in what we say, how we say it, and who we are.

LESSON 8.2

The Spiritual Harvest Process

While addressing problems in the church at Corinth, Paul offers a revealing truth about the nature of evangelism.

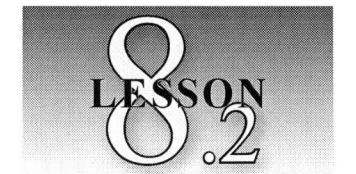

8.2.1 OBJECTIVE
Recognize the potential in any person to respond to the gospel.

First Corinthians 3:4-8 is most often referenced for teaching concerning local church division. In Corinth, believers were either aligning themselves as those "of Paul" or those "of Apollos." It is natural to have a special affection and respect for a person God used to help lead us into a relationship with Christ. Paul does not say this is evil, just human. He writes,

> For when one says, "I am of Paul," and another, "I am of Apollos," are you not mere men? What then is Apollos? And what is Paul? Servants through whom you believed, even as the Lord gave opportunity to each one. I planted, Apollos watered, but God was causing the growth. So then neither the one who plants nor the one who waters is anything, but God who causes the growth. Now he who plants and he who waters are one; but each will receive his own reward according to his own labor. (1 Corinthians 3:5–8)

6 Is it wrong to express affection and respect for specific spiritual leaders?

Paul was not rebuking the believers for having special affection and respect for him and Apollos. Both were spiritual fathers to the Corinthians. What Paul is communicating is that if that relationship is all people see, they do not understand the nature of how God gathers the spiritual harvest. The Corinthians were only believers because the Lord gave opportunity, and Paul and Apollos were servants through whom they believed. Three evangelism principles can be gleaned from this passage.

The Potential Is in the Soil

We can never tell from the appearance of people whether they will be truly productive soil for the gospel. Some of those who appear responsive will not last, and some who appear unresponsive are only initially so. In the end they may not only produce life but are also a means of multiplying the message.

Too often people analyze the demographics of a certain area and try to predict where a fruitful field will be in which to sow the gospel. God is working in ways that are not visible or obvious to us. We must be obedient to His call to proclaim the message everywhere, even in places that do not appear to be responsive. God does not waste the efforts of His laborers. He does not send them to fields where no harvest will be gathered. Some fields are harder than others. Wherever we are sent by the Lord of the harvest, there is good ground in which the message will grow and multiply.

The Privilege Is the Servant's

In the spiritual harvest of God's kingdom, God causes the growth. We enter into the work of the Holy Spirit. Evangelism is not only a human effort to persuade nonbelievers to come to Christ. Evangelism involves God's servants planting and watering the message in every way possible, knowing that God is the harvester. He gives us the privilege of entering into His work.

When I have the privilege of witnessing to someone and leading him or her in a prayer to receive Christ, I learn that God has almost always used other people in the preparation process. John Wesley referred to this activity of the Holy Spirit as **prevenient grace**.

After teaching the Parable of the Sower, Jesus explained that "the message about the kingdom" is the seed in the spiritual harvest" (Matthew 13:1–19, NIV). The Holy Spirit prepares the soil (people's hearts) to receive the message. The servant's role in evangelism is to enter into the Holy Spirit's work in people's lives. Jesus said to His disciples, "The saying is true, 'One sows and another reaps.' I sent you to reap that for which you have not labored; others have labored and you have entered into their labor (John 4:38).

Paul said in 1 Corinthians 3:6, "I planted, Apollos watered, but God was causing the growth." God's servants plant and water the seed. God causes the growth.

God's work in the spiritual harvest is distinguished from that of His human servants. The time factors Paul describes in this process are different for God's work and for our work. When Paul and Apollos planted and watered the seed (the message), the Greek verb tenses indicate specific time frames. For a period of time, Paul planted the seed. For another period of time, Apollos watered it. When Paul describes God's activity in this process, the verb tense in Greek reveals that God did not work only after the seed was planted and watered but all along God was causing the growth.

In a responsive conversation with a nonbeliever, we cannot always share what we might consider to be a complete presentation of the gospel. But few people make a decision for Christ because of a single encounter, and we can still guide a responsive conversation, even if we do not control it. We are planting and watering the message. God is causing the growth. The Holy Spirit brings people to decision.

Before we sow the seed of God's message into the lives of people, the Holy Spirit has gone before us to prepare the soil of their hearts to receive the seed.

---

7 What do the different types of soil in the Bible's planting analogies tell us about people?

8.2.2 OBJECTIVE
Define one's responsibility and privilege to communicate God's Word to the lost.

8 What is the believer's function in the task of evangelism?

8.2.3 OBJECTIVE
Explain how to rely on God to continually be at work in unbelievers' lives.

In the case of Paul and Apollos in Corinth, the Holy Spirit preceded Paul's work. He worked while Paul ministered in Corinth and while Apollos ministered. He continued to work beyond the time Paul and Apollos were present.

God is the one who begins the work of salvation in each life, and He is the one who completes it. Jesus is the author and finisher of our faith, according to Hebrews 12:2. As Paul reminds us so clearly, "He who began a good work in you will perfect it until the day of Christ Jesus" (Philippians 1:6).

The Power Is in the Seed

When Paul speaks of his work of planting and Apollos' work of watering, he is talking about the seed, which Jesus explained is the message of God.

Paul said, "I am not ashamed of the gospel, because it is the power of God for the salvation of everyone who believes: first for the Jew, then for the Gentile" (Romans 1:16, NIV).

The primary power in evangelism is not in the messenger. The primary power is in the message.

"For the word of God is living and active and sharper than any two-edged sword, and piercing as far as the division of soul and spirit, of both joints and marrow, and able to judge the thoughts and intentions of the heart" (Hebrews 4:12).

The New Testament reveals four kinds of power in God's Word.

1. The Power of Regeneration

The Greek word translated "regeneration" is *palingenesia*. *Palin* means "again." *Genesia* is derived from *genesis*, means "existence" or "birth." *Regeneration* means "existing again." That is the nature of the new birth. It is starting a whole new life by God's supernatural work.

Peter wrote, "For you have been born again not of seed which is perishable but imperishable, that is, through the living and enduring word of God" (1 Peter 1:23).

Paul taught that "Therefore if anyone is in Christ, he is a new creature; the old things passed away; behold, new things have come" (2 Corinthians 5:17).

2. The Power of Sanctification

Paul wrote to the Ephesians, "Husbands, love your wives, just as Christ also loved the church and gave Himself up for her, so that He might sanctify her, having cleansed her by the washing of water with the word, that He might present to Himself the church in all her glory, having no spot or wrinkle or any such thing; but that she would be holy and blameless" (Ephesians 5:25–27).

God uses His Word to confront us with the truth about ourselves and expose things in our life that need to be purged or cleansed. God's Word cleanses our lives and penetrates our motives (Hebrews 4:12).

3. The Power of Transformation

God uses His Word not only to cleanse us, but also to change us. The change is radical, not merely a psychological adjustment. Paul told the Romans in 12:2 that we are transformed by the renewing of our mind. In 2 Corinthians 3:18, he says that this transformation process is step by step making us more like Jesus from "glory to glory."

4. The Power of Multiplication

In the Parable of the Sower Jesus said that when the seed of God's message lands upon good ground, it produces thirty, sixty, and one hundred times as much grain. The power of God's Word changes individual lives and multiplies through

---

8.2.4 OBJECTIVE
Describe four ways in which God's Word impacts a life.

9 What is the source of power in the presentation of the gospel?

10 What types of power are attributed to God's Word?

those lives to change others. As Jesus revealed in the Parable of the Mustard Seed, what begins as a small work can grow to enormous proportions. The power of God's message multiplies through countless lives once it is received by a person whose heart is productive soil.

LESSON 8.3

Paul's Principles

Evangelism is God's work. We are privileged to partner with the Holy Spirit to reach the spiritually lost. Witnessing is not merely human persuasion.

Effective witness involves the principles of **dependence** and **discipline**. We must discipline ourselves to do our part in personal evangelism while depending on God to do what only He can.

Many years ago I heard this truth succinctly communicated by C.M. Ward, who for twenty-three years was *Revivaltime* speaker on the Assemblies of God's national radio broadcast. He said, "God will do for you what you can't do for yourself. He will not do for you what you can."

The principles of dependence and discipline characterize Paul's teaching. Paul's epistle to the Colossians includes instruction concerning how believers can actively and effectively share their faith with nonbelievers.

Paul's Mission

8.3.1 OBJECTIVE
Identify Paul's evangelism message, method, and means.

Early in his Colossian epistle, Paul succinctly states his personal mission: "We proclaim Him, admonishing every man and teaching every man with all wisdom, so that we may present every man complete in Christ. For this purpose also I labor, striving according to His power, which mightily works within me" (Colossians 1:28–29).

11 What three components describe Paul's mission?

In these two verses, Paul expresses three missional elements:

1. *The message.* He says, "We proclaim him" (NIV). When Paul communicates, his message is Jesus.

2. *The method.* Paul talks about both "warning every man and teaching every man" (KJV). We must warn the spiritually lost in the light of sin's eternal consequences. Earlier in Colossians 1, Paul says that salvation means we have been delivered "from the domain of darkness, and transferred to the kingdom of his beloved Son, in whom we have redemption, the forgiveness of sins" (1:13–14, NASB). Paul also speaks of teaching every man with all wisdom so that each person may be presented before God complete in Christ. Evangelism includes discipleship. The objective of evangelism is not only a decision but that a person becomes complete in Christ. Evangelism and discipleship cannot be separated from one another.

3. *The means.* Notice that Paul expresses a combination of dependence and discipline. "I labor, striving according to His power, which mightily works within me" (Colossians 1:29, NASB). Notice that Paul advocates the human effort of discipline ("*I* labor, striving") that depends on God ("according to *His* power").

Dependence and Discipline

8.3.2 OBJECTIVE
Explain the relationship in evangelism between dependence and discipline.

The character combination of dependence and discipline is found throughout the New Testament to apply to every aspect of the Christian life. The principle is even illustrated throughout the Old Testament when God worked miraculously. He often required some sort of action on the part of the person in whose life He was working. We must do what we can, and God will do what we cannot. When we do our part in the natural realm, God will manifest the supernatural.

In the Old Testament, God required the Israelites to march around the walls of Jericho. The marching didn't bring the walls down; God did. He worked the miracle after they did what He ordered. In the New Testament, Jesus' first miracle occurred when He required servants to fill six water pots; then He turned the water into wine.

We must do what is possible. God will accomplish what is impossible. The same is true in evangelism.

The combination of the principles of discipline and dependence are evident in Paul's teaching to the Philippians, chapters 2, 3 and 4. He communicates this truth in Philippians 2:12–13: "So then, my beloved, just as you have always obeyed, not as in my presence only, but now much more in my absence, *work out your salvation* with fear and trembling; for it is *God who is at work in you*, both to will and to work for His good pleasure."

Paul is not saying that salvation is earned by works. Rather, he is saying that believers are to live out the results of God's inner work. The conjunction *for* makes this clear. The reason our salvation can be worked out in our lives is only because God first works within us, to shape our desires and our actions to be pleasing to Him.

In Philippians 3:12, Paul says, "I press on so that *I may lay hold of that* for which also *I was laid hold of by Christ Jesus*." Consistent with what Paul says in Colossians about laboring and striving, he says he presses on to lay hold of that for which Christ Jesus first laid hold of him. One depends upon the other. Laying hold involves discipline that is based on dependence of first being laid hold of by Christ Jesus.

"I can do all things through Him who strengthens me," Paul says in Philippians 4:13. He shows that we are called to discipline ourselves to do what our Lord has commanded. Our actions are dependent on "Him who strengthens me."

God's Part and Our Part

Nothing holds more Christians back from being effective witnesses than the misconception that we are responsible to persuade nonbelievers to become Christians. Only God can open a heart and move someone to decision. We do what we can—share a clear message, communicate it with sincerity and conviction, and live exemplary lives that give credibility to our words.

Teaching believers to be effective witnesses demands that they understand the difference between their part in evangelism and God's part.

Whether we came to Christ through a sermon or one-on-one witnessing, most of us can remember that even before we heard the message, God prepared our hearts to receive the truth. Just as God prepared us, He is preparing people around us to receive the message.

Paul wrote in Ephesians 2:8–9, "For by grace you have been saved through faith; and that not of yourselves, it is the gift of God; not as a result of works, so that no one may boast." The next verse (v. 10) explains that God saved us by grace for a purpose: "For we are His workmanship, created in Christ Jesus for good works, which God prepared beforehand so that we would walk in them."

God is preparing us for good works. He is also preparing good works for us. Before we were born, He had a specific purpose for each of us. Part of that plan is

---

12 What does it mean to apply both dependence and discipline in one's walk of faith?

8.3.3 OBJECTIVE
Describe the role of personal will and action in relation to God's activity.

13 What is the best way to describe the partnership between God and the believer during a witnessing opportunity?

that God has divine appointments for us, both with strangers and those we know well—friends, family members, neighbors and co-workers. Those encounters will happen whether we are ready or not.

Understanding God's work in evangelism is essential to having the faith to do our work. We will fail in our part if we're trying to do His part. He is God. We are not. He assigned our part to us, and He does not command anything that we cannot do with His help.

Although God has chosen to involve us in the evangelism process, our part is possible only because the Holy Spirit is working in people even before we share the message.

We have no excuses. God will do what we cannot, if we will do what we can.

Response Evangelism

In Paul's letter to the Colossians, his final instructions conveyed how Christians should relate to nonbelievers, whom he appropriately calls "outsiders." This simple, yet profound, teaching is the foundation for what I call *response evangelism*:

> Devote yourselves to prayer, keeping alert in it with an attitude of thanksgiving; praying at the same time for us as well, that God will open up to us a door for the word, so that we may speak forth the mystery of Christ, for which I have also been imprisoned; that I may make it clear in the way I ought to speak. Conduct yourselves with wisdom toward outsiders, making the most of the opportunity. Let your speech always be with grace, as though seasoned with salt, so that you will know how you should respond to each person. (Colossians 4:2–6)

In these verses, Paul asks the Colossians to pray for his personal effectiveness in proclaiming the message of Christ and also instructs them how to be effective in communicating Christ to outsiders. His teaching in these five verses reveals two major principles and six practices. The two principles are *dependence* and *discipline*. As in all of Christian living, the combination of dependence and discipline is essential to effective witnessing. While dependence and discipline are distinct from one another, they should not be separated from each other. Each is essential, and they should also interact.

The next chapter is devoted to six practices based on Paul's teaching in Colossians 4:2–6. The principle of dependence applies most in the first two practices and discipline is the major emphasis in the remaining four. But each of the six practices involves dependence and discipline; both always apply.

Disciplined Dependence

The first two practices of *praying for open doors* and *sharing Christ clearly* are in the form of a prayer request from Paul. Dependence on God's help is the major emphasis of both. While prayer is an expression of dependence, it also takes discipline to pray. Both practices involve discipline.

Dependent Discipline

Although the last four practices are instructions, or commands, Paul gives the Colossians, each conveys our dependence on God's help to be effective. We need His wisdom from above and the Holy Spirit's guidance to seize and build opportunities. We depend on the Spirit's help to speak with grace and sensitivity and know how to respond individually to people.

8.3.4 OBJECTIVE
Describe the function of response evangelism.

14 For what does Paul rely on the Colossians to contribute to the effectiveness of his ministry?

15 Besides speaking, what communication skill is vital to response evangelism?	The response evangelism approach involves not just speaking but listening and being ready to answer people's questions and relate to their spiritual needs. It demands more than learning a witnessing routine, because we do not control the conversation.

Jesus promised, in John 16:8, that the Holy Spirit would convince the world concerning "sin and righteousness and judgment." We are responsible to share the message, but the Holy Spirit convinces and persuades the heart of the listener.

Response evangelism is possible because God takes the initiative in people's lives and continues to work in the evangelism process. When we understand His work in evangelism, it enables us to be bold, dependent on His persuasive work. We can also be patient, trusting His timing rather than pushing people to a premature decision. This frees us from anxiety and allows us to be neither hesitant nor hasty.

Response evangelism acknowledges God's sovereignty and depends on His activity. This allows us to fulfill our role in the evangelism process—responding to people while depending on the Holy Spirit's help.

Test Yourself

Circle the letter of the *best* answer.

1. Both Peter and Paul emphasized which three components of effective evangelism?
   a) What the believer says, how the believer says it, and whether the believer lives accordingly
   b) The speaker, the listener, and the message
   c) God, the speaker, and the message
   d) Pentecostal baptism, the fruit of the Spirit, and the gifts of the Spirit

2. *Lifestyle evangelism* is
   a) a subtle deviation from the Great Commission and a satanic tool to keep Christians silent.
   b) a necessary, but not exclusive, focus on developing friendships with nonbelievers and living consistent Christian lives.
   c) the outgrowth of the "What Would Jesus Do?" movement.
   d) ministry to people addicted to immoral lifestyles.

3. What three factors communicate our message as much as our words?
   a) Appearance, personal hygiene, level of alertness
   b) Clarity of speech, knowledge of vocabulary, grammatical skill
   c) Emotions, attitudes, actions
   d) General knowledge, acquired education, personal experience

4. The Holy Spirit is effective in the believer's witness by
   a) empowering the choice of words, the manner in which words are used, and the life that backs them up.
   b) preserving the believer from all illness and poverty.
   c) giving the believer knowledge of every unbeliever's need.
   d) signs and wonders.

5. When cautioning the Corinthians regarding their focus on human ministers, Paul
   a) warned that they had left their first love.
   b) reminded them that God is the Source of all spiritual growth.
   c) recommended that they elect Apollos as their bishop.
   d) condemned the practice outright.

6. The believer's central task in personal evangelism is to
   a) present the arguments for Christ's divinity in irrefutable terms.
   b) confront unbelievers with the despicable nature of their personal sin.
   c) quote from memory the pertinent biblical references to salvation.
   d) obey God's leading in sharing and nurturing the Word at every opportunity.

7. God's Word exercises what four types of power?
   a) Law, prophetic record, wisdom literature, the Gospels
   b) General influence, specific guidance, special revelation, correction
   c) Regeneration, sanctification, transformation, multiplication
   d) Conviction, condemnation, pronouncement of judgment, damnation

8. The three components of Paul's mission were his
   a) knowledge of the Law, acceptance of grace, and reliance on the Spirit.
   b) Jewish heritage, Gentile familiarity, and Roman citizenship.
   c) message, method, and means.
   d) Damascus road encounter, temporary blindness, and multiple persecutions.

9. What two factors are vital in personal witnessing?
   a) Dependence and discipline
   b) Salvation and sanctification
   c) Speaking in tongues and interpreting tongues
   d) Personal charisma and biblical education

10. When describing his ministry to the Colossians, Paul invited them to
    a) sacrificially plant a financial seed of faith.
    b) claim their own miracle by making a monthly faith pledge.
    c) participate with him by supporting him in prayer.
    d) be tentmakers with him.

Responses to Interactive Questions
Chapter 8

Some of these responses may include information that is supplemental to the IST. These questions are intended to produce reflective thinking beyond the course content and your responses may vary from these examples.

1 What three elements of a comprehensive gospel witness do both Paul and Peter identify?

They identify the need for correct content in personal evangelism as well as the need to back up that content with an effective manner of communication and a lifestyle consistent with the message presented.

2 How can the valuable concept of *lifestyle evangelism* be misused?

Lifestyle evangelism rightly emphasizes the critical need to form friendships with nonbelievers and to live credible Christian lives but should never be used as an excuse to avoid verbally sharing the gospel.

3 What is a key component to giving our words vitality?

We must be thoroughly convinced of the truth of our message and allow that conviction to be obvious.

4 Why is Christian character vital to the communication of the gospel?

Whether or not our lives back up the truth of the gospel can have a dramatic effect on whether or not a person will believe the gospel.

5 What role does the Holy Spirit play in our effective gospel witness?

The Holy Spirit guides us in the words we use, helps us to convincingly communicate those words, and conforms our lives to the truth of the gospel.

6 Is it wrong to express affection and respect for specific spiritual leaders?

It is natural to honor people God has used to lead us into a relationship with Christ, but we should understand the supreme role of God himself in that process.

7 What do the different types of soil in the Bible's planting analogies tell us about people?

We cannot always assess if people are ready to respond to the gospel (good ground) but should communicate the truth to as many as possible.

8 What is the believer's function in the task of evangelism?

The believer is to communicate God's Word, or plant and water the seed, in obedience to God who causes the growth.

9 What is the source of power in the presentation of the gospel?

God's Word, the seed referenced in Paul's analogy, is that source of power.

10 What types of power are attributed to God's Word?

God's Word regenerates, sanctifies, transforms and multiplies.

11 What three components describe Paul's mission?

Paul communicated the message of Jesus, using the method of warning and teaching, and relying on the means of dependence and discipline.

12 What does it mean to apply both dependence and discipline in one's walk of faith?

The believer is dependent on God to do what only God can do but is to be disciplined in obeying God to take the actions God asks of us.

13 What is the best way to describe the partnership between God and the believer during a witnessing opportunity?

Through a variety of circumstances, God divinely prepares the heart to receive the truth of the gospel. He asks the believer to obediently communicate the content of the gospel to the lost.

14 For what does Paul rely on the Colossians to contribute to the effectiveness of his ministry?

Paul asks the Colossians to pray for his effectiveness in proclaiming the message of Christ.

15 Besides speaking, what communication skill is vital to response evangelism?

The believer needs to be listening and ready to answer the questions and recognize the spiritual needs of the lost.

CHAPTER 9

Paul's Evangelism Practices

In March of 1973, nineteen-year-old Maria Lourdes committed her life to Christ on the first night of missionary Bernhard Johnson's evangelistic crusade in Porto Alegre, Brazil. The next night she was filled with the Holy Spirit. On her first Sunday morning in church, the pastor's sermon challenged the people to personal witnessing. Maria realized that she had not yet told anyone about her new faith in Christ. So, she prayed, "Lord, before I go to bed tonight, I will tell someone what You have done for me."

Maria was determined to witness to someone on the forty-minute bus ride home from church. No one sat beside her. As she ran home from the bus stop, she felt she had failed God.

When she opened the door to her apartment, the Holy Spirit impressed her to go to the telephone. She opened the telephone book, closed her eyes, and put her finger down on the page. Her finger landed on the name Johnny Sousa. She dialed the number. After the sixth ring, a gruff voice answered.

"Who is this?"

Maria didn't know what to say. All that came to her mind was the song the choir sang in the stadium crusade. Maria started to sing into the telephone, "Just as I am, without one plea."

Something changed in Johnny Sousa's voice. "Please don't hang up," he replied. "I'll be right back." A minute later, he came back on the line. "My wife Clara's standing next to me, and we're holding the telephone so we can both hear. Would you please sing that song again?"

Maria sang "Just as I Am" three times, then shared her testimony and explained why Jesus gave His life for us. She asked Johnny and Clara Sousa if they wanted to receive God's forgiveness. Over the telephone, she led them in prayer to receive Christ.

Then Johnny Sousa told her their story. He and Clara had been married seven years, could have no children, and were too poor by government standards to adopt a child. Six months earlier, Johnny had lost his job, and they were down to their last few cents. They expected to be evicted the next day.

"My wife and I got so desperate this morning that we took the last money we had and bought poison. We agreed to drink the poison and die together. I mixed it and gave one glass to my wife. I picked up the other. We began raising the glasses. When the poison was just about to touch our lips, the telephone rang."

Johnny Sousa's story didn't end the night he and Clara received Christ. God called them into the ministry, and he became an Assemblies of God pastor. His congregation in Santa Rosa, Brazil, eventually grew to more than thirty thousand members.

The Holy Spirit searches people's hearts and knows when someone is ready for the gospel. He guides circumstances and will use believers as vessels of God's message of forgiveness, hope and everlasting life. We need to be ready for God to use us as He works in people's lives.

Lesson 9.1   Pray for Open Doors

Objectives

9.1.1 Explain the relational approach to prayer modeled by Christ.
9.1.2 Explain why human argument alone is incapable of changing human desire to conform to God's desires.
9.1.3 Commit to pray regularly and specifically for every aspect of the evangelistic process.
9.1.4 Describe the importance of depending on the Holy Spirit's ability to change the human heart.

Lesson 9.2   Share Christ Clearly

Objectives

9.2.1 Describe the importance of relying on the Holy Spirit to help during evangelism opportunities.
9.2.2 Outline a simple, clear presentation of the gospel.
9.2.3 Emphasize the person of Jesus Christ when evangelizing.
9.2.4 Validate a verbal witness with evidence of a personal relationship with God.

Lesson 9.3   Be Wise with Outsiders

Objectives

9.3.1 Describe the growing chasm between modern culture and Christian thought.
9.3.2 Outline an approach to nonbelievers based on a compassionate attitude toward their ignorance of the gospel.
9.3.3 Translate Christian terminology into expressions easily grasped by those outside the church culture.
9.3.4 Connect any presentation of the gospel with a person's interests.

Lesson 9.4   Make the Most of Opportunities

Objectives

9.4.1 Propose ways to be alert to opportunities to address people's spiritual needs.
9.4.2 Express Christ's heart of compassion for the lost.
9.4.3 Describe how to prepare to seize opportunities to share the gospel or spiritual comfort.
9.4.4 Prayerfully develop opportunities to their fullest potential.

Lesson 9.5   Speak with Grace

Objectives

9.5.1 Explain why any gospel presentation is more than the words spoken.
9.5.2 Speak of God's grace and Christ's sacrifice, rather than focusing on someone's sin.
9.5.3 Validate your spoken witness with kindness.

Lesson 9.6   Respond Individually

Objectives

9.6.1 Recognize and emulate Jesus' commitment to touching individual lives.
9.6.2 Distinguish between evangelizing a group and an individual.
9.6.3 Explain why relationship is the foundation for individual ministry.
9.6.4 Demonstrate Jesus' self-sacrificing approach to meeting others' needs.

Pray for Open Doors

Prayer is essential in evangelism. Unless God works in hearts and lives, our work will not produce lasting results. Our responsibility is to share the message and pray for God to do what only He can do in the evangelism process.

Our Model Is Jesus

Our greatest example concerning prayer is our Lord Jesus taught and modeled a life of prayer. His commitment to prayer made a powerful impact on His disciples. When they asked Him in Luke 11:1, "Lord, teach us to pray," it was not a casual inquiry. Something was different about Jesus' prayer life, and it instilled in them the desire to pray like Him. They had witnessed prayer in the temple and practiced it themselves. But Jesus prayed to Jehovah as His Father and taught them that He was their heavenly Father. He demonstrated that prayer is not a ceremony, but a relationship with an all-powerful and caring God who hears and answers.

Jesus exemplified what Paul instructed the Colossians to do. He was devoted to prayer. He made His disciples aware that God is always present; He sees the sparrow fall and knows how many hairs are on our head (Matthew 10:30; Luke 12:7). By instruction and by example, Jesus taught His disciples that in normal daily living and in crisis, we need to get alone with God: "But you, when you pray, go into your inner room, close your door and pray to your Father who is in secret, and your Father who sees what is done in secret will reward you" (Matthew 6:6).

Paul explained that Jesus, "although He existed in the form of God, did not regard equality with God a thing to be grasped, but emptied Himself, taking the form of a bond-servant, and being made in the likeness of men" (Philippians 2:6–7). In His earthly life, Jesus obeyed the Father and depended upon the guidance and power of the Holy Spirit. The Holy Spirit will also open doors of opportunity and enable us to effectively share the message of Christ.

Not Merely Human Persuasion

Evangelism is, in some respects, a process of persuasion. In 2 Corinthians 5:11, Paul wrote, "Knowing the fear of the Lord, we persuade men." Evangelism is different from normal human persuasion. Paul also wrote, "My message and my preaching were not in persuasive words of wisdom, but in demonstration of the Spirit and of power" (1 Corinthians 2:4). Though Paul certainly had persuasive ability, he understood that earthly wisdom and human persuasion were inadequate to reach the Corinthians with the gospel of Christ.

The reason human persuasion alone will not lead someone to a decision for Christ is found in the nature of persuasion itself. For persuasion to be effective, it must appeal to human desires. People do what they want to do. To move people to a decision, they must see that the decision will result in gratifying a desire. This is the objective of advertising.

People living in sin do not have the human desire to deny themselves, follow Christ, and do God's will. It requires a special work of the Holy Spirit in our minds and hearts to bring us to an understanding of and willingness to obey the truth.

People are not naturally inclined to believe the gospel because sin blinds them to the truth. Paul says, "The god of this world has blinded the minds of the unbelieving so that they might not see the light of the gospel of the glory of Christ" (2 Corinthians 4:4). He also says, "A natural man does not accept the things of the Spirit of God, for they are foolishness to him; and he cannot

---

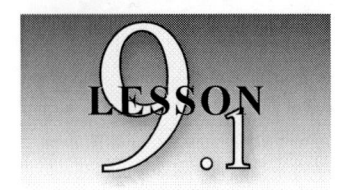

9.1.1 OBJECTIVE
Explain the relational approach to prayer modeled by Christ.

1 What key aspect of Jesus' prayer life set it apart as the believer's supreme example?

9.1.2 OBJECTIVE
Explain why human argument alone is incapable of changing human desire to conform to God's desires.

2 Why is human persuasion unequal to the task of evangelism?

3 What influence contributes to people's inability to believe the gospel?

understand them, because they are spiritually appraised" (1 Corinthians 2:14). Without God's help, a person cannot understand or respond to the truth. That is why no one can come to Christ through human persuasion alone.

We must pray because we are dependent on God for opportunity and to bring understanding to hearers' minds and to move their hearts to decision.

How We Should Pray

Believers should pray regularly in three ways.

1. We should pray specifically and regularly for nonbelievers we know. As I was growing up, my parents led us in daily prayer for family members and friends who were nonbelievers. Over the years we have had the joy of seeing many for whom we prayed come to Christ. Their conversions happened in ways that showed they were responding as a result of believing prayer. It may take many months, and even years of consistent prayer, but God persistently works in the lives of those for whom we regularly pray. It is helpful to keep a prayer list in your Bible to remind you of people for whom you are committed to pray.

2. We should pray for divine appointments. God wants to use us to plant and water the seed of Christ's message in the lives of casual acquaintances and even strangers.

3. We should pray for each other, that God will open doors of opportunity, just as Paul requested the Colossians to pray for him in 4:3.

In Erie, Pennsylvania, three teenage girls formed a prayer group that God used in a dramatic way. Each girl wrote the names of two or three school friends on a card as a reminder of her commitment to pray for friends to receive Christ during the Easter season. As they read their friends' names to each other, one girl commented about a name on another student's list. "You know she will never become a Christian!" she exclaimed. The girl who had written the name promptly crossed it off. The third girl said, "I don't think you should cross off her name. That's like saying God can't save her." So the name was rewritten on the prayer card. Now the girl's name appeared twice on the card, once with a line through it, once without.

The three girls joined in prayer for all of the names on their cards and especially for the one they had discussed. One week later, while riding a bus to a ball game, that girl received Christ through the witness of the girl who had written her name twice on her prayer card!

A Lifestyle of Prayer

A revealing example of the necessity of the Holy Spirit's work in evangelism is found in Acts 16. When Paul and his companions went to a riverbank outside Philippi to pray on the Sabbath day, they sat down and began speaking to a group of women. "A woman named Lydia, from the city of Thyatira, a seller of purple fabrics, a worshiper of God, was listening; and the Lord opened her heart to respond to the things spoken by Paul" (Acts 16:14).

Paul spoke the message, but the Lord opened Lydia's heart! The truth is, none of us can open a heart, not even the apostle Paul.

As I walked through the Billy Graham Center in Wheaton, Illinois, I read quotations by Billy Graham displayed on the walls. He said, "If God should take His hand off me, I would have no more spiritual power. The whole secret of the success of our meetings is spiritual, it is God answering prayer. I cannot take credit for any of it."

9.1.3 OBJECTIVE
Commit to pray regularly and specifically for every aspect of the evangelistic process.

4 What three practices should characterize the believer's evangelistic prayers?

9.1.4 OBJECTIVE
Describe the importance of depending on the Holy Spirit's ability to change the human heart.

5 How vital is the Holy Spirit to the ministry of the believer?

Anyone who has been involved in evangelism knows that it is a spiritual activity, and human persuasion alone cannot accomplish the task. We can do our part. Unless God works in people's hearts, we will not see lives changed. Billy Graham knows that and so should every person who obeys our Lord's command to be His witnesses.

We have the privilege and responsibility of sharing the message. Only God can open a heart.

LESSON 9.2

9.2.1
OBJECTIVE

Describe the importance of relying on the Holy Spirit to help during evangelism opportunities.

6 What double function does Paul identify in the help God offers during evangelism?

Share Christ Clearly

Just as we are dependent on God to open the heart of a person with whom we share Christ's message, we must also depend on Him to help us communicate that message clearly.

Paul's prayer requests teach that we are dependent on God at both ends of the communication process. We need the Holy Spirit's help to open a door for the message to be effectively received. We also need His help to deliver the message.

Paul wrote the Colossians, "Devote yourselves to prayer, keeping alert in it with an attitude of thanksgiving; praying at the same time for us as well…so that we may speak forth the mystery of Christ, for which I have also been imprisoned; that I may make it clear in the way I ought to speak" (4:2–4).

We Need the Spirit's Help

At the end of Ephesians, Paul gives an exhortation and prayer request that is similar to the Colossians passage:

> With all prayer and petition pray at all times in the Spirit, and with this in view, be on the alert with all perseverance and petition for all the saints, and pray on my behalf, that utterance may be given to me in the opening of my mouth, to make known with boldness the mystery of the gospel, for which I am an ambassador in chains; that in proclaiming it I may speak boldly, as I ought to speak. (Ephesians 6:18–20)

7 What does Paul's prayer request reveal about his priorities in personal evangelism?

Paul asked the Colossians to pray for clarity of speech for him. He asked the Ephesians to pray for him to be bold. In Ephesians, his desire was to speak the message "boldly, as I ought to speak." In Colossians he asked believers to pray that he would make the message "clear in the way I ought to speak." For Paul, boldness and clarity were not options, but necessities.

9.2.2
OBJECTIVE

Outline a simple, clear presentation of the gospel.

Clear, Not Clever

The priority is to be clear, not clever.

I question the value of some Christian bumper stickers and billboards. Limited space requires brief messages. Since it is necessary to capture people's attention while driving by, the messages tend to focus on the clever and confrontational. Often this comes at the expense of clarity. In the case of bumper stickers, it is an appropriate irony that the message is usually moving away from people.

Paul said his message was the "mystery of Christ." (See Ephesians 3:4 and Colossians 4:3.) The central issue in evangelism is that people must decide what Christ's sacrifice on the cross means for them personally.

8 Must an unbeliever first understand the Bible's inspiration in order to be saved?

It helps when an unbeliever believes the Bible is the Word of God, but the Bible itself does not require that someone believes in the verbal plenary inspiration of the Scriptures to be saved. God's Word does require true faith in the heart and confession with the mouth (Romans 10:9–10).

Some salvation presentations begin by focusing on the inspiration of the Scriptures so a person has a biblical foundation from which to start. For many people, the process works in reverse. First, they must be confronted with the person and work of Christ. The Word must be proclaimed. The Holy Spirit will convince a person of its truth.

The simple two-point presentation in Chapter 7 of who Jesus was and why He gave His life (from the analysis of Peter's preaching) can be effectively shared by any believer.

Our message to nonbelievers must be clear and simple. The primary focus must be Jesus. The life of Jesus Christ is history's turning point. The world's calendar is hinged on His birth. He is thought of by many as a teacher, a philosopher, or even a prophet, but every person must be confronted by who Jesus is. All people must be given an adequate witness and the opportunity to make a choice of accepting or rejecting His offer of forgiveness of sin and everlasting life and then submitting to His lordship.

When Jesus dealt with Nicodemus and the Samaritan woman at the well, He brought them to a revelation of who He was. In our encounters with people, we must do the same. We must not merely communicate truth concerning what we believe. We must communicate Jesus Christ the Person, who is our Savior and Lord.

The Spirit's Message

In John 16:14, Jesus promised that the Holy Spirit would glorify Him. It is the Christ-centered message the Holy Spirit will honor and use.

In Acts 1:8, after the outpouring of the Holy Spirit on the Day of Pentecost, the first Christians boldly and clearly witnessed about Jesus as He promised they would.

In Acts 2, the multitude was amazed because they heard those who had been filled with the Holy Spirit speaking in the languages of the nonbelievers who were gathered. When they asked, "What does this mean?" Peter, filled with the Holy Spirit, stood and explained that what had happened was the fulfillment of Joel's prophecy in the Old Testament concerning the outpouring of the Holy Spirit (Acts 2:12–36). Then he clearly and boldly preached about Jesus Christ, and about three thousand people were added to the Church that day.

In Acts 3, Peter and John were going to the temple to pray, and a man lame from birth was healed at the temple gate. Peter again used the opportunity to proclaim Jesus, and about five thousand believed the message.

In Acts 4, the priests, captain of the temple guard, and the Sadducees were so disturbed that they put Peter and John in jail. The next day the rulers, elders, scribes, and high priests challenged them: "By what power, or in what name, have you done this?" (Acts 4:7). Then Peter, filled with the Holy Spirit, spoke boldly about Jesus: "There is salvation in no one else; for there is no other name under heaven that has been given among men by which we must be saved" (Acts 4:12).

Notice that when the Church was born on the Day of Pentecost and in the days following, the message of the Christians focused on the person Jesus Christ. As they boldly and clearly proclaimed Jesus, great numbers believed. Today this same message—Jesus—must be clearly communicated to the spiritually lost of this world.

9.2.3 OBJECTIVE
Emphasize the person of Jesus Christ when evangelizing.

9 What message is consistently presented to unbelievers in the book of Acts?

9.2.4 OBJECTIVE
Validate a verbal witness with evidence of a personal relationship with God.

Not Just Words

Communicating the message of Christ effectively is not just an issue of the words we speak. Sharing Christ in a compelling way will be directly connected to our personal relationship with Him.

Clarity of message also relates to the consistency and credibility of our personal Christian lives. If there is a difference between what we say and how we live, we send mixed signals that hinder the effectiveness of our witness.

10 What must accompany any verbal presentation of the gospel?

When Peter instructs us in 1 Peter 3:15 to be ready to give a reason for the hope that is within us, he did not necessarily mean we will have all the right intellectual and philosophical arguments at our disposal. What really matters is that we are able to effectively communicate our hope. Our hope need not always be articulate, but it must always be evident.

Effective personal evangelism is not merely about what we know but about whom we know. Our personal relationship with Jesus is an integral part of our witness. Making the message clear involves what we say, how we say it and who we are.

Sometimes we may be at a loss for what to say, but if our manner and character reflect the love of Christ, we will be more effective than if we say the right words with a manner inconsistent with the message of Christ.

The text for this lesson was one of Paul's prayer requests. He needed the Spirit's help to share Christ clearly, and so do we.

LESSON 9.3

9.3.1 OBJECTIVE
Describe the growing chasm between modern culture and Christian thought.

Be Wise with Outsiders

Devote yourselves to prayer, keeping alert in it with an attitude of thanksgiving; praying at the same time for us as well, that God will open up to us a door for the word, so that we may speak forth the mystery of Christ, for which I have also been imprisoned; that I may make it clear in the way I ought to speak. *Conduct yourselves with wisdom toward outsiders*, making the most of the opportunity. Let your speech always be with grace, as though seasoned with salt, so that you will know how you should respond to each person. (Colossians 4:2–6, emphasis added)

I had a unique opportunity to witness to an Indian guru on a flight from Los Angeles to Honolulu. I recognized his face and confirmed who he was in conversation, noting that he had advised wealthy celebrities and rock musicians.

The swami was surprisingly cordial. When I turned the conversation first to spiritual things and then to Jesus Christ, I was pleasantly surprised at the respect with which he spoke of Jesus. As I probed what he believed, I was puzzled to discover that he believed in Christ's bodily resurrection, but he said he could not believe in His virgin birth. At first, I was bewildered by this contradiction, because the virgin birth is just as critical to the Christian faith as the Resurrection.

While gurus are not our typical audience, many in U.S. secular culture are just as far, and in some cases further, in their understanding of who Jesus is and His saving work on the cross. At least the swami believed in Jesus' death and bodily resurrection, which is more than many North Americans believe. Today, more than ever, we must understand the increasing variety of contexts, cultures, and philosophies with which we have to contend in Christian evangelism. "Conduct yourselves with wisdom toward outsiders," Colossians 4:5 says.

9.3.2
OBJECTIVE
Outline an approach to nonbelievers based on a compassionate attitude toward their ignorance of the gospel.

11 Why is the biblical term *outsider* appropriate for a nonbeliever?

12 Why are predetermined witnessing programs often inadequate to the task of connecting the lost with the gospel?

9.3.3
OBJECTIVE
Translate Christian terminology into expressions easily grasped by those outside the church culture.

13 What is one approach that lays a clear foundation for the nonbeliever to recognize his or her spiritual need?

Communicating with Outsiders

After telling the Colossians to devote themselves to prayer and requesting prayer for his own work in evangelism, Paul instructs them to act wisely toward outsiders. The word *outsiders* is significant. Most people have experienced feeling outside a particular group. The insiders have jokes and expressions we don't understand. We are left out because the meanings are inside the group.

Paul's term outsider is an appropriate and practical way of describing a nonbeliever's relationship to the church. Most nonbelievers with whom we will share Christ today are further outside the Christian context than ever. Christians must now communicate the message of Christ with intercultural sensitivity, much like missionaries to other countries who learn to communicate across barriers of language and culture.

Most Christians are familiar with terms for non-Christians such as *nonbeliever* and *sinner*, but the term *outsider* has not been used as much. Jesus uses the term in Mark 4:11, and Paul uses it in three of his epistles. *Outsider* is a helpful expression to understand the communication challenge we face in evangelism.

When we converse with nonbelievers, we are communicating from a church culture to a secular culture. If we have spent much of our lives in the church, we have acquired perceptions, values, and vocabulary that those outside church do not understand.

Witnessing programs and evangelism approaches that depend on a predetermined routine often assume a basic understanding of Judeo-Christian concepts and values. In today's society, we cannot assume that our audience has that shared understanding.

When I served as a missionary in the Samoan Islands, I had to learn a new language. Part of being a missionary—one who is sent—is crossing language barriers. Chasms of understanding must be bridged. We might think we witnessed to someone, but if the message was not communicated in understood terms, we failed. I could travel halfway around the world to communicate the gospel and fall one foot short of my goal, if I cannot clearly and effectively communicate the message in a language that a person understands. We cannot assume people know and understand our Christian terminology. Having to take time to give Christian explanations to our theological vocabulary can be a distraction from presenting a simple, clear witness of Jesus Christ.

Clarity

Several common Christian words illustrate the clarity challenge. The first is the word *salvation*, along with the related word *saved*. Asking, "Are you saved?" to someone from a non-Christian background can confuse them because the concepts are unknown or, at least vague, to them. Perhaps our first communication should be that God has a purpose and plan for every life. He loves us and His plan for our lives is for our good. In Ephesians 1:5–9, Paul writes:

> He predestined us to adoption as sons through Jesus Christ to Himself, according to the kind intention of His will, to the praise of the glory of His grace, which He freely bestowed on us in the Beloved. In Him we have redemption through His blood, the forgiveness of our trespasses, according to the riches of His grace which He lavished on us. In all wisdom and insight He made known to us the mystery of His will, according to His kind intention which He purposed in Him.

Notice that the intention of God's will is kind, but His best purpose for our lives cannot be realized unless we first deal with our sin and need for forgiveness.

Sin is a better known and understood term than the word *saved*. While people may have misconceptions about sin, they usually understand right and wrong and the concept of forgiveness, because of human relationships.

Another example of Christian terminology is the word *repent*. If a person is from a Roman Catholic background, the word *repent* could bring to mind the concept of *penance*. Telling a person, "You need to repent," can mislead them, depending on their history. *Repentance* means to "change direction," turning away from sin and turning to God. It is a spiritual change of mind and heart. A clearer explanation is to say, "You need to have your heart and life changed."

14 How has the term *Christian* been misappropriated?

Even the words *Christian* and *born again* cause difficulties. The word *Christian* has acquired connotations that can be a distraction in witnessing. There are political connotations to the word in many countries and increasingly in the United States. I prefer to use the term *believer* or *follower of Christ*.

In recent decades in America, *born again* has become a commonplace term. Unless you explain what Jesus taught about being born again, the description can be confusing or misleading. Even when Jesus first used the expression *born again* with Nicodemus, it provoked a question from the Jewish religious leader:

> That which is born of the flesh is flesh, and that which is born of the Spirit is spirit. Do not be amazed that I said to you, 'You must be born again.' The wind blows where it wishes and you hear the sound of it, but do not know where it comes from and where it is going; so is everyone who is born of the Spirit." Nicodemus said to Him, "How can these things be? (John 3:6–9)

Jesus went on to explain what He meant by *being born of the Spirit*. A clearer description is to talk of a *spiritual birth* or having our *heart changed* rather than being *born again*. Even an expression such as *starting a new life* is effective to introduce the truth that only God can change our hearts and give fresh starts.

These are just a few examples. A thoughtful examination of our vocabulary is essential to becoming more effective witnesses.

9.3.4
OBJECTIVE

Connect any presentation of the gospel with a person's interests.

Interest

Communicating with anyone requires getting and keeping the person's attention. We must be interesting.

For nonbelievers to be interested in what we have to say, our conversation should address their interests and concerns. People's interests differ, but one subject in which almost all people are interested is themselves. We must listen to them and learn about them.

15 What is the broader meaning of the word *missionary*?

Jesus said to His disciples, "As the Father has sent Me, I also send you" (John 20:21). The word *missionary* does not occur in the Bible. It comes from the Latin term *missio*, which means "sent." Paul expressed the task before us: "Whoever will call on the name of the Lord will be saved. How then will they call on Him in whom they have not believed? How will they believe in Him whom they have not heard? And how will they hear without a preacher? How will they preach unless they are sent?" (Romans 10:13–15).

When most people read this text, they probably think of missionaries going to other countries. God wants to send all of us outside the church to penetrate the spiritual darkness of our communities with the light of Christ's message.

Lesson 9.4

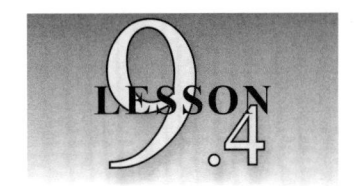

Make the Most of Opportunities

I had a layover waiting for my connecting flight, so I decided to get my shoes shined. I am sure I have connected in that airport more than two hundred times over the years, and I have had my shoes shined there often. The shoeshine stand is a busy one. This day, only one man was shining shoes. Usually as many as four people work there, and a line is always waiting. This day only one other customer came at the time I did for a shoeshine. I arrived first but offered to let the other man go first. Had I gone first, I might have missed an evangelism opportunity.

After the other gentleman left, I was alone with the shoeshiner. I asked about his family, and he told me that he was divorced from his wife who had repeatedly been unfaithful to him.

We continued talking after he finished the shoeshine. I asked about his spiritual life. I told him God's plan for his life could not happen unless he was in right relationship with God through Christ. After a fifteen-minute conversation, I asked if he was prepared to invite Jesus Christ into his life and offered to pray with him. He accepted, and I put my hand on his shoulder and led him in a prayer to receive Christ into his heart.

Devote yourselves to prayer, keeping alert in it with an attitude of thanksgiving; praying at the same time for us as well, that God will open up to us a door for the word, so that we may speak forth the mystery of Christ, for which I have also been imprisoned; that I may make it clear in the way I ought to speak. Conduct yourselves with wisdom toward outsiders, *making the most of the opportunity*. Let your speech always be with grace, as though seasoned with salt, so that you will know how you should respond to each person. (Colossians 4:2–6, emphasis added)

Divine Appointments

God ordains divine appointments for each of us who will let Him work through us. In God's planning, we will experience opportunities to witness to strangers and casual acquaintances.

When Jesus encountered the Samaritan woman at the well, He could have listed many reasons not to spend time with her. He was tired. It was in the noonday heat. Publicly conversing with the woman would not have been good for His reputation. She was slow to understand and raised objections. The overwhelming, compelling reason for Him to spend time with her was her spiritual need. After His conversation with the woman, He said to His disciples, "My food is to do the will of Him who sent Me and to accomplish His work. Do you not say, 'There are yet four months, and then comes the harvest?' Behold, I say to you, lift up your eyes and look on the fields, that they are white for harvest" (John 4:34–35).

Opportunities are framed in time. The saying, "Opportunity doesn't knock twice," is true. Each opportunity is unique, because people and circumstances are different. Opportunities should be approached in two ways—to seize them and to build them.

Seize Opportunities

We need to be spiritually alert to seize opportunities. In Colossians 4:2, Paul tells believers to devote themselves to prayer, "keeping alert in it with an attitude

---

9.4.1 OBJECTIVE
Propose ways to be alert to opportunities to address people's spiritual needs.

16 What was Jesus' motivation for reaching out to the Samaritan woman?

9.4.2 OBJECTIVE
Express Christ's heart of compassion for the lost.

of thanksgiving." If we are not alert in prayerful dependence on God, we can miss these divine appointments. God is working in our everyday circumstances.

17 Why is a prayer life and spiritual discipline critical to our evangelistic effectiveness?

Many believers feel inadequate to witness because they think they cannot retain all necessary information. They cannot remember all the Scriptures they think they should. Even if they could, they are not confident to recall them when needed. Two simple practices can be powerful in every believer's witness: sharing a personal testimony and praying with people.

18 What are two vital tools in personal evangelism?

Every believer has a personal testimony. Sharing our personal experience and relationship with Jesus Christ with sincerity and conviction can be the most compelling witness with some people.

Another way we can seize opportunities for witness is praying for someone in their presence. I have had this opportunity many times as I travel. When people express problems, ask them for the privilege of praying with them. If we truly believe God answers prayer, we should practice our belief by praying with and for people, trusting God to answer. It is important to be sensitive to the surroundings and not embarrass people by praying with them in a public way that attracts attention.

Hearing a believer pray can have a significant effect on nonbelievers. When we pray for their needs, people can usually tell we are sincere and have a relationship with God. And when God answers prayer, it can be the means of opening hearts to the message of Christ.

Build Opportunities

9.4.3 OBJECTIVE
Describe how to prepare to seize opportunities to share the gospel or spiritual comfort.

The second way of making the most of opportunities is to build them. Those who called Jesus "a friend of sinners" meant it as an insult. God the Father sent His Son Jesus to seek and save the lost. Jesus said, "As the Father has sent Me, I also send you" (John 20:21). If we are to reach people as Jesus did, we will become friends of sinners, too.

19 Why is personal evangelism really a long-term commitment?

Opportunities for prayer or a salvation decision will not usually come the first time we talk with someone. By taking time to become friends with people, the opportunity to plant and water the seed will happen.

When my wife Ruth and I moved to a different part of our city, we found a café where we went for hamburgers and ice cream. Lori, the owner, was friendly, and we developed a casual friendship with her.

One day, while taking our order, she expressed her frustration about a circumstance in her life. What was unusual about this evening is that Ruth and I were the only customers there. Normally, the café was busy. I have learned to be "spiritually suspicious" when I am in circumstances where other people usually would be, yet I find myself alone with someone. Sometimes that is a clear signal that God has brought about that circumstance for His purposes.

We finished our order, and Lori went back to the kitchen. I told Ruth, "I should have prayed with her right then. When she comes back, I am going to ask her if she will let us pray with her." Before she returned with the food, another man entered the café. I was frustrated. "Lord, let him leave so we have the chance to pray with Lori," I prayed. The man picked up an order of ice cream and left. I thanked the Lord.

When Lori returned to the table, I said, "Lori, God cares about you and your life. Would it be all right if we prayed with you right here and now?" She nodded her head, and I prayed with her for God to take control of her circumstances and lead her life into His will.

Paul's Evangelism Practices

We will not have the opportunity in every circumstance to lead someone in a sinner's prayer, but we can respond to them in times of need, building and seizing opportunities for witness.

Inconvenient Opportunities

9.4.4 OBJECTIVE
Prayerfully develop opportunities to their fullest potential.

Sometimes opportunities will be inconvenient. As the apostle Paul taught, we must be prayerfully alert and sensitive to God's guidance in situations that might appear natural but are divine appointments He has brought about to work through us.

Ecclesiastes 11:4 says, "He who watches the wind will not sow and he who looks at the clouds will not reap." This verse about physical harvest illustrates a principle that applies to spiritual harvest. Every time will not be convenient or perfect in which to sow the seed.

20 What caution must believers keep in mind when looking for opportunities to share the gospel?

Personal evangelism will seldom happen on our schedule. While many have been reached through door-to-door evangelism, our personal schedule is not always going to coincide with people's needs to which we can respond.

Often divine appointments will be occasions when God calls upon us to sacrifice time. People are busy. If we want to accomplish the good work God has prepared for us, it will interrupt our schedule, require us to slow down, and let God use us in a way that could count for eternity. This may mean going out of our way to meet a person at a time that is convenient for them.

When we pray for open doors, we should not be surprised when opportunity knocks. We should be alert in prayer and ready to respond.

LESSON 9.5

Speak with Grace

Many Christians seem to believe the most critical issue in personal witnessing is knowing what to say. Knowing what to say is not enough.

Communicating Christ clearly involves both clarity and sincerity. Our message is not only what we say, but also *how* we say it and who we *are*.

Devote yourselves to prayer, keeping alert in it with an attitude of thanksgiving; praying at the same time for us as well, that God will open up to us a door for the word, so that we may speak forth the mystery of Christ, for which I have also been imprisoned; that I may make it clear in the way I ought to speak. Conduct yourselves with wisdom toward outsiders, making the most of the opportunity. *Let your speech always be with grace, as though seasoned with salt,* so that you will know how you should respond to each person. (Colossians 4:2–6, emphasis added)

More Than Words

9.5.1 OBJECTIVE
Explain why any gospel presentation is more than the words spoken.

Our emotions, attitudes, and actions are just as much a part of our message as our words. How we say things and who we are will not be determined by completing a study course. These elements of our message come from our character. Effective personal evangelism is rooted in spiritual life. In a culture increasingly skeptical of Christianity, it is more critical. The content of our message will be hindered if our manner and lives are inconsistent with our words.

21 Why is it vital that one's lifestyle be consistent with one's spoken testimony?

The apostle Peter expressed this concept when he said we should always be prepared to give a reason for the hope that we have, but "with gentleness and respect" (1 Peter 3:15, NIV).

For many people, what will be compelling is our testimony of the difference Christ makes in our lives and that our lives are consistent with our message. Sometimes when the best intellectual arguments supporting Christianity are inadequate, our consistent personal testimony is effective.

One of the greatest tests of Christian character is how we treat someone who has no power over us and can do nothing for us. All people have a deep, personal need for genuine love.

Paul said in Romans 5:8, "But God demonstrates His own love toward us, in that while we were yet sinners, Christ died for us." God's love is not in response to anything we have done. It is the fruit of His character. Our mission is to communicate this unconditional love to spiritually lost people.

Paul said our speech should always be with grace, which we can demonstrate in three ways.

22 How must the believer's actions toward others mirror God's actions toward him or her?

A Message of Grace

9.5.2 OBJECTIVE
Speak of God's grace and Christ's sacrifice, rather than focusing on someone's sin.

We need to communicate a message of grace. The message of God's grace is centered in the person and work of Jesus Christ, which makes accessible God's love and forgiveness.

In the early part of his letter to the Colossians (1:28), Paul says, "We proclaim Him, admonishing every man and teaching every man with all wisdom, so that we may present every man complete in Christ." The message we proclaim is Jesus, but that message includes a warning. *Warning* is the word used in the New King James Version and is a simpler meaning of *admonishing*. Paul also says, "He rescued us from the domain of darkness, and transferred us to the kingdom of His beloved Son, in whom we have redemption, the forgiveness of sins" (Colossians 1:13–14).

Paul's statement is reminiscent of Jesus' words to him on the Damascus road: "For this purpose I have appeared to you, to appoint you a minister and a witness . . . to open their eyes so that they may turn from darkness to light and from the dominion of Satan to God, that they may receive forgiveness of sins and an inheritance among those who have been sanctified by faith in Me" (Acts 26:16, 18).

Evangelism is not for the purpose of inviting people to join a group of nice people with higher-than-average moral standards. We are challenging others to change their kingdom adherence—from Satan's kingdom of darkness to our Lord's kingdom of marvelous light. (See 1 Peter 2:9.) As sensitive as Jesus was in His dealings with Nicodemus and the Samaritan woman, He still proclaimed the truth that sin must be dealt with and hearts changed.

The issue of sin should be addressed in the context of the good news of Christ's forgiveness and the offer of eternal life. It is not our responsibility to convince people they are sinners. That is the Holy Spirit's work. Jesus promised that when the Holy Spirit came, He would "convince the world concerning sin and righteousness and judgment" (John 16:8, RSV).

23 How must the believer deal with the issue of sin when sharing the gospel?

When witnessing to strangers, I have found that it is usually not an obstacle for people to understand they have sinned. Although many do not understand how they have sinned against God, they do understand that they have sinned against other people. God has put within each person a conscience, the capacity to understand right and wrong. We all know what we do not want others to do to us. When we do to others what we don't want them to do to us, our conscience tells us that we have sinned.

We have been given the privilege of sharing the good news of Christ's forgiveness. We are called by our Lord to be witnesses, not prosecuting attorneys.

A Gracious Manner

9.5.3 OBJECTIVE
Validate your spoken witness with kindness.

We need to demonstrate a manner that is gracious. This may seem obvious, but some Christians apparently miss it. An important part of effective witnessing is just being nice!

As salt seasons food, a spirit of grace should season our conversation with nonbelievers. Communicating the grace of Christ is demonstrated through words and actions. We must not compromise the truth, but we can communicate the truth with kindness.

Our attitude toward sinners should be gracious, as God has been gracious to us. We have no right to be self-righteous, thinking ourselves to be better than others. We are all sinners being saved by grace. We need the Holy Spirit's help to enable us to be gracious rather than judgmental.

Paul says, "For what have I to do with judging outsiders? Do you not judge those who are within the church? But those who are outside, God judges" (1 Corinthians 5:12–13).

24 What is one of the greatest hindrances to effective personal evangelism?

Few things will distract nonbelievers from the truth more than if they perceive the messenger as insincere. Sincerity is increasingly required in a culture where people have seen and experienced Christians' hypocrisy.

Much of our interpersonal communication is nonverbal. If a contradiction exists between what someone says and the way it is said, we will believe the way it is said. An apology can be perceived as either sincere or sarcastic, depending on the way the words are spoken. Voice inflection and facial expressions can contradict our words. Many we are trying to reach in the United States have a negative history with the church and are defensive or hostile to Christian witness. Others are emotionally scarred and have become insensitive to spiritual issues. The Christian with personal grace will help counteract the mixed signals from those whose lives are inconsistent with their message.

In a culture that is resistant, and even hostile to Christianity, our message must be accompanied by godly, blameless Christian living. The validity of our message is connected to the credibility of our lives. If our lives are not credible, the likelihood of a salvation decision among those we are trying to reach will suffer and, in many cases, fail.

Gracious Acts

We need to demonstrate acts of grace. Jesus said, "You are the salt of the earth . . . You are the light of the world . . . Let your light shine before men in such a way that they may see your good works, and glorify your Father who is in heaven" (Matthew 5:13–14, 16).

25 Why is it wrong to universally condemn benevolent deeds as evidence of giving in to a secular, social gospel?

Communicating the grace of Jesus Christ is much more than sharing His message in words. Our Lord commanded us to let our good works be evident to the world around us so that God will be glorified.

Around the middle of the last century in the small town of Shawano, Wisconsin, Albert Kallies beat a man to death in a bar fight. After he was arrested and jailed, a newspaper article recorded that he had a wife and six children. A local pastor visited the woman's home, a small two-bedroom house next to the railroad coal chute and water tower. The pastor did not preach to the woman or even invite her to church. He simply brought two boxes of groceries to her home. People from the church continued to take groceries to the family. The woman and her children came to church and eventually received Christ.

Albert Kallies was convicted of manslaughter and sentenced to eight years in the state penitentiary. His oldest son, Bruce, faithfully visited his father in prison and Albert also received Christ as his Savior.

After serving five years, Albert was released from prison on probation. Years later, he died in a tragic hotel fire while rescuing another man.

Bruce Kallies later became the associate pastor of First Assembly of God in Rochester, Minnesota. The young pastor who reached out to the Kallies family was Paul Hoff, who served thirty-five years as an Assemblies of God missionary in Bolivia, Argentina, and Chile before retiring in 2001.

What would happen in our communities if multitudes of Christians did whatever they could to penetrate their surroundings with words, manners, and actions of grace?

LESSON 9.6

Respond Individually

Paul concluded his exhortation to the Colossians with this reminder: "Let your speech always be with grace, as though seasoned with salt, so that you will know how you should respond to each person" (4:6).

The Power of Response

9.6.1 OBJECTIVE
Recognize and emulate Jesus' commitment to touching individual lives.

A study of the Gospels reveals a startling fact about the nature of Jesus' public ministry. Many of His most significant teachings and miracles were in response to people and circumstances. It would seem that the Son of God—on a mission to save the world and knowing His time is short—would have a focused, strategic plan for proclaiming His message to as many people as possible. Yet, Jesus spent ninety percent of His life in preparation for public ministry and never traveled far from His hometown. He devoted most of His time to twelve men. He did not record His teachings on parchment or stone. The One who had the most and best to say and do simply said and did it. He spoke the Word and left it to the hearers to record. He didn't write it on a temporary medium but on the only permanent one available, the hearts of His followers.

26 What was Jesus' primary approach to ministry?

Perhaps more surprising, the One who came to earth with the greatest mission responded to people most considered insignificant. Much of His ministry was defined by interruptions. His miracles witnessed to who He was, but His motivation to work the miracles seems to have been as simple as meeting an individual's need. Many of His parables were a response to someone's question. Jesus, the Son of God, lived an earthly life that was responsive to common people—fishermen, shepherds, women, and children.

Jesus shaped His words to fit the occasion and in response to people who asked questions, some penetrating and some simple. Even to simple questions from ordinary people, He responded with profound truth, unfolding the mysteries of the universe. He revealed the nature of an infinite God in words and images even the illiterate people of His day could understand.

His life challenges us to respond as He did to people in our world who are seeking peace, forgiveness and hope.

9.6.2
OBJECTIVE
Distinguish between evangelizing a group and an individual.

27 How can a focus on souls rob the believer of effective outreach?

More Than Souls

Often, the vocabulary many Christians use concerning evangelism focuses on *souls* rather than *people*. While each person is a living, eternal soul, the emphasis of Colossians 4:6 is focused on people as individuals. The end goal of evangelism is not merely to produce a soul count. It is being a vessel communicating God's grace to a person God knows intimately and loves deeply.

Souls are not just statistics. Paul said, "From now on we regard no one from a worldly point of view" (2 Corinthians 5:16, NIV). Every person should be viewed in the light of eternity. To be effective in reaching people, we must understand that every soul is a person, and each person is unique. Relevance is an individual issue.

Learning the thinking processes, values, concerns, interests, and desires of people in various cultures and generations is helpful. But, generalizations can be misleading. Baby boomers or busters, Gen X-ers, members of a post-Christian or postmodern culture, millennials or mosaics—these profiles and stereotypes are useful tools, but they are not personal realities. No single mold fits every person within a particular generation, ethnic, or cultural group.

When Paul says we are to respond to each person, he implies that we will respond differently, because each person is an individual. Paul was committed to identifying with anyone who was spiritually lost. He wrote in 1 Corinthians 9:19–20, 22: "Though I am free and belong to no man, I make myself a slave to everyone, to win as many as possible. To the Jews I became like a Jew, to win the Jews. . . . To the weak I became weak, to win the weak. I have become all things to all men so that by all possible means I might save some" (NIV).

This missionary apostle could not be content just to preach the gospel to crowds. His heart reached out to individuals to such an extent that he considered himself a slave to each one. Whether or not a person responded, Paul gave his best to each, to win as many as possible.

9.6.3
OBJECTIVE
Explain why relationship is the foundation for individual ministry.

28 What are the two implications of Paul's focus on individual evangelism?

All Kinds of Individuals

Chapter 8 in this course emphasized Paul's evangelism objective in Colossians 1:28: "that we may present every man complete in Christ." The Greek word translated "every" has two implications.

1. We should warn and teach each person individually, so that each person will be presented complete in Christ.
2. *Every man* also means "some of every kind" of person. This speaks of the variety of individuals to whom we must relate. We are called to reach outsiders, people who are different from us. Christian witness should not only be to our kind of people. The Holy Spirit will enable us to effectively communicate with many kinds of people.

While the basic physical, social, and spiritual needs of people are the same, the paths by which we arrive at those needs wind through personal interests and concerns. How can we really know people's individual interests? The answer is simple. Building relationships and friendships with outsiders is the primary method by which we can respond individually. When Paul says that our gracious conversation will enable us to know how to respond to individuals, he implies that we will learn how to respond.

Paul's exhortation seems overwhelming. How can we possibly know enough to be able to respond individually to each person we encounter?

We will not effectively reach outsiders unless we get to know them where they are. The most important research is done by listening to people. That will happen only if we spend time with them with the intention of knowing and understanding them. Only then can we effectively share the message of Christ. God's timeless truth must be communicated in a timely manner, with the right words for the right occasion. In many situations, a preplanned message would be uninteresting and irrelevant and presume that others will respond to us. We should respond to them.

Most people who come to Christ through personal evangelism are not reached by strangers but by someone they know. Most of our witness will be among people with whom we have ongoing relationships. In these relationships, memorizing an evangelistic routine will not be adequate. We can't just keep repeating the same things to people we know. We must be ready to respond to them in a variety of ways.

29 How do most people come to faith in Christ?

In Jesus' Steps

If we are to follow in Jesus' steps, we should care about people as individuals, knowing that each is known and loved by our heavenly Father. We must connect with them, not only in their cultural context but also in their personal lives.

Jesus gave no less than His best to both Nicodemus and the Samaritan woman. How He dealt with these two people affirms the worth of each individual. Jesus dealt with each differently, tailoring the conversation to individual understanding and interests. For both, He was the answer to their deepest spiritual needs.

Jesus related to people individually and addressed their personal needs, confusion, and pain. He always had time for people. He had time to go with Zaccheus to his house and time in the heat of the day to converse with the Samaritan woman. He had time for children. He had time to rescue the woman caught in adultery. Even in His hour of suffering, when it would have been natural to be occupied with self-interest, He had time for Peter. As the rooster crowed, He gave Peter a look—not an I-told-you-so look—that conveyed love and forgiveness. On the cross, Jesus bore pain none of us will ever know. He still had time to forgive a dying thief and ensure that His mother would be cared for.

Jesus always had time for people. To reach people in the way He commanded us, we must value them as Jesus did and be committed to spending time with them. No one Jesus met was beneath His attention.

The most quoted verse in the Bible, John 3:16, was not part of Jesus' sermons. It was spoken softly in the night during a conversation with Nicodemus, as Jesus responded to the Pharisee's searching questions.

Everyone—our friends and family members, our neighbors, and co-workers, every person we meet—will spend eternity in heaven or hell. Every person should be given an adequate witness of the gospel and the opportunity to make a decision concerning Christ's offer of salvation.

People who are headed toward eternal judgment deserve more from us than canned answers to serious, heart-searching questions. People are not statistics, not merely souls to be won for the Kingdom. They are individuals with distinct personalities—unique creations for whom God has a personal purpose and plan.

Jesus taught in Matthew 10:29–30 that a sparrow does not fall to the ground without our heavenly Father's notice, and the hairs of our head are numbered. He values each person for whom His Son gave His life.

People who are spiritually lost deserve what those who came in contact with Jesus received—a personal response.

9.6.4
OBJECTIVE
Demonstrate Jesus' self-sacrificing approach to meeting others' needs.

30 How should the reality of eternity impact the believer's commitment to personal evangelism?

Test Yourself

Circle the letter of the *best* answer.

1. Human persuasion is an inadequate means of evangelism because
   a) it relies on convincing people to do something based on existing human desires.
   b) the Holy Spirit must be at work in the listener.
   c) the Holy Spirit must be at work in the speaker.
   d) all of the above.

2. The believer should pray which three ways for evangelistic needs?
   a) Bind Satan, rebuke personal pride, claim all lost souls for Christ
   b) Specifically and regularly for nonbelievers, for divine appointments, that other believers will be effective witnesses
   c) Prophesy, pray in tongues, proclaim the triumph of the gospel
   d) Fast, wear sackcloth, tithe

3. A person's acceptance of the Bible as God's inspired Word
   a) is essential for salvation.
   b) has no impact on a decision to be saved.
   c) can be valuable but does not supplant the central truth of believing in Jesus Christ.
   d) is fully expanded the moment he or she comes to salvation.

4. From a biblical viewpoint, Christians who call nonbelievers *outsiders*
   a) recognize the need to communicate the gospel in terms the lost will understand.
   b) are exclusionist hypocrites.
   c) have fallen back into the Law's dichotomy of separating Jews and Gentiles.
   d) recognize that many people are predestined never to enter God's kingdom.

5. In today's culture, the term *Christian*
   a) is recognized as a description of someone who follows Jesus Christ.
   b) should never be used.
   c) has lost all specific meaning.
   d) should be used with synonyms such as *believer* or *follower of Christ*.

6. What two tools are vital to personal evangelism?
   a) Sharing a personal testimony, praying with people
   b) Knowing Hebrew, knowing Greek
   c) Word of knowledge, word of wisdom
   d) A crucifix, a tract

7. Opportunities for witnessing and praying with people usually come
   a) during the first conversation and must be pursued.
   b) over time as a relationship develops.
   c) as elderly family members approach death.
   d) when the believer publicly reads the Bible.

8. All people have a deep, personal need for
   a) an uncompromising explanation of their sinful condition.
   b) genuine love.
   c) a personal copy of the Bible.
   d) a tract.

9. Jesus' primary approach to ministry was to
   a) share the gospel with the largest crowds He could gather.
   b) travel widely proclaiming the kingdom of God.
   c) chastise the Sadducees and Pharisees.
   d) connect with individuals and tailor His teachings and miracles to respond to their needs.

10. Most people come to faith in Christ in response to
    a) reading a clever bumper sticker or church sign.
    b) finding a tract on their windshield.
    c) the personal witness of someone they know.
    d) anointed pleas for seed-faith pledges.

Responses to Interactive Questions
Chapter 9

Some of these responses may include information that is supplemental to the IST. These questions are intended to produce reflective thinking beyond the course content and your responses may vary from these examples.

1 What key aspect of Jesus' prayer life set it apart as the believer's supreme example?

Jesus prayed to God as His Father, demonstrating that prayer is not ceremony but active relationship.

2 Why is human persuasion unequal to the task of evangelism?

Human persuasion appeals to human desires that may not agree with God's desires.

3 What influence contributes to people's inability to believe the gospel?

Satan, "the god of this world," blinds the mind of the lost.

4 What three practices should characterize the believer's evangelistic prayers?

Believers should pray specifically and regularly for nonbelievers they know. They should pray for divine appointments. They should pray for other believers that God will open doors of opportunity to them.

5 How vital is the Holy Spirit to the ministry of the believer?

The Holy Spirit must be at work through the believer for any ministry to be effective. The Spirit both empowers the evangelist and opens the heart of the lost.

6 What double function does Paul identify in the help God offers during evangelism?

God helps the unbeliever become receptive to the gospel. He assists the believer to communicate the message.

7 What does Paul's prayer request reveal about his priorities in personal evangelism?

Paul understood that boldness and clarity were necessities in any gospel witness.

8 Must an unbeliever first understand the Bible's inspiration in order to be saved?

Although it is valuable if an unbeliever accepts the Bible as God's Word, the crux of any salvation decision is the belief in Jesus Christ as God's Son and one's personal Savior and confession of that belief.

9 What message is consistently presented to unbelievers in the Book of Acts?

The message of the early Christians focused on the Person, Jesus Christ.

10 What must accompany any verbal presentation of the gospel?

A compelling gospel witness must be by a living, evident relationship with Christ.

11 Why is the biblical term *outsider* appropriate for a nonbeliever?

The term correctly describes the nonbeliever's disconnect not only with the Christian faith, but with the culture and terminology of the church.

12 Why are predetermined witnessing programs often inadequate to the task of connecting the lost with the gospel?

A predetermined approach to evangelism often assumes a basic understanding of Judeo-Christian concepts and fails to communicate with the spiritually ignorant nonbeliever.

13 What is one approach that lays a clear foundation for the nonbeliever to recognize his or her spiritual need?

Communicating God's purpose and plan for every person's life can direct the nonbeliever's attention to the more elusive concept of salvation.

14 How has the term *Christian* been misappropriated?

Social and political overtones have crowded out, in some people's minds, the term's personal identification of the believer with Christ.

15 What is the broader meaning of the word *missionary*?

The term really means "sent one" and is not limited to a presentation of the gospel on foreign soil. All believers are sent outside the church to share the good news.

16 What was Jesus' motivation for reaching out to the Samaritan woman?

Jesus thrived on the opportunity to meet someone's spiritual need.

17 Why is prayer life and spiritual discipline critical to our evangelistic effectiveness?

Through prayer and discipline, we hone spiritual alertness to the opportunities God creates for us to touch the lost.

18 What are two vital tools in personal evangelism?

Sharing a personal testimony and praying with people can be effective evangelistic practices in every believer's life.

19 Why is personal evangelism a long-term commitment?

Evangelism is most effective when it is built on a relationship developed over time rather than on a presentation that is memorized for instant delivery.

20 What caution must believers keep in mind when looking for opportunities to share the gospel?

Even divine appointments do not usually come in convenient packages. Believers must be careful not to overlook the opportunities for witness that God provides.

21 Why is it vital that one's lifestyle be consistent with one's spoken testimony?

Today's society is increasingly skeptical of Christianity, and the believer's life must back up the believer's witness.

22 How must the believer's actions toward others mirror God's actions toward him or her?

Just as God's love is not in response to anything the believer has done, the believer must genuinely love even those who can do nothing for him or her in return.

23 How must the believer deal with the issue of sin when sharing the gospel?

It is essential to identify the lost's sinfulness in the context of Christ's offer of forgiveness and eternal life.

24 What is one of the greatest hindrances to effective personal evangelism?

Any form of insincerity or inconsistency between the believer's lifestyle and message will fatally compromise the impact of the gospel.

25 Why is it wrong to universally condemn benevolent acts as evidence of giving in to a secular, social gospel?

Jesus commanded believers to let their good works be evident to the world so God would be glorified.

26 What was Jesus' primary approach to ministry?

Jesus connected with individuals and tailored His teachings and miracles to respond to their needs.

27 How can a focus on souls rob the believer of effective outreach?

While every person is an eternal soul, the concept of the soul can become an impersonal substitute for the real needs of real people.

28 What are the two implications of Paul's focus on individual evangelism?

The Greek word translated "every" in Paul's stated objective of presenting "every man complete in Christ" refers to individual people and to every type of person in a multicultural environment.

29 How do most people come to faith in Christ?

Most people who make a salvation decision do so in response to the personal witness of someone they know as opposed to the testimony of a stranger.

30 How should the reality of eternity impact the believer's commitment to personal evangelism?

Everyone, both close and distant in relationship to the believer, will spend eternity in heaven or hell. That truth should motivate the believer to move beyond canned or rehearsed references to the gospel and direct all energy to a coherent, living presentation of the good news.

Chapter 10

Motivation for Evangelism

An Assemblies of God pastor in a communist country served four separate prison terms for preaching the gospel, leading many of his fellow prisoners to Christ. In his fourth imprisonment, he led forty-two of his cellmates to Jesus, as well as two prison guards. One of the forty-two was a young drug dealer. He was filled with the Spirit and called to the ministry.

This convert was released from the prison four months after the pastor. He journeyed to the pastor's town to attend the underground Pentecostal Bible school. Only two weeks remained in the semester, so he could not receive credit, but he could sit in the classes.

Then students had a one-month break. One of the requirements for entrance into the Bible school was to lead five nonbelievers to Christ. The young man journeyed to his hometown, a communist stronghold where not one religious house of worship existed. All such buildings had been destroyed by the communists. Three weeks later, he called the pastor and asked if the pastor would come and baptize those he had led to Christ.

"Do you have five?" the pastor asked.

"No," the young man replied.

"Then I will not come," the pastor said. "It is a long train journey to your town, and until you have five converts I will not come."

The young man interrupted, "Oh, no, Pastor, I have more than five."

The pastor did not ask how many people the young man had led to Christ. Two days later, he took the train to the young man's city and baptized 753 believers!

The young man had not taken a personal evangelism course. He simply shared the story of Jesus, and the Holy Spirit convinced nonbelievers of the message.

Lesson 10.1   Motivation Levels

Objectives

10.1.1 Explain why self-confidence is not a key to successful evangelism.
10.1.2 Identify a personal obligation to share the gospel with the lost.
10.1.3 Describe how to nurture an eagerness to communicate God's truth.
10.1.4 Dedicate mind and emotions in an unashamed commitment to the task.

Lesson 10.2   Maintaining Motivation

Objectives

10.2.1 Describe the lifelong nature of the zeal God desires for every believer.
10.2.2 Outline a personal commitment to maintaining spiritual fervor.
10.2.3 Explain the priority of focusing on the Person of Christ and the reality of eternity.
10.2.4 Identify and apply three keys to maintaining devotion to God.

Motivation Levels

The Confidence Factor

Why don't more Christians tell others about Jesus Christ? Many think the most common reason is apathy, that Christians just don't care. For most people, the problem is lack of confidence.

Most followers of Christ want to be effective witnesses. Many feel inadequate, intimidated or even fearful about sharing their faith in Christ, especially with someone who doesn't have a Christian background. Most people look for confidence within themselves, which is not the believer's source.

The Early Church believers are an inspiring and instructive example of confidence. After the Holy Spirit was poured out on the Day of Pentecost, a man who had been lame all his life was healed. Those who knew him were "filled with wonder and amazement at what had happened to him" (Acts 3:10).

Because of this miracle and the resulting commotion, Peter and John were arrested and put in jail. The religious leaders and rulers questioned them, "By what power, or in what name, have you done this?" (Acts 4:7). Peter, filled with the Holy Spirit, declared the powerful testimony of Christ, concluding with: "There is salvation in no one else; for there is no other name under heaven that has been given among men by which we must be saved" (Acts 4:12).

The Scriptures then record, "Now as they observed the confidence of Peter and John and understood that they were uneducated and untrained men, they were amazed, and began to recognize them as having been with Jesus" (Acts 4:13).

The confidence of Peter and John was evident and troubling to the religious leaders who said, "But so that it will not spread any further among the people, let us warn them to speak no longer to any man in this name" (Acts 4:17). Peter and John responded, "We cannot stop speaking about what we have seen and heard" (Acts 4:20).

When Peter and John returned to the other believers and reported what had happened, they didn't look for a way to escape the persecution. They first acknowledged God's greatness, saying, "O Lord, it is You who made the heaven and the earth and the sea, and all that is in them" (Acts 4:24).

They recognized the nature of the problem. They didn't take the persecution personally, but prayed instead, "For truly in this city there were gathered together against Your holy servant Jesus, whom You anointed, both Herod and Pontius Pilate, along with the Gentiles and the peoples of Israel, to do whatever Your hand and Your purpose predestined to occur" (Acts 4:27–28).

They did not see their problem as persecution but as part of God's larger plan. They concluded their prayer, "And now, Lord, take note of their threats, and grant that Your bond-servants may speak Your word with all confidence, while You extend Your hand to heal, and signs and wonders take place through the name of Your holy servant Jesus" (Acts 4:29–30).

After they prayed, "the place where they had gathered together was shaken, and they were all filled with the Holy Spirit and began to speak the word of God with boldness" (Acts 4:31).

The confidence with which the first Christians shared the message of Christ was not based on their own persuasive ability. It came from knowing who Jesus is, their understanding of what God was doing, and the power of the Holy Spirit.

Being an effective witness, or evangelist, is not an issue of how much someone knows. Why is it that more new believers are active in sharing

---

LESSON 10.1

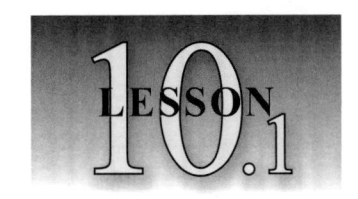

10.1.1 OBJECTIVE
Explain why self-confidence is not a key to successful evangelism.

1   What mistake do many followers of Christ make in regard to personal evangelism?

2   What was the early church's source of confidence when sharing the message of Christ?

Christ with nonbelievers? They are highly motivated to share the difference Christ has made in their lives.

Part of the problem is a matter of education. I believe the greater issue is motivation. People need to see more believers engaged in evangelism. I believe they need a little training and much encouragement.

Paul's Unique Letter to the Romans

Paul's letter to the Romans is unique among his correspondence in the New Testament. Because Paul had never visited Rome, he wrote a more complete theology than he did to any of the other churches. His other letters exhorted and taught concerning particular, unique problems in those specific churches.

It is to our benefit that Paul had not visited Rome, because it provided him an occasion to be thorough in communicating the saving work of Jesus Christ.

In Romans 1:14–16, Paul writes about his ministry of proclaiming the gospel to lost people. His teaching is instructive concerning motivation: "I am under obligation both to Greeks and to barbarians, both to the wise and to the foolish. So, for my part, I am eager to preach the gospel to you also who are in Rome. For I am not ashamed of the gospel, for it is the power of God for salvation to everyone who believes, to the Jew first and also to the Greek."

Paul uses three words to describe three levels of motivation. The words are *obligated, eager,* and *unashamed.*

Obligated

First, Paul says that he is obligated. The Greek word Paul used here is *opheiletes*, which is often translated "a debtor" or "one who owes." This word, when used literally, described a financial obligation. A debt is not an option. If a person has a loan on a house, the bank does not send a monthly suggestion in case the borrower has a little something extra to tuck in an envelope and send to the bank. A debt is a firm contract that cannot be escaped unless it is either paid or forgiven.

Paul's debt to all spiritually lost people, which he describes as being to "Greeks and barbarians, both to the wise and to the foolish," includes everyone. The mission to which the Lord committed Paul was not an option. In Paul's speech before King Agrippa in Acts 26:16–20, Paul says he was not "disobedient to the heavenly vision but kept declaring" Jesus' offer of forgiveness of sins.

Paul understood that his obligation to the spiritually lost was always upon him. Nowhere do the Scriptures record that believers have been released from the same obligation. Paul expressed our debt to the Lord in 2 Corinthians 5, which is among his most personal epistles. In it he opens the motives of his heart:

> We must all appear before the judgment seat of Christ, that each one may receive what is due him for the things done while in the body, whether good or bad. Since, then, we know what it is to fear the Lord, we try to persuade men . . . for Christ's love compels us, because we are convinced that one died for all, and therefore all died. And he died for all, that those who live should no longer live for themselves but for him who died for them and was raised again . . . and he has committed to us the message of reconciliation. We are therefore Christ's ambassadors, as though God were making his appeal through us. (10–11; 14–15; 19–20)

The book of Acts contains four accounts of angelic appearances. In Acts 8, an angel appeared to Philip and directed him to the road between Jerusalem and Gaza, where he proclaimed Christ to the Ethiopian. In Acts 10, an angel appeared

---

10.1.2 OBJECTIVE
Identify a personal obligation to share the gospel with the lost.

3 Why is Paul's sense of obligation an example to every Christian?

and told Cornelius to send for Simon Peter to explain the message of Christ to him. The results were that the Ethiopian and Cornelius believed on Jesus.

Do angels know the gospel? If so, why did not the angel take the message to the Ethiopian? Since the angel spoke directly to Cornelius, why did not he share the message of Christ? Angels are not responsible to proclaim the gospel. Instead, that work is the responsibility of the church. God, in His wisdom and mercy, has determined that we who have experienced Christ's salvation have the privilege of sharing it with others who do not know.

10.1.3 OBJECTIVE
Describe how to nurture an eagerness to communicate God's truth.

Eager

The second word Paul uses in this passage is *eager*. The Greek word used here is *prothumon*, the root of which is *thumos*. The primary meaning of *thumos* relates to passion, anger, or other strong feeling. *Prothumos* is translated "ready" or "willing" in the King James Version. The word is found twice in the Gospels. Both occurrences are in descriptions of the same event, when Jesus was praying in Gethsemane. He said to Peter, James and John, "The spirit is *willing* but the flesh is weak" (Matthew 26:41; Mark 14:38, emphasis added).

It is one thing to recognize a debt or obligation. It is another to be excited about paying it.

4   Why is recognition of an obligation only partial motivation for sharing the gospel?

Why are new believers generally much more active than most Christians in sharing their faith? It is because they are still passionate about sharing the peace they have found in Christ and the joy of their salvation.

The joy of salvation does not have to diminish as believers continue in Christ.

10.1.4 OBJECTIVE
Dedicate mind and emotions in an unashamed commitment to the task.

Unashamed

The third word Paul uses in this passage to describe his motivation is *unashamed*.

To be obligated is to know and understand we have a responsibility. It doesn't speak to our emotions. Eagerness, on the other hand, is an issue of the heart and the emotions—a passion and readiness to do something. To be unashamed is an issue of heart and mind, involving both emotion and intellect.

5   How does emulating Paul's unashamed commitment to share the gospel touch the believer's entire life?

Paul's unashamed view of the gospel was grounded in his knowledge of what Christ had done for him. The reason Paul was unashamed in his ministry of sharing the gospel was not because of self-confidence in his education under Gamaleil, one of the foremost rabbis of the day. It was not because of his eloquence in rhetoric, which was significant, or his passion, which was evident. His confidence was in the power of the gospel itself—"because it (the gospel) is the power of God unto salvation" (Romans 1:16).

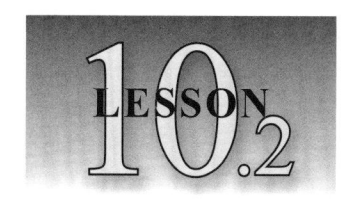

LESSON 10.2

Maintaining Motivation

In the first chapter of Romans, Paul speaks to levels of evangelism motivation. In chapter 12 he speaks of maintaining motivation.

Perhaps you have heard someone described as "a zealous new Christian." Why is the word *zeal* so often associated with new Christians? Probably because it seems that most Christians' spiritual fervency diminishes in time. What about a zealous old Christian?

10.2.1 OBJECTIVE
Describe the lifelong nature of the zeal God desires for every believer.

6 How does the popular view of the zealous Christian differ from the scriptural mandate to be zealous?

10.2.2 OBJECTIVE
Outline a personal commitment to maintaining spiritual fervor.

10.2.3 OBJECTIVE
Explain the priority of focusing on the Person of Christ and the reality of eternity.

7 What two factors radically influenced Paul and energized his faith?

8 How would applying Paul's worldview today impact the life of the believer?

My Grandfather VanDover was a zealous old Christian. The grace of Jesus and the fire of the Holy Spirit ignited a fervency in his heart that never diminished. Grandpa was a bartender and a drunkard who dealt cards and raked the poker table in a gambling house. Grandmother received Christ in meetings preached by P.T. Emmett, an Assemblies of God pastor. Not long after, Pastor Emmett drove to Grandpa's bar and asked him to step outside, where he challenged him to commit his life to Christ and become a Christian husband and father. Grandpa was saved that week and took off his poker apron for the last time.

Until Grandpa VanDover went home to be with the Lord at age eighty two, he never lost the joy and wonder of his salvation. I frequently took him out for lunch during the final years of his life. If a server gave him thirty seconds, he was thirty seconds into his testimony of how God saved a drunken bartender over forty years before.

Paul encouraged the Roman believers to "never be lacking in zeal, but keep your spiritual fervor, serving the Lord" (Romans 12:11). The Greek word translated "zeal" is *spoude*, which speaks of earnestness or diligence. The Greek word translated "fervor" here (*zeo*) has a temperature connotation. It means "boiling" when referring to liquids and "glowing" when referring to solids. The Revised Standard Version accurately translates the expression for *spiritual fervor* as "aglow with the Spirit."

Paul lived his admonition to the Roman Christians. After his encounter with the Lord on the Damascus road, he was never the same. The fire in his soul never seemed to diminish. While this is not the norm for most Christians, it is God's will. The New Testament is clear that the spiritual life of the church was designed by God to be a constant flow of God's Spirit within and through His people.

A hymn familiar from my Pentecostal youth says, "Revive us again; fill each heart with Thy love, May each soul be rekindled with fire from above" (Mackay 1863, 302). We don't really have a problem obtaining the fire; our problem is retaining the fire. Paul reminded Timothy to "kindle afresh the gift of God which is in you" (2 Timothy 1:6).

Second Corinthians contains a passage that reveals Paul's inner motives. In 2 Corinthians 5:1–15, two factors are at the heart of Paul's zealous, fervent life:

1. Paul focused on the eternal rather than the temporal.
2. Paul nurtured personal devotion to Jesus Christ.

In the first few verses of 2 Corinthians 5, Paul rejoiced in the reality of our eternal "dwelling from heaven." For Paul, the earthly body does not even merit being called a building. Rather, it is a tent, a temporary dwelling.

Because of his devotion to Christ and his eye on eternity, whether he lived or died was not the point, he says in 2 Corinthians 5:8–9. His beautiful expression at the end of 2 Corinthians 5:4 explains what death means for the Christian: "What is mortal will be swallowed up by life." Paul's preference for being absent from the body was not pessimistic escapism but a positive faith that was focused on his Lord. He preferred death to life because death means to be at home with the Lord. For this reason, he could say, "For to me, to live is Christ and to die is gain" (Philippians 1:21).

In 2 Corinthians 5:9 Paul reveals his single ambition to be pleasing to Jesus. Why? "For we must all appear before the judgment seat of Christ, that each one may be recompensed for his deeds in the body, according to what he has done, whether good or bad." The judgment seat of Christ is an awesome event to face. Paul said, "Therefore, knowing the fear of the Lord, we persuade men" (2 Corinthians 5:11). His objective to please the Lord was related to his knowledge of Jesus' future judgment of all who follow Him.

In the same passage Paul relates his motive to the "fear of the Lord," but his motivation was the "love of Christ." The Greek word used here (*sunecho*) is translated in different versions as "constraineth" (KJV), "compels" (NIV), and "controls" (NASB). This word refers to something that literally takes over. In the Gospels it describes those who were controlled by different diseases, such as Peter's mother-in-law who was controlled by a fever. Paul was saying that the love of Christ had taken control of his life the same way a disease or fever takes control of a body. His zeal was a result of Christ's love, not his own will or emotions.

9   How does the love of Christ transcend mere emotional warmth?

The compelling love of Christ was not a sentimental or emotional feeling for Paul. He had concluded that Jesus died for all so that we who live should no longer live for ourselves but for Him who died and rose again on our behalf. (See 2 Corinthians 5:14.) The Greek word translated "concluded" here means to make an intellectual and ethical judgment. Paul's fervency was not the product of emotionalism.

The foundation of Paul's fervency was his wholehearted devotion to Jesus. To him the issue was simple—life is a response to the sacrifice of our Lord. He said it clearly in Romans 12:1: "Therefore, I urge you, brothers, in view of God's mercy, to offer your bodies as living sacrifices, holy and pleasing to God—this is your spiritual act of worship."

When Paul admonished Timothy to "kindle afresh" the gift of God within him, he was telling Timothy that the fire of his spirit was burning low and that he could and must do something about it.

How can we kindle our zeal? As with Paul, we must focus on Jesus and eternity. The personal realization of our Lord's sacrifice for us and His grace in our lives sparks the flame of spiritual passion in our hearts. The great old hymn "My Faith Looks Up To Thee" says, "May thy rich grace impart strength to my fainting heart, My zeal inspire; As thou has died for me, O may my love to thee Pure, warm, and changeless be A living fire!" (Palmer 1830, 287).

Remember, our problem is not as much obtaining the fire but retaining the fire. How do we retain spiritual fire? By maintaining the fire.

10.2.4 OBJECTIVE
Identify and apply three keys to maintaining devotion to God.

As a Boy Scout, I learned that to maintain a fire, I needed three things:

1. A constant supply of wood
2. A free flow of air
3. Continual clearing of ashes

The same is true spiritually. To maintain the zeal of devotion to the Lord, we need three similar things.

10   How can the believer maintain zealous devotion to God?

1. A constant, fresh supply of the Word
2. A free flow of the Spirit in our prayer life
3. Continuous cleansing from sin and self-will

Paul feared that the passion for Christ would diminish in the Corinthian believers. He said, "I am afraid that, as the serpent deceived Eve by his craftiness, your minds will be led astray from the simplicity and purity of devotion to Christ" (2 Corinthians 11:3).

People who long for revival in our churches must first seek God in their personal lives. We need to sing again with understanding and conviction, "O Holy Ghost, revival comes from Thee; Send a revival, start the work in me!"

My Grandfather Hurst lived a rich, full life as a Pentecostal preacher. He retired from the pastorate early to care for my grandmother who was slowly dying from cancer. Even in retirement, he was zealous, daily searching the Word and praying. He never stopped growing spiritually. When he went home to be with the Lord at age eighty nine, his final utterances were a prayer in tongues and a song: "Oh, how I love Jesus, Because He first loved me!" The controlling focus of His life to the end was Jesus.

As with Paul, we must keep our eyes on Jesus and eternity. The simplicity and purity of devotion to Christ will enable us to obey Paul's exhortation, "Never be lacking in zeal, but keep your spiritual fervor, serving the Lord" (Romans 12:11, NIV).

Motivation for Evangelism

Test Yourself

Circle the letter of the *best* answer.

1. Most Christians who are reluctant to share the gospel are struggling with
   a) spiritual apathy.
   b) a skewed understanding of God's elect.
   c) hidden sin.
   d) lack of confidence and a belief that confidence is self-produced.

2. The early church confidently shared the message of Christ because
   a) of their faith in and relationship to each Person in the Trinity.
   b) of the miracles performed by the apostles.
   c) Jesus' teachings were popular among the common people.
   d) they expected Christ's soon return.

3. Paul described his obligation to share the gospel as a debt owed to
   a) the Gentiles, since Peter and others would minister to the Jews.
   b) all spiritually lost people, regardless of race or class.
   c) the Pharisees, to whom he could relate as a scholar.
   d) those who gave faith pledges to his ministry.

4. Paul's evangelistic obligation was backed up by
   a) deep theological training as a Pharisee.
   b) ordination from the original church in Jerusalem.
   c) his eagerness to share the gospel with the lost.
   d) his regret for having helped stone Stephen.

5. A believer who unashamedly carries the gospel to the lost will
   a) fast and pray until the Holy Spirit identifies an audience.
   b) experience complete sanctification as a second work of grace.
   c) engage mind and emotions in full commitment to the task.
   d) always be ridiculed and persecuted.

6. In general, Christians with a reputation for spiritual fervor and zealous evangelistic desire
   a) are new believers.
   b) are under twenty.
   c) are women.
   d) have gone to Bible college.

7. Paul's spiritual zeal was fed by his focus on
   a) The inadequacy of the Law and on the gifts of the Spirit.
   b) The eternal versus the temporal and his personal devotion to Jesus Christ.
   c) Reaching the Gentiles and ministering in Rome.
   d) Miracles and the end-time.

8. Paul's view of life and death
   a) gave him favor with the Sadducees.
   b) created a fatalistic tone in his epistles.
   c) caused many early Christians to wait in futility for Christ's return.
   d) saw the former as service to Christ and the latter as the opportunity to be with Him.

9. The love of Christ constraining a believer refers to
   a) its powerful influence on the believer's life and the outgrowth of obedient witnessing.
   b) Christ's determination to save the elect.
   c) the Christian's inability to sin as long as he or she loves Christ.
   d) the Holy Spirit's control of the believer's tongue during Pentecostal baptism.

10. What three disciplines nurture spiritual zeal?
    a) Love, joy, and peace
    b) Church membership, tithing, and lay ministry
    c) Study in the Word, reliance on the Holy Spirit, and rejection of sin
    d) Psalms, hymns, and spiritual songs

Responses to Interactive Questions
Chapter 10

Some of these responses may include information that is supplemental to the IST. These questions are intended to produce reflective thinking beyond the course content and your responses may vary from these examples.

1   What mistake do many followers of Christ make in regard to personal evangelism?

They look for confidence within themselves when sharing the gospel.

2   What was the early church's source of confidence when sharing the message of Christ?

Early Christians found confidence in their knowledge of and relationship to God.

3   Why is Paul's sense of obligation an example to every Christian?

The Bible makes it clear that all who have been saved are compelled by Christ's love to share the message of salvation with the lost.

4   Why is recognition of an obligation only partial motivation for sharing the gospel?

Recognition of the obligation must be followed by an eagerness to fulfill that obligation.

5   How does emulating Paul's unashamed commitment to share the gospel touch the believer's entire life?

An unashamed gospel witness involves both a mental acknowledgment of the truth and an emotional commitment to sharing it.

6   How does the popular view of the zealous Christian differ from the scriptural mandate to be zealous?

Zealous faith is most often associated with new Christians, while the Bible commands believers to maintain that zeal throughout life.

7   What two factors radically influenced Paul and energized his faith?

Paul maintained a focus on the eternal and a personal devotion to Jesus Christ.

8   How would applying Paul's worldview today impact the life of the believer?

Christians who focus on Christ and on eternity are able to lead fulfilled lives with no fear of death.

9   How does the love of Christ transcend mere emotional warmth?

Christ's love is an active force that takes control of the believer's life.

10   How can the believer maintain zealous devotion to God?

Faithful study of God's Word, praying in the Spirit, and cleansing from sin and self-will.

UNIT PROGRESS EVALUATION 3

Now that you have finished Unit 3, review the lessons in preparation for Unit Progress Evaluation 3. You will find it in Essential Course Materials at the back of this IST. Answer all of the questions without referring to your course materials, Bible, or notes. When you have completed the UPE, check your answers with the answer key provided in Essential Course Materials. Review any items you may have answered incorrectly. Then you may proceed with your study of Unit 4. (Although UPE scores do not count as part of your final course grade, they indicate how well you learned the material and how well you may perform on the closed-book final examination.)

UNIT 4

Pastoral Leadership in Evangelism

In every community, God sees individuals with an eternal destiny. God called Moses to lead His people out of bondage in Egypt and into the Promised Land. He still sees souls that are in bondage. He sees the sheep that are not yet of His fold (John 10:16), so He sends a shepherd to lead a congregation in reaching the spiritually lost of a community.

God called Steve and Lauri Funderburk to leave a larger church to pastor a congregation of just fifty-two people in Wetumpka, Alabama. God gave Steve a clear vision concerning what needed to happen for the church to reach its community for Christ. Steve kept the vision to himself and waited for God's time to share it with the congregation.

For three years he simply shepherded and cared for the people of Bethel Assembly. During this time, the church experienced little numerical growth. Then the day came when the Holy Spirit released Steve to share his vision with the congregation. He had spent three years establishing a relationship with the people. Now, they responded to the vision, trusting the pastor who had faithfully ministered to them. The church began to grow in every way—in salvation decisions, Sunday morning attendance, Holy Spirit baptisms, water baptisms, and missions giving.

When the church passed 120 in attendance, many of the original church members felt uncomfortable. They thought the congregation had grown beyond a family church. They told Steve they would be more comfortable in a small church, and the majority of them left. But they parted ways with good relationships. Steve still goes fishing with former members and eats vegetables from their gardens.

At the time of this writing, Bethel Assembly has more than three hundred in Sunday morning attendance. People regularly come to Christ and the church continues to grow.

Had Steve immediately shared his vision with the congregation, they would not have been ready to follow his leadership. Leaders need the guidance of the Holy Spirit, not only concerning what to do but also when. The vision must be from God. The method must be from God. And the timing must be from God.

The key to a local church's mission is a committed, spiritually equipped pastor who is led by the Holy Spirit.

Chapter 11   The Pastor's Role in Evangelism

Lessons
11.1   Modeling and Motivating Evangelism
11.2   Mobilizing and Maintaining Evangelism
11.3   Partnering and Planting in Evangelism

Chapter 12   Evangelism in the Pulpit

Lessons
12.1   The Power of the Preached Word
12.2   Preparation for Proclamation
12.3   Call to Decision

Chapter 13   **From Decision to Disciple**

Lessons
13.1   Initial Follow-Up
13.2   Discipling
13.3   Components and Means of Discipling

Chapter 14   **World Missions**

Lessons
14.1   Our Worldwide Mission
14.2   World Missions in the Local Church

Chapter 15   **The Church in Mission**

Lessons
15.1   The Redemptive Mission of the Church
15.2   Fulfilling the Mission

CHAPTER 11

The Pastor's Role in Evangelism

Thomas Trask, general superintendent of the U.S. Assemblies of God at the time of this experience, one day asked me to go with him immediately to St. John's Hospital in Springfield, Missouri. On the way he explained. Eddie was a mutual business acquaintance. A colleague told Brother Trask that Eddie had suffered a heart attack, and doctors were not sure if he would live.

We walked into Eddie's room in the coronary care unit. After a few words of greeting and inquiry, Brother Trask said with great kindness, "Eddie, I'm not trying to scare you, but the doctors say they're not sure if you'll make it."

"I know," Eddie replied. "They told me."

"Randy and I had to come and talk with you today," Brother Trask continued. "I have to know that you're ready for heaven."

I wish I had a videotape of the ensuing conversation. With a gracious and passionate demeanor, Brother Trask gently but clearly led Eddie to the point of decision.

"Are you ready to surrender your life to Christ?" he asked. When Eddie replied that he was, Brother Trask added, "Then I'm going to ask Randy to lead us in prayer, and you and I will follow him."

I led in a sinner's prayer as Brother Trask and Eddie responded. Then Brother Trask prayed for Eddie's new life in Christ and for his physical recovery. Eddie lived and went back to work, a new man. About a year later, Eddie died and went to be with the Lord.

It has been an inspiration to me for many years to observe Brother Trask. He models a life of personal evangelism with a heart for the lost that moves him to action. In the same way, a local church pastor should be an example of someone who is loving and reaching the lost.

Lesson 11.1   Modeling and Motivating Evangelism

Objectives

11.1.1   Explain the role of evangelism within the home and the importance of creating regular evangelistic invitations within the church.

11.1.2   Outline the role of sermons and testimonies in communicating evangelism.

11.1.3   Pursue evangelism opportunities within the community, and support world missions as an example to the congregation.

11.1.4   Identify and describe the primary motivators in sharing the good news.

Lesson 11.2   Mobilizing and Maintaining Evangelism

Objectives

11.2.1   Identify the church's primary means of witness.

11.2.2   Take advantage of annual seasons and one-time events when the gospel can be highlighted.

11.2.3   Propose a creative spectrum of emphases to mobilize believers' witness.

11.2.4   Describe how the church maintains long-term evangelism.

Lesson 11.3   Partnering and Planting in Evangelism

Objectives

11.3.1   Explain the function of the evangelist as described in the New Testament.

11.3.2   Describe how partnering with evangelists can meet needs within the church and spur believers to personal evangelism.

11.3.3   Identify criteria for selecting evangelists.

11.3.4   Explain the evangelistic potential of church planting.

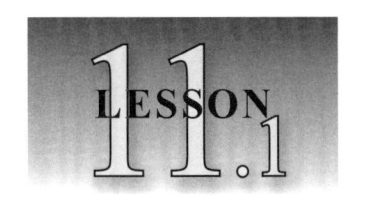

LESSON 11.1

11.1.1
OBJECTIVE

Explain the role of evangelism within the home and the importance of creating regular evangelistic invitations within the church.

1   What foundational teaching principle does the modeling concept embody?

Modeling and Motivating Evangelism

The apostle Paul told his young disciple and friend Timothy, "Do the work of an evangelist" (2 Timothy 4:5). Timothy was called and gifted for pastoral ministry, yet his model and mentor exhorted him to do the work of an evangelist.

No two ministers are alike. Not everyone in itinerant ministry is primarily an evangelist. On the other hand, many pastors minister in their communities as gifted evangelists. Unfortunately, some have taught designations concerning spiritual gifts that are too rigid and categorical. Stereotypes of ministry are limiting and cause some to fall short of their calling.

Paul is an example of a blend of spiritual gifts. He functioned first as an apostle, but he also was an evangelist, a prophet and a pastor-teacher. From his perspective of ministry in a variety of roles, Paul exhorted Timothy to do the work of an evangelist.

Modeling

Evangelism in a local church begins with the pastor. Before a pastor can motivate his congregation to do outreach, he must first model evangelism. I have ministered many years in itinerant ministry and have observed hundreds of Pentecostal pastors and churches. I have never seen a praying church that does not have a praying pastor. I have never seen a giving church that does not have a giving pastor. A worshiping church has a worshiping pastor. A missions-minded church has a missions-minded pastor. Eventually, what the pastor is, the congregation becomes.

Luke opens the book of Acts in 1:1 with an instructive phrase about our Lord: "Jesus began both to do and teach." The order is significant. The tendency of modern education is to teach first and then expect students to do what they have been taught. Jesus did first, then He taught. Our Maker became our Model. Paul understood this and wrote, "Be imitators of me, just as I also am of Christ" (1 Corinthians 11:1). In Philippians 4:9, Paul said, "Those things, which ye have both learned, and received, and heard, and seen in me, do."

Children do what their parents do much more often than they do what their parents say. The greatest leaders in history led by example more than by command. Almost all of us can think of people who influenced us and can see this principle at work. The old adage is true: "The most important lessons are caught rather than taught." This is especially true in evangelism.

The modeling principle is evident throughout the Scriptures. Consider the relationships between such people as Moses and Joshua, Elijah and Elisha, and Jesus and His disciples. Similar modeling relationships continued in the New Testament church with Barnabas and Paul, Paul and Silas, and then Paul and Timothy.

How does today's pastor model the ministry of evangelism?

In the Pastor's Family

A pastor's family who is fully committed to the Lord can exemplify a home that represents well the life of Christ. Evangelizing and discipling our children are a major part of the ministry God gave us. Modeling a lifestyle of evangelism begins in the home.

Before the Congregation

One of the most important ways a pastor can model evangelism in his church is by giving regular public invitations to salvation. Even when no one responds to a salvation invitation, people in the congregation witness their pastor's concern, passion, and commitment to reaching the lost. They observe not only what the pastor does, but also how he does it. Invitations to commitment and any other evangelism effort in the church service should be done with conviction, faith and earnestness. The pastor's attitude about reaching the lost will be apparent to the congregation.

In the Community

The most effective evangelistic pastors make a direct personal impact on people outside the church. Building relationships with nonbelievers in the community and being interested in them will provide opportunities to share the gospel. When they are in spiritual need, they will more likely respond to an invitation to church or for personal counseling. When a pastor encounters people in his everyday activities and learns they do not regularly attend a church, it should be natural for him invite them to visit his church. Pastors should acquire the same nickname as the Chief Shepherd, who became known as "a friend of . . . sinners" (Matthew 11:19).

One of the most powerful aspects of evangelism is simply praying with someone for a need. Pentecostal people believe that God answers prayer. We should practice our belief by praying with and for people in the community. Just hearing a born-again believer pray has a significant effect on a nonbeliever. And when God answers prayer, it can be the means of opening hearts to the gospel.

---

2   Why is a godly home a model of evangelism?

11.1.2 OBJECTIVE
Outline the role of sermons and testimonies in communicating evangelism.

11.1.3 OBJECTIVE
Pursue evangelism opportunities within the community, and support world missions as an example to the congregation.

3   What is a simple way to begin the evangelism process with some people?

In the Pastor's World

A direct correlation exists between a pastor's heart for the lost in his own community and his vision for the lost of the world. When a congregation can observe a pastor's burden for the world's lost multitudes, it affects how believers view the lost of their own community. An expansive vision and burden for world missions will bear fruit in the local church. A church that commits to supporting missionaries and praying for the lost around the world will have an increased vision for reaching people in their immediate surroundings.

Motivating

11.1.4 OBJECTIVE
Identify and describe the primary motivators in sharing the good news.

Christian bookstores and Internet sites offer an abundance of good materials and books concerning personal evangelism. Yet, in most churches—even evangelical and Pentecostal churches—both attendance and salvation decisions are declining, while the population is growing.

On the other hand, multitudes of people in countries overseas are coming to Christ, and churches are growing. These believers have few resources, but they have the Bible and a passionate motivation to share Christ.

The motivating power for evangelism comes from the Holy Spirit. Believers in a local congregation need encouragement and training. In motivating believers for outreach, we cooperate with the work of the Holy Spirit.

A pastor cooperates with the Holy Spirit when he or she strategically and regularly preach the Word regarding evangelism. Preaching a sermon concerning evangelism once or twice a year is not enough to keep a congregation focused on outreach.

4 What is one of the most effective tools for communicating evangelism principles to a congregation?

An effective way of motivating is personal testimonies, both from the pastor and people in the congregation. If the pastor models evangelism in his everyday life, he will have testimonies to share publicly. It is best not to publicly name people to whom the pastor has witnessed, but testimonies discreetly shared will encourage a congregation to follow this example.

Testimonies by other church members are most effective when selected and directed by the pastor. In one service, a pastor invited evangelism testimonies from the congregation. Only one testimony out of six was appropriate. If people are encouraged to tell their pastor about their witnessing experiences, he can ask certain ones to share a testimony with the congregation. Testimonies are most effective if they are used selectively and sparingly.

These two factors are powerful motivators:

1. A Response to Christ's Sacrifice

5 What should be the effect of a personal frame of reference regarding Christ's sacrifice?

   To effectively evangelize, we need a genuine realization that Christ died for us. Our Christian service is a logical and "reasonable" response to the sacrifice of our Lord (Romans 12:1, KJV). Paul took the Lord's sacrifice personally. That was the secret to the powerful motivation he had to reach the unreached. (See Galatians 2:20.) His personal motivation came from the logical conclusion that "One died for all . . . and He died for all, that those who live should no longer live for themselves, but for Him who died for them and was raised again on their behalf" (2 Corinthians 5:14–15, NIV).

2. The Work of the Spirit

   Evangelism is primarily a work of the Holy Spirit. Convicting nonbelievers of their sin is not our work, but the Holy Spirit's. We are witnesses for Christ, but the Spirit is the One who wins people to Christ. He is the One who convinces nonbelievers of sin and leads them to confession and repentance. The Spirit also empowers believers to express effectively, through both word and action, the truth and reality of Jesus in their lives.

The pastor who keeps his congregation focused on the Lord's sacrifice and the power of the Holy Spirit will be effective in inspiring his church in its mission of evangelizing the lost.

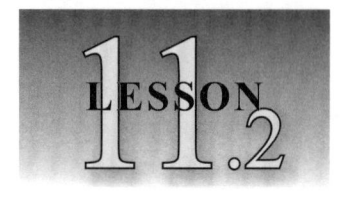

LESSON 11.2

11.2.1 OBJECTIVE
Identify the church's primary means of witness.

Mobilizing and Maintaining Evangelism

Mobilizing

Motivating people to evangelism—stirring their desire to reach the lost—is one thing. Mobilizing them to ministry is another.

Christ gave pastors to the church "for the equipping of the saints for the work of service, to the building up of the body of Christ" (Ephesians 4:12). Mobilizing members of a congregation in evangelism, especially personal evangelism, is one of a pastor's most important biblical responsibilities in equipping believers for ministry. Many believers are regularly stirred by the Spirit to share their faith and spiritual experience with nonbelievers. What they need from the pastor is encouragement, training and opportunities to help them translate motivation into action.

Personal Evangelism—the Number One Priority

While many people who find Christ do so in a local church service, the impact of personal evangelism and witness outside the church building is paramount. Christian parents often lead their children to Christ. A personal invitation to attend a church service or another church event can result in a person coming to Christ. However, outreaches that minister to needs in the community can also open doors for personal evangelism. By far, the highest priority in a church's evangelistic outreach is the personal witness of its members in the community at large.

Many approaches to training for personal evangelism are available. But the volume of content in many resources can be overwhelming and intimidating, discouraging Christians from getting involved in evangelism training courses. The response evangelism approach in Chapter 8, based on Paul's instructions to the Colossians, is a simple, biblical, and practical approach that will help believers in their relational witness.

Both focused personal evangelism classes and churchwide emphases can be used in teaching personal evangelism from a biblical perspective. Units 2 and 3 of this course offer teaching appropriate to both contexts. A pastor should keep the cause of personal evangelism regularly before his people. Simple practices should be encouraged on an ongoing basis by mentioning them occasionally from the pulpit. These four practices will help any Christian who wants to be active in personal witness:

6 What four practices offer a solid start to personal evangelism?

1. Believers should be encouraged to share from their own experience—how they know their sins were forgiven, that they are new creations in Christ, and that they have an eternal home in heaven.

2. Believers should learn to avoid religious arguments and controversies. The focus should instead be on a person's relationship with God, on whether he or she has found the peace of knowing God's forgiveness, and has assurance of everlasting life.

3. While community witness is important, believers should also be exhorted to find opportune ways to invite people to church where they can experience God' presence, receive the ministry of the Word, and be challenged to a decision to receive and follow Christ.

4. Believers should be encouraged to seize opportunities to pray with nonbelievers. Many nonbelievers may pray at times, but it can be awkward and uncomfortable for them. As born-again believers, how we pray in the presence of a nonbeliever is a testimony to the living relationship we have with our Lord.

Above all, believers need to be reminded that God is the One who saves people. The Holy Spirit is the One who convinces of sin. Jesus is the One who builds His church. We simply take part in the work God is doing in people's lives.

Seizing Seasons

Certain seasons of the year afford appropriate opportunities for outreach. Other open doors occur because of one-time events. A church that focuses on evangelism should be prayerfully alert to seize the moment when any opportunity arises to reach people for Christ.

Christmas and Easter offer two of the most opportune times for evangelism. Two activities that can enhance this are prayer circles and Bible-reading programs.

1. Prayer circles offer opportunities to put Matthew 18:19–20 into practice. Church members join in groups of two to four to pray regularly for specific friends and family members who do not know Christ. On a designated Sunday, these groups gather and write down on a Bible marker the names of one to three friends or family members who do not know Christ. The group then agrees in prayer for them. Participants try to join in prayer with their prayer circle partners by phone during the week and for a few moments at church before or after services. They also can put their prayer into action in a variety of ways, including giving an evangelism gift book or a video of Christ's life and inviting the nonbelievers to special church services.

Individual prayer cards also can be used for people who prefer to pray alone, rather than praying in a group.

2. Involving church families in Bible-reading disciplines for the same time period also is effective. The most appropriate Bible reading program for the Easter and Christmas seasons involves reading through the life of Christ, either one of the Gospels or a harmonized version from all four Gospels. This can be done over varying lengths of time, but an effective method is a forty-day program prior to Easter and a twenty-five-day program leading up to Christmas.

Scripture readings for these programs can be compiled in a variety of ways. For the forty-day period before Easter, people may follow through on the program more easily if the readings are done only on weekdays, requiring just thirty readings. At Christmas, one selection daily from December 1 through Christmas Day is effective.

Other special seasonal outreaches can be incorporated, such as July 4, when a patriotic emphasis might attract some people who wouldn't come to Christmas and Easter services. Memorial Day can focus on veterans and Labor Day on various occupations. Any season or event that captures the interest and involvement of people is an opportunity for outreach. For many churches, Friend Day is especially effective. Friend Day gives a reason for church members to

---

11.2.2 OBJECTIVE

Take advantage of annual seasons and one-time events when the gospel can be highlighted.

7 What are two effective tools for enhancing seasonal evangelism opportunities?

invite friends and also gives people a reason to come. The bond of friendship creates a wonderful opportunity for a Christian to invite a nonbeliever to church.

By All Means

The apostle Paul includes a challenging phrase in his letter to the Corinthians. "I have become all things to all men, so that I may by all means save some" (1 Corinthians 9:22). It is impossible in this lesson to list the wide variety of means available to mobilize a congregation to various forms of evangelistic outreach.

Even if people are motivated, most find it easier to become involved in evangelism if they are presented with a simple plan or program in which to participate. Following are three examples and suggestions:

1. Ministries to meet specific spiritual needs. Developing ministries that focus on unique spiritual needs of groups, such as single parents, the divorced, or the unemployed, can reach people with the gospel in their time of greatest need.

2. Community prayer ministry. One pastor saw great evangelistic response by focusing on specific prayer needs of the neighborhood surrounding the church. Groups of two from the church walked through these neighborhoods, praying for the residents house by house as they walked. After doing this for three weeks, they visited the homes and told the residents they were from the Assemblies of God church. They explained that they believe God answers prayer and then asked if their congregation could pray for any specific needs. Many people shared prayer requests. The congregation prayed for those requests, and a few weeks later the prayer teams returned to the houses. They asked the people if the Lord had answered their prayers and invited them to attend church services. The first Sunday after this visit, fifty-two people received Christ as Savior.

3. Special sermon series. Preaching a special sermon series is a productive approach to evangelism. Expository messages are the most evangelistically effective, but try to choose titles that are representative of the biblical content yet appeal to the interest of the general public. Printing fliers or brochures for congregation members to distribute to their friends works well.

These are just a few examples of ideas that have been used to reach nonbelievers. Seek the Holy Spirit's guidance and be open to the creativity of people within the congregation for opportunities that are unique to your local church and community. As with the apostle Paul, commit to reaching the spiritually lost "by all means."

While we should prioritize the most effective means of evangelism that result in the greatest long-term results, we also should be open to "all means" of reaching the spiritually lost.

Maintaining Evangelism

Regaining lost momentum in evangelism and church growth is harder than establishing it initially.

More than anything else, maintaining evangelism in a local church involves exhorting and teaching church members to establish and maintain long-term relationships with nonbelievers, especially family members and friends. They need to be there for people in times of need and in major crises. Sometimes a relationship with a nonbeliever requires many years of nurturing before the Holy Spirit opens the door to lead that person from an acquaintance with the gospel to a life-changing decision concerning the claims of Christ.

11.2.3 OBJECTIVE
Propose a creative spectrum of emphases to mobilize believers' witness.

8 What common denominator characterizes every means used to communicate the gospel?

11.2.4 OBJECTIVE
Describe how the church maintains long-term evangelism.

After more than twenty years of ministry in hundreds of churches, I have concluded that the following four characteristics can make a church effective in both reaching and retaining people:

1. *A church of the Word*. Strategies for attracting people to church will ultimately fail if the Word of God is not presented in power. The seed for planting the harvest is always the message of the gospel. If a local church has a reputation in the community as a place where the Word of God is preached with power and effectiveness, people will come to hear it, and their lives will be changed.

2. *A church of the manifest presence of the Holy Spirit*. The Spirit's presence empowers a church as nothing else can. Even nonbelievers can sense something different about a Pentecostal church. The pastor and congregation should pray for the moving of the Holy Spirit in church services.

3. *A church on a mission*. The local church that focuses on reaching the lost of its community and the world is a place where people can find their reason for being. Paul taught in Ephesians 2:8 that we are saved by grace, not by works. He goes on to say that we are God's workmanship created in Christ Jesus for good works. A church on a mission affords people the opportunity to live out God's purpose in their lives.

4. *A church that loves*. Many people will stay in a particular church if they can find just one friend!

9 What four characteristics make a church especially effective in reaching and retaining people?

Evangelism is an activity that a pastor can model, motivate, mobilize, and maintain. We must never forget that it is first and foremost a work of the Holy Spirit. Spirit-filled believers are privileged to have a part in the miracles God works in people's lives to bring them "out of darkness into His marvelous light" (1 Peter 2:9).

10 What must remain in sharpest focus for the evangelistically minded church?

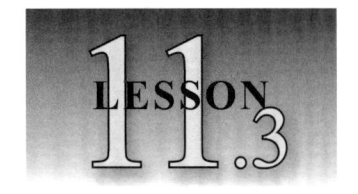

Although this chapter suggests ways to lead a church in evangelism, nothing is more important than a pastor who seeks the Spirit's creative direction for his life, his church, and his community. The Holy Spirit knows how to reach each community, and He knows the spiritual gifts and resources of every pastor and local church. A pastor who seeks the Spirit's creative direction will find it!

LESSON 11.3

Partnering and Planting in Evangelism

Partnering with Evangelists

Any pastor would do well to ask him- or herself: "Can I lead my congregation in evangelism by myself?" The obvious answer is no. God has given a diversity of gifts in the Body, yet no matter how gifted a person is, he or she cannot reach everyone.

When the Christian leaders in Jerusalem heard about the great number of people turning to the Lord in Antioch, they sent Barnabas to the city. Luke records in Acts 11:23–26:

> When he arrived and witnessed the grace of God, he rejoiced and began to encourage them all with resolute heart to remain true to the Lord; for he was a good man, and full of the Holy Spirit and of faith. And considerable numbers were brought to the Lord. And he left for Tarsus to look for Saul; and when he had found him, he brought him to Antioch. And for an entire year they met

with the church and taught considerable numbers; and the disciples were first called Christians in Antioch.

Barnabas saw spiritual needs he felt inadequate to meet. He saw potential in Paul's ministry that suited the needs of the Antioch church. It was a divinely ordered connection, but God used Barnabas to make it happen.

Just as Barnabas brought Paul to Antioch, a pastor can benefit greatly by partnering with an evangelist to maximize the effectiveness of a local church's outreach.

The Evangelist in the New Testament

The New Testament contains only three references to the ministry of the evangelist:

1. "And He gave some as apostles, and some as prophets, and some as evangelists, and some as pastors and teachers" (Ephesians 4:11).

   Among the ministry callings listed by Paul is the evangelist. The word *evangelist* comes from the Greek word *euangelistas*, which means "a bringer of good news."

2. "On the next day we left and came to Caesarea, and entering the house of Philip the evangelist, who was one of the seven, we stayed with him" (Acts 21:8).

   Philip is the only individual named as an evangelist in the New Testament. In Acts 8 God used him to bring the Ethiopian eunuch to faith, providing an example of what an evangelist does. In modern culture, most people think of evangelists as those who preach to large crowds. Philip's example is a one-on-one personal evangelism encounter.

3. "But you, be sober in all things, endure hardship, do the work of an evangelist, fulfill your ministry" (2 Timothy 4:5).

   Paul told Timothy to "do the work of an evangelist." Timothy was undoubtedly a pastor-teacher, but Paul wanted to ensure that the young man did not function only in that gifting. Paul wanted Timothy to proclaim the message to nonbelievers and see the lost come to Christ.

Itinerant Ministry

The term *evangelist* has commonly been used to describe anyone in itinerant ministry. Many itinerant ministers are evangelists, but no scriptural prescription determines that an evangelist must travel. An evangelist can be placed within a local church, and his or her entire ministry may be localized in one community. The important issue is how the ministry functions.

An itinerant evangelist is basically a multichurch associate pastor. Whether an evangelist comes to minister for a weekend or an extended period, he or she is there to supplement and complement the senior pastor's ministry. Often, the Holy Spirit will guide the evangelist to minister the Word in ways that confirm the pastor's ministry. The evangelist can be a voice of confirmation to the congregation concerning the ongoing leading of the Lord through their pastor's pulpit ministry.

God uniquely gifts itinerant ministers to serve the church. Many evangelists are specialists who master a certain biblical subject and bring a fresh perspective. Some are gifted to pray with people in faith to receive the Holy Spirit baptism. Others specialize in Bible prophecy or other teaching ministries. Some are, in the biblical sense, exhorters to motivate the church to godly living and evangelism. Some equip the body for evangelism and discipleship. The model closest to the New Testament evangelist is one who preaches to the lost and leads people to receive Christ.

11.3.1 OBJECTIVE
Explain the function of the evangelist as described in the New Testament.

11 How does the New Testament describe an evangelist?

11.3.2 OBJECTIVE
Describe how partnering with evangelists can meet needs within the church and spur believers to personal evangelism.

12 What are the geographical parameters of an evangelist's ministry?

11.3.3 OBJECTIVE
Identify criteria for selecting evangelists.

13 Why must great care be taken in partnering with an evangelist?

Choosing a Partner in Evangelism

A pastor would not take a haphazard approach to bringing an associate pastor on staff in a church. Neither should inviting an evangelist be a casual decision. A pastor should do research and prayerfully seek the Lord's guidance to find an evangelist who is a fit to the pastor's ministry and local congregation and community. As Barnabas wisely discerned that Paul would be a blessing to Antioch, the Holy Spirit can guide a pastor to finding the right evangelists with whom to partner in ministry.

Planting in Evangelism

A local church committed to fulfilling the Great Commission and with a passion for reaching the spiritually lost will use all means of outreach and prioritize the most effective ones.

The most effective means of reaching the spiritually lost is motivating and mobilizing believers to personal witness. On a larger scale, one of the most effective means of making an impact on a community is to plant a church.

As with any new ministry, the church leadership should seek the Lord for the method and timing of the church plant. Above all, God's help is needed to supply the pastor who will lead the new congregation.

11.3.4 OBJECTIVE
Explain the evangelistic potential of church planting.

14 What are the primary church planting models and how do they function?

Church Planting Models

A variety of **church planting models** can be used to plant a church. The following five are from the Assemblies of God Church Planting Department.

1. Mother Church Model

   The mother church releases people and resources as part of the initial startup for the new church. The church planter may be a staff member or someone hired to plant the new church. People and finances are released for a predetermined length of time. Afterward, people may return to the mother church should they desire. The daughter church is usually, but not always, in the same community as the church that planted it.

2. Internal Church Plant Model

   The host church provides its facilities to be used by a church plant. The church plant meets at different times or in a different part of the host church facility. The church plant may use some of the host's existing ministries in order to shore up weak areas. For example, teens from the church plant might attend the host church's youth group. Sometimes the host church also provides resources and people to help the new church. The church plant may or may not be expected to pay rent or part of the utilities. This model works well in reaching people of a different ethnicity than the host church. The church plant may or may not eventually secure its own facilities.

3. Satellite Model

   In the satellite model, the sending central church sends a pastor and people to another location in its geographic area (town or city) to start a new work. The satellite church shares the vision and ministry style of the central church. The calendar and ministry goals of the satellite church are established by the central church. The satellite church reproduces the ministries of the central church in another geographic area.

4. Cathedral Model

   In the cathedral model, the sending cathedral church sends a church planter and people to another location in its geographic area (town or city) to start a new work. The branch church has its own vision and ministry style. The branch church benefits from the strength, stability, and maturity of the cathedral church.

5. Sectional Model

   In the sectional model, a number of churches, usually within a specific section or district, agree to plant a church together. A sectional committee or leadership team identifies the location for the new church. A sponsor church may provide a staff member to be the planter, while other sponsor churches provide people, finances, material, and various other needs. The sectional committee or the designated pastor may serve to oversee the new church. The goal is for the church plant to become fully autonomous and self-supporting.

A Vision for Church Planting

If planting a church seems too overwhelming for your congregation, consider partnering with another church as a cooperative project.

Extensive research has shown that the congregation of a new church plant tends to be much more active in personal evangelism. A new church, by its nature, depends on people inviting others to attend. A church plant will almost always reach people who likely would never come to the mother church. Church planting applies the multiplication principle of the gospel.

The essential key to planting a church is not in the amount of financial resources or the attractiveness of programs. It is having divinely called and equipped spiritual leadership—a pastor to lead the congregation effectively. Increasingly, mother churches tend to install their staff members as pastors of the churches they plant.

Every pastor should prayerfully consider the prospect of planting a church in his or her long-term plans. It may take years before such an endeavor is feasible, but it should be a consideration in the vision of every church.

15 How does establishing a church plant affect the level of personal evangelism in a church?

The Pastor's Role in Evangelism

Test Yourself

Circle the letter of the *best* answer.

1. Modeling, a powerful teaching tool, works by
   a) demonstrating a truth to the student through the teacher's actions before theory is taught.
   b) creating a theorem, or verbal model, of the truth to be absorbed.
   c) pairing students in teams throughout a teaching session.
   d) interviewing students on past life experiences and then connecting those experiences with the material to be studied.

2. One of the simplest and most effective ways to begin personally sharing the gospel is to
   a) begin talking about eternal damnation.
   b) describe how fast your church is growing.
   c) pray with someone about a personal need.
   d) summarize the key evidences for God's existence.

3. Two tools for keeping a congregation motivated to share the gospel are
   a) Friday night visits to local bars and Saturday morning prayer walks.
   b) naming unsaved loved ones from the pulpit and phoning church members to remind them to pray for their families.
   c) regular targeted sermons on evangelism and personal testimonies about evangelism.
   d) a churchwide point system and cash prizes for inviting people to church.

4. Four practices that offer a solid start to personal evangelism are
   a) sharing personal experience, avoiding controversy, inviting to church, and praying for needs.
   b) sharing personal experience, inviting to church, praying for needs, and identifying besetting sins.
   c) inviting to church, following up with phone calls, requiring reasons for missed church services, and insisting on daily accountability.
   d) gospel tracts on doors, Scripture yard signs, public Bible reading, and gospel bumper stickers.

5. Prayer circles, when used evangelistically, usually involve
   a) groups of believers agreeing to pray regularly for a list of people needing salvation.
   b) holding hands and forming a circle around a visitor who expresses a need.
   c) similarities to community prayer walks.
   d) the pastor and one other church staff member.

6. The seed for planting the harvest is always
   a) a personal testimony or anecdote.
   b) the Word of God.
   c) identifying personal lostness.
   d) the Romans Road.

7. The New Testament mentions evangelists
   a) three times but gives a clear picture of the evangelist's ministry.
   b) in each of the Gospels and uses Jesus to illustrate the ministry.
   c) in each book and uses a variety of Greek words to explain the meaning.
   d) only once, and the passage is textually questionable.

8. A good way for a pastor to view the evangelist's role in ministry partnership is
   a) as a diversion from regular church activity.
   b) as a visiting dignitary.
   c) in the role of an associate pastor.
   d) in the context of the worldwide Church.

9. Which three church planting models maintain the strongest link between the plant and host churches?
   a) Mother, internal, satellite
   b) Satellite, mother, sectional
   c) Internal, satellite, cathedral
   d) Sectional, internal, cathedral

10. A church plant tends to
    a) decrease personal evangelism, since members are preoccupied with financial needs.
    b) leave the level of personal evangelism unchanged.
    c) increase personal evangelism, since members invite people to the new church.
    d) decrease personal evangelism, since some see the church plant as a threat.

Responses to Interactive Questions
Chapter 11

Some of these responses may include information that is supplemental to the IST. These questions are intended to produce reflective thinking beyond the course content and your responses may vary from these examples.

1 What foundational teaching principle does the modeling concept embody?

The best teaching occurs when a truth is lived out first and followed by instruction.

2 Why is a godly home a model of evangelism?

Children who follow Christ are evidence of a clear presentation of the gospel and Christian integrity within the home.

3 What is a simple way to begin the evangelism process with some people?

Praying with someone for a personal need opens the door to a more complete presentation of the gospel.

4 What is one of the most effective tools for communicating evangelism principles to a congregation?

Strategic and regular sermons on evangelism will connect in the congregation's minds the evangelism concept with the primacy of God's Word.

5 What should be the effect of a personal frame of reference regarding Christ's sacrifice?

People who see themselves as the direct beneficiaries of Christ's sacrifice should live for Him rather than themselves. This translates into a commitment to obey Christ in sharing the gospel.

6 What four practices offer a solid start to personal evangelism?

Believers who share from their own experience, avoid religious arguments, invite people to church, and pray with nonbelievers for personal needs build a foundation on which a clear gospel presentation can be offered.

7 What are two effective tools for enhancing seasonal evangelism opportunities?

Prayer circles help believers organize and agree in prayer for the lost, while Bible-reading programs give believers a motivational foundation from which to present the gospel.

8 What common denominator characterizes every means used to communicate the gospel?

Whether it is a targeted needs ministry, organized prayer outreach, sermon series or drama, the church must have a heart of compassion for the lost of its community. No evangelistic undertaking can function effectively without a love for the lost.

9 What four characteristics make a church especially effective in reaching and retaining people?

A church must be grounded in the Word of God, manifest the Holy Spirit's active presence, be focused on the mission of reaching the lost, and be known for its genuine love.

10 What must remain in sharpest focus for the evangelistically minded church?

Believers must remember that evangelism is first and foremost a work of the Holy Spirit. The Spirit's work should be acknowledged and sought in every method used to reach the lost.

11 How does the New Testament describe an evangelist?

In the New Testament's three references to the evangelist, the position is defined as a ministry gift that is focused on proclaiming the message of Christ to nonbelievers and is illustrated through one-on-one ministry.

12 What are the geographical parameters of an evangelist's ministry?

While the popular concept of the evangelist is that of a traveling minister, an evangelist can also function within the local church as key person who helps facilitate outreach to the community.

13 Why must great care be taken in partnering with an evangelist?

The evangelist makes an impact on a church much like a church staff member, and similar care must be taken in choosing an evangelist as in staffing a church.

14 What are the primary church planting models and how do they function?

The Mother Church Model sends people and resources from a mother church to start a new church, offering temporary resources. The Internal Church Plant Model creates a church plant within the facilities of the host church. The Satellite Model creates a church plant that continues to represent the central church in a new location. The Cathedral Model creates a church plant with a ministry style distinct from the central church. The Sectional Model creates a church plant through a partnership of host churches.

15 How does establishing a church plant affect the level of personal evangelism in a church?

Personal evangelism is generally more active in a church plant since those involved in planting a church necessarily become involved in personal outreach to bring people to the new church.

Evangelism in the Pulpit

During a weekend of ministry in New Zealand, more than 1,200 people attended the Sunday morning service. When I gave a salvation invitation, only one man came forward.

Two years later, I was preaching again in New Zealand, this time in the city of New Plymouth, in the southern part of the island. After the service, a woman approached me and said, "I wanted to meet you because you were a real blessing in my life a couple of years ago."

I said, "But, I've never been to this church. I've never even been to this town."

"It wasn't here," the woman explained. "I was in Auckland on vacation. I was a new Christian trying to share my faith with a family there. They have been my friends for many years, but I was getting nowhere witnessing to them. They were unresponsive. The husband was even hostile, claiming to be an agnostic. Sunday morning we were driving down the freeway to a late breakfast. Suddenly the husband, who was driving, turned off the freeway into the driveway of Takapuna Assembly of God.

"He turned to me and said, 'Let's forget about breakfast. Instead, let's go to church. I will listen to this preacher, whoever he is. If I do, will you leave me alone?'"

The woman told me, "That was the Sunday you were there. In your sermon you answered all the questions he asked that I couldn't answer. Do you remember a man coming forward to receive Christ? That man was my agnostic friend."

I said, "Thank you. You have made my day."

She said, "I'm not finished. The next day, he was on his way to work on the same freeway. Coming from the opposite direction, a car had a blowout on a front tire. The car swerved across the median and had a head-on collision with his. He was killed instantly and went to be with the Lord."

When we preach the Word of God, we have no way of knowing how the Holy Spirit will use the proclaimed Word to rescue someone—to change a life and bring them out of darkness into His marvelous light (1 Peter 2:9).

Lesson 12.1   The Power of the Preached Word

Objectives
12.1.1 Explain the priority of the authority of God's Word in pulpit ministry.
12.1.2 Describe the divine inspiration of God's Word, and apply it as the infallible, authoritative rule of faith and conduct.
12.1.3 Cite the role of God's Word and the Holy Spirit in sermon preparation.
12.1.4 Communicate the Word of God under the Holy Spirit's anointing in a culturally and age-relevant manner.

Lesson 12.2   Preparation for Proclamation

Objectives
12.2.1 Dedicate yourself to in-depth study of the Scriptures to discern original meaning and current application.
12.2.2 Identify those expressions that most directly and simply present God's Word to an audience.
12.2.3 Organize, illustrate, and present your sermon with clarity and exegetical soundness.
12.2.4 Interweave a clear invitation to salvation regardless of the material presented.

Lesson 12.3   Call to Decision

Objectives

12.3.1 Identify and apply the three components of a Pentecostal service.

12.3.2 Identify the principles of a Holy Spirit directed altar call.

12.3.3 Describe how to communicate with those making first-time commitments to Christ in a way that ensures their understanding.

12.3.4 List and explain the different reasons people have for responding to an altar invitation.

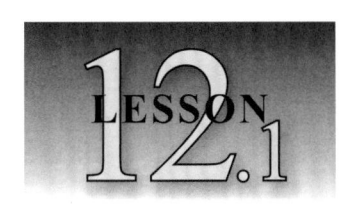

12.1.1
OBJECTIVE

Explain the priority of the authority of God's Word in pulpit ministry.

1   What is the primary nature of evangelistic preaching?

The Power of the Preached Word

The reason this chapter is included in this course is because, along with effective personal evangelism, biblical preaching is one of the most vital factors in the evangelistic effectiveness of the local church.

Tragically, an increasing number of pulpits are filled by preachers who do not seem to understand the power of God's Word to transform lives. For a variety of reasons, including a desire to be more interesting or relevant, many pastors and evangelists have exchanged exposition of the Scriptures for sermonizing. By doing so, they are forsaking both their God-given privilege as His messenger and their responsibility to spiritually feed His people.

A common misconception is that evangelistic preaching means delivering a sermon that is primarily directed to the nonbeliever in what is often called a salvation message.

The inspired Word of God is, as the writer to the Hebrews described it in 4:12, "living and powerful, and sharper than any two-edged sword, piercing even to the division of soul and spirit, and of joints and marrow, and is a discerner of the thoughts and intents of the heart" (NKJV). Effective evangelistic preaching is first and foremost expository Bible preaching. When God's Word is accurately proclaimed, the Holy Spirit will bring understanding to the mind of the hearer and activate faith in the heart to believe and respond.

In more than thirty years of preaching ministry, I have never preached a biblical sermon that could not be concluded by an invitation for nonbelievers to accept Christ. Sound expository biblical preaching that is centered upon Christ can always be evangelistic. The proclamation of God's inspired Word provides the truth, releasing the Holy Spirit to work in the minds and hearts of listening nonbelievers.

The Word at Work

Paul wrote to the church at Thessalonica: "We also constantly thank God that when you received the word of God which you heard from us, you accepted it not as the word of men, but for what it really is, the word of God, which also performs its work in you who believe" (1 Thessalonians 2:13).

Notice that Paul stated that the Word of God "performs its work" in those who believe. The preacher must clearly understand the nature and power of God's Word. The Word is not just a resource for sermons.

Every Pentecostal preacher should be of the same mind as Peter when he wrote,

As each one has received a special gift, employ it in serving one another as good stewards of the manifold grace of God. Whoever speaks, is to do so as *one who is speaking the utterances of God*; whoever serves is to do so as one who is serving *by the strength which God supplies*; so that *in all things God may be glorified through Jesus Christ*, to whom belongs the glory and dominion forever and forever. (1 Peter 4:10–11, emphasis added)

2 What is the proper place of the Word in relation to the speaker of the Word?

The Bible preached and taught correctly demands servants of the text, people who are, as Martin Luther expressed it, "under the Word." The pulpit must be used to teach under the authority of God's Word, not to convey personal opinion. People do not assemble to hear what the preacher thinks but what God thinks.

The messenger of God's Word has a responsibility to proclaim the whole truth. We would do well to learn from our own legal system, which was established on biblical principles. When the truth is sought from a witness in court, the witness is required to pledge to "tell the truth, the whole truth, and nothing but the truth." Preachers and teachers of God's Word should subscribe to the same pledge.

For this reason Paul was able to say, "I testify to you this day that I am innocent of the blood of all men. For I did not shrink from declaring to you the *whole purpose* of God" (Acts 20:26–27, emphasis added).

As Paul mentored young Timothy, he told him, "Be diligent to present yourself approved to God as a workman who does not need to be ashamed, accurately handling the word of truth. (2 Timothy 2:15). To accurately handle the Word of truth—preaching the Bible as it requires—we must address these issues: **inspiration**, **illumination**, and application.

12.1.2 OBJECTIVE
Describe the divine inspiration of God's Word, and apply it as the infallible, authoritative rule of faith and conduct.

Inspiration

God used human writers as His messengers, but they left us with His message. As they wrote, the Holy Spirit "breathed" (God's word choice) the truth of God through what they said. The writers did not pen God's Word simply from their own initiative or from their natural knowledge and wisdom. Peter said, "No prophecy was ever made by an act of human will, but men moved by the Holy Spirit spoke from God" (2 Peter 1:21).

The Assemblies of God doctrinal statement makes this clear in its first fundamental truth: "The Scriptures, both the Old and New Testaments, are verbally inspired of God and are the revelation of God to man, the infallible, authoritative rule of faith and conduct."

3 In light of the divine inspiration of God's Word, what function did its human writers play?

God used the experiences, thoughts, and vocabulary of the prophets and apostles. Furthermore, He directed their thoughts. When we study God's Word to understand what the writers' inspired meaning was, we must recognize that they were writing beyond themselves. Although God used human writers, His Spirit is the author of the Bible.

12.1.3 OBJECTIVE
Cite the role of God's Word and the Holy Spirit in sermon preparation.

Illumination

To fully and accurately proclaim the truth of the Bible, a preacher needs the illumination of the Spirit, just as the authors needed His inspiration when committing God's message to writing. Jesus promised the Holy Spirit would guide us "into all truth" (John 16:3, NIV). In prayer, Jesus said, "Thy word is truth" (John 17:17, KJV). The Holy Spirit helps us to understand the truth beyond our natural ability. The apostle John said, "You have an anointing from the Holy One, and all of you know the truth" (1 John 2:20).

4 What role does the Holy Spirit play in the proclamation of God's Word?

The Bible provides abundant evidence that it is God's Word, but a person is persuaded of the Bible's divine authority by an inward work of the Holy Spirit. He alone can convince a person's heart of the truth. A wonderful thing happens when a regenerated believer reads God's Word. The same Holy Spirit who inspired the writers will open the understanding of those who read it. The Holy Spirit guided the writers of His Word by inspiration. The same Holy Spirit guides those who hear, read, and study God's Word by illumination.

One who proclaims the Word of God must experience the message of truth beyond mental comprehension. We are saved not because we have accurate views of Christ's redemptive work but because we are joined by a living faith to Him who accomplished that redemption. This experience separated the apostles' teaching from the teaching of the rabbis. The apostles were not from among the priests and teachers of Jerusalem. They were not Levites or scribes. They were, as the Scriptures record in Acts 4:13, "uneducated and untrained men." None of the original apostles attended the school of Gamaliel or were taught by the other great Jewish teachers. Until Jesus' call, they were fishermen and tax collectors, simple and ordinary men. Yet thousands devoted themselves to their teaching. Even the finely robed rabbis sat and listened to these common men who spoke as prophets, because the apostles had been baptized, as John the Baptist prophesied, with the Holy Ghost and fire.

Application

12.1.4 OBJECTIVE
Communicate the Word of God under the Holy Spirit's anointing in a culturally and age-relevant manner.

Inspired Scripture is "God-breathed." The purpose of breath is to create and sustain life. Genesis 2:7 records that when God breathed into man, he became a living soul. Of all preachers, Pentecostals should always be aware that God's Word, proclaimed by the enabling of the Spirit, produces and sustains life in its hearers.

The writer of Hebrews said, "We must pay much closer attention to what we have heard, so that we do not drift away from it" (2:1). Drifting takes no conscious effort or strategy. The currents and winds of social trends and fads, in the church as well as in the world, are always in motion. As preachers, we will be pressured by those who view the Word of God as the words of men. We must keep a straight course and not drift from our position on that Word.

Preaching the Bible as the Word of God requires that the Holy Spirit's message be communicated effectively, without compromise or distortion. The preacher's challenge is to do this with vocabulary, concepts, and symbols that are relevant to the culture and generation of the receiving audience.

5 How does true anointing differ from the popular concept of anointing?

In Pentecostal circles, speaking of the Holy Spirit's **anointing** on preaching is common. However, many inaccurately equate an anointing with volume, demonstrative emotion or perspiration. Our popular use of the term is extrabiblical. True anointing describes a divine phenomenon in which we preach beyond ourselves, outdoing ourselves because of the Spirit's touch, presence, and activity in our preaching. Two other words in the New Testament better describe this: *energeo*, which refers to God's "working" in His human agents, and *zoopoieo*, which is translated "quicken," "give life," or "make alive."

The anointing has as much to do with what is happening to the hearer as it does to the speaker. Pentecostal preaching with the energizing touch of the Spirit should produce the results we read about in Acts 2. When Peter preached with the Spirit's empowering on the Day of Pentecost, Luke records, "Now when they heard this, they were *pierced to the heart*, and said to Peter and the rest of the apostles, 'Brethren, what shall we do?' Peter said to them, 'Repent and each of you be baptized in the name of Jesus Christ for the forgiveness of your sins; and you will receive the gift of the Holy Spirit'" (Acts 2:37–38, emphasis added). Spirit-energized preaching pierces to the heart and results in repentance, forgiveness, and transformed lives.

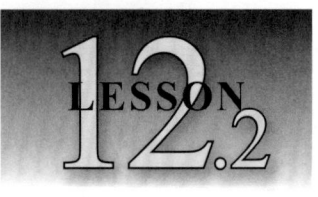

Preparation for Proclamation

The church calendar includes several occasions, such as Christmas, Easter and Mother's Day, when nonbelievers are more likely to be present. A pastor also may schedule special Sunday events, such as Friend Day, when congregation members are encouraged to bring nonbelieving friends. At such times, the message will most likely address nonbelievers. A church that focuses on fulfilling the Great Commission should view every Sunday as an opportunity for nonbelievers to come to Christ.

When accurately and relevantly applied, God's truth will minister to both believers and nonbelievers in the same audience. The inspired nature of God's Word and the active work of the Holy Spirit bring understanding to the mind of the hearer. Preaching that is primarily addressed to nurture an audience of believers can, at the same time, stimulate spiritual hunger in nonbelievers. The preacher who focuses on evangelism will always have both audiences in mind, and each should be considered during the preparation and the delivery of the message.

Simply defined, *homiletics* is "the art of preaching." The preacher's calling is not as an artist, to display his own creative capabilities. Paul's term of choice in 2 Timothy 2:15 is "workman"—a laborer. To accurately convey God's message, the laborer—the servant of the text—must accurately handle the revelation God provided. The Bible is not only a well of truth but also the water. Paul admonished Timothy that as God's messengers, we must be wholehearted and diligent in the way we handle the word of truth that has been delivered to us. The archaic meaning of *study* used in the King James Version of the passage is not misleading, but it falls short of the strength of Paul's call to devotion and diligence in the task.

While the application of God's Word cannot be dealt with extensively in this lesson, five issues are given attention regarding sermon preparation: exposition, simplification, organization, illustration, and invitation.

Exposition

Spin is defined as "a special point of view, emphasis, or interpretation." More than in any other context, biblical interpretation should be a no spin zone. Jesus addressed the Pharisees concerning their distortion of the truth when He said, "'Rightly did Isaiah prophesy of you hypocrites, as it is written: 'this people honors me with their lips, but their heart is far away from me. But in vain do they worship me, teaching as doctrines the precepts of men.' Neglecting the commandment of God, you hold to the tradition of men . . . you are experts at setting aside the commandment of God in order to keep your tradition'" (Mark 7:6–9).

Exposition requires the hard work of correctly interpreting a Bible passage and then explaining the interpretation in a way that is relevant to the hearers' needs. Bible interpretation (**exegesis**) must be done carefully, according to the principles of **hermeneutics**. In most cases, when a preacher does not preach expository messages, the reason is not because of an inability to learn how to do effective exposition. Rather, it is due to an unwillingness to commit the time required. That commitment will come only from a personal love of God's Word and an understanding of the necessity of expository preaching.

Simplification

Expository preaching encompasses much more than style. Unfortunately, many well-meaning proponents narrowly define expository preaching as a running commentary on the text without going the second mile of simplifying truth to

---

12.2.1 OBJECTIVE
Dedicate yourself to in-depth study of the Scriptures to discern original meaning and current application.

6 What danger must be avoided when expositing, or explaining, biblical truth?

12.2.2 OBJECTIVE
Identify those expressions that most directly and simply present God's Word to an audience.

Evangelism in the Pulpit 157

7 Why is simplification of a text not to be confused with dumbing it down?

make it most accessible. This simplification does not mean to dumb it down, but make it more easily understood. The expositor will work to organize and illustrate the content of the text in a way that applies the truth in a fresh, relevant, and provocative way to a contemporary audience, especially to nonbelievers who are present. By reading the Gospels and examining Jesus' communication with people, we find that He always used vocabulary and word pictures that came from people's daily lives. He identified and connected with them, using language they could understand and concepts to which they could relate. Jesus should be our model.

Organization

12.2.3 OBJECTIVE
Organize, illustrate, and present your sermon with clarity and exegetical soundness.

In preaching, it is imperative that we strive to excel to edify, according to 1 Corinthians 14:12. However, to view preaching as an art has its hazards. For some, the primary emphasis in homiletics focuses on the organizational structure of a sermon. Some homileticians contrive such clever outlines that clarity suffers. If the homiletical structure of a sermon draws attention to itself and away from the text, its purpose is defeated.

8 What must be the preacher's focus when organizing a sermon's structure?

Structure should always serve, but never overshadow, the text. **Alliteration** that flows naturally can create greater understanding as well as make text memorable. Alliteration that is exaggerated or strained does the opposite.

In addition to guiding the human authors of sacred Scripture in their choice of vocabulary and imagery, the Holy Spirit influenced structure. He inspired the Bible to be written a book at a time, so it should be studied a book at a time. Structure that is discovered within the text will naturally serve to explain the text.

The preacher who is a conscientious laborer will not obscure the structure of the text with his own. Whenever the structure of a message can be discovered in the text, it will be especially effective, since it comes directly from the inspired content.

Illustration

12.2.4 OBJECTIVE
Interweave a clear invitation to salvation regardless of the material presented.

Both in preaching and teaching, illustrations have value in a variety of ways. They bring clarity and make a lesson or truth memorable. Whenever possible, illustrations should be found from Scripture. Augustine said, "The New Testament is in the Old Testament concealed and the Old Testament is in the New Testament revealed." Often, Old Testament narrative stories offer appropriate and powerful illustrations of New Testament truths. The Gospels illustrate the epistles, and the epistles amplify lessons taught in the Gospels.

9 Illustration of a text serves what purpose?

Illustrations from contemporary life are helpful in applying scriptural truth in a relevant way. They reveal both the timeless and timely nature of God's truth to the nonbeliever. Nonbelievers need to see the application of the Scriptures in everyday life. Again, Jesus is our best example. His stories always related to His audiences' contexts and lives. Consequently, the preacher who is effective in applying God's Word in practical ways to people's lives will be first and foremost a student of the Word, the truth of which is as relevant today as when it was first recorded. An effective preacher will also be a student of his own time and culture.

Invitation

10 How does the Holy Spirit assist in the integration of a salvation invitation with the presentation of any text?

In 2 Corinthians 5:11, Paul wrote, "Knowing the fear of the Lord, we persuade men." Evangelism involves persuasion, of course, but in his first letter to the Corinthians, Paul wrote, "My message and my preaching were *not in persuasive words* of wisdom, but in demonstration of the Spirit and of power" (1 Corinthians 2:4, emphasis added). Though Paul certainly had persuasive ability, he understood that earthly wisdom and human persuasion were inadequate to reach the Corinthians with the gospel of Christ.

A great miracle occurred on the Day of Pentecost. The response of the crowd that resulted in salvation was not because of the sound from heaven like a rushing mighty wind, or the tongues like fire resting on the 120, or the unknown languages spoken by locals. Rather, it was in response to the Spirit-empowered Word that was preached.

A friend of mine, David Petts, was studying for a master's degree in philosophy at Oxford University. One day, during a tutorial about seventeenth-century French scientist René Descartes' **ontological argument**, my friend's professor attacked his Christian faith. My friend's faith was shaken, and he prayed to God for help. In desperation, he opened his Bible, where he saw these words: "I have more understanding than all my teachers: for thy testimonies are my meditation" (Psalm 119:99, KJV). Faith flooded his heart. He realized that unbelieving hearts and minds will always create evidence for their unbelief, but the truth of God's Word is unshakable.

As with those whom the Holy Spirit inspired to write the text, we need the Holy Spirit's help both to understand God's Word and to communicate its truth with quickened or energized (what Pentecostals would term anointed) application. A good preacher is in command of the message. A great preacher lets the message be in command of him.

In today's multicultural environment, absolutes are increasingly denied and tolerance represents a virtue. The world needs messengers bearing God's truth, which is universal, applying to all cultures, because it is above culture, being from heaven. A world in despair needs the "hope of the gospel" (Colossians 1:23). God's Word, which transcends all human philosophy and thought, is the antidote to human sinfulness, rebellion, and lostness.

The pulpit has never been the place for lazy laborers. To effectively preach and teach the Bible as the Word of God requires both discipline and dependence. The discipline of thorough exegesis, following strict hermeneutics, is essential. We must also exercise conscious and focused dependence upon the Holy Spirit to illumine our understanding and help us apply the truth with relevance to our audiences, especially nonbelievers. The desperate spiritual needs of people demand preachers who are diligent to preach the Bible as the Word of God, so that it will perform its work (1 Thessalonians 2:13).

Call to Decision

A critical aspect of evangelism is the public call to decision. The pastor who has a heart for reaching the spiritually lost should provide opportunity for public salvation responses.

Clarence St. John pastored twenty-one years in Hibbing, Minnesota. He faithfully gave public salvation invitations every Sunday for seven years before seeing a breakthrough. Then fifty people came forward for salvation in one year. Two years later, even after moving into a new building, the church still had to go to two morning services. In one year, 377 people came forward for salvation.

When a pastor commits to giving public calls to decision, the sovereign Holy Spirit will guide and send nonbelievers to the church to respond.

the third person. Do not say, "There may be someone here who does not know Christ." Rather, say, "You are here this morning, and you are not a follower of Christ."

Following is a simple invitation that includes both first-time converts and backsliders: "Everyone, please bow your head in prayer. You are here this morning and don't have the peace of God in your soul that if you died today, or the Lord returned today, you are ready to stand before Him. You may have followed Christ at one time, but you have turned away from Him and you are not living for Him. You need to return to Him this morning and have your sins forgiven. Or maybe you never have received Christ as your Savior. You may have attended a church somewhere, but you have not personally asked Him to forgive your sins, come into your heart, and change your life. You can leave here today knowing that peace. In either of these cases, I am asking for the privilege of praying with you personally this morning. If I am speaking to you, please raise your hand so I know who you are."

3. Have the congregation stand.

If you are going to call people forward to the altar, first have the entire congregation stand. It is more difficult for someone to get past people and out to the aisle, if everyone is seated.

4. Have altar counselors ready.

Have trained altar counselors ready to step to the altar to pray with those who are responding to the salvation invitation.

Ensuring Understanding

12.3.3 OBJECTIVE
Describe how to communicate with those making first-time commitments to Christ in a way that ensures their understanding.

When people are called to a public decision for Christ, it is imperative that they understand what they are doing. The altar counselor or speaker who prays with those who respond can help ensure that understanding.

Even if an altar call is worded specifically as a salvation invitation, believers who are going through personal struggles or have failed the Lord in some way often respond. Believers need to understand that even though they may have sinned or failed, it does not mean that they have fallen from grace or become a nonbeliever again.

14 What caution must be taken when interviewing those who are making spiritual decisions at an altar?

To determine whether the person is making a first-time decision or a recommitment, ask, "Have you known the Lord before?" Using the phrase "knowing the Lord" is recognizable to a Christian but someone who has never followed Christ will hesitate to say so. Do not ask, "Have you been a Christian before?" If a person was raised in a liturgical church or is a nominal Christian, they will answer yes.

Once the determination is made whether a person is making a first-time decision or a recommitment, consider these two basic approaches:

1. First-time decisions

Ask, "Are you sure you understand what you are doing?" Then take them at their word and proceed. Praying with a person who is making a salvation decision must not be considered a ritual. This is especially the case when someone is from a nominal Christian background. I usually say, "God wants to hear your prayer." Pause, then say, "But, would it help if I led you in a prayer?" Usually people will appreciate your help. Say, "It is not enough just to say the words. You have to mean your prayer from your heart. Try to put into words what you want to say."

Remember that the Holy Spirit is dealing with new believers and you need to help them in their prayer relationship.

2. Recommitments

OBJECTIVE 12.3.4
List and explain the different reasons people have for responding to an altar invitation.

If someone is making a recommitment, say something such as, "If you have known the Lord, you already know what to do. Possibly you have even prayed and asked God for forgiveness before you came to the altar. Just because you have sinned does not mean that you are out of relationship with God, but you have done the right thing by coming forward. You knew something needed to be made right between you and God."

Sometimes it is difficult to ascertain when a believer is making a recommitment after totally backsliding or just suffering from the normal sins and failures. Only God knows the heart. The important thing is, regardless of the spiritual condition of the people responding to the invitation, they are recommitting their lives to the Lord. They should meet a positive response at the altar.

15 In the final analysis, why is it more important to focus at the altar on the fact of response than on the exact nature of a response?

First Assembly of God in Griffin, Georgia is a thriving church that is especially committed to evangelism. Pastor Randy Valimont has instituted regular training concerning altar calls. Every other month, all Sunday school teachers receive instruction on how to conduct two altar calls every Sunday morning—a salvation invitation and an invitation to seek the Holy Spirit baptism. Often these Sunday school teachers are late to the worship service, because they are praying with students in the Sunday school rooms for those two reasons. Salvation decisions and Holy Spirit baptisms are a regular and common occurrence in this church.

Altar calls can be given in a variety of ways. Whenever possible, invite people forward to pray in the altar area and make life commitments. On some occasions, it may be more appropriate to have people make decisions at their seats, such as at funerals and other special events. The important issue is that people should be guided in making a decision at critical moments in the service when the Holy Spirit is dealing with their hearts.

Even after inviting people forward for salvation decisions, people who are hesitant and remain in their seats can be led to a decision. In the introduction to Chapter 8, John Blanchard made a critical life decision without going forward in response to the invitation given by Paul Cantelon. He eventually had an impact on the lives of many tens of thousands.

What is most important is that, in every way possible, we should cooperate with the Holy Spirit to help bring people to decisions that will count for eternity.

Test Yourself

CHAPTER 12

Circle the letter of the *best* answer.

1. Effective evangelistic preaching prioritizes
   a) biblical exposition.
   b) definitions of *sin*, *grace*, *repentance*, and *salvation*.
   c) personal testimony.
   d) careful interpretation of key words in the original languages.

2. When sharing truth from God's Word, the speaker must keep in mind that
   a) he or she is under the Word.
   b) every translation of the Word has weaknesses that must be considered.
   c) the meaning of the Word is tied to the reader's life experience.
   d) literary and historical criticism of the Word are integral to sermon preparation.

3. The inspired writing of God's Word is best explained as
   a) God's complete influence on everything written, with the writers' thoughts and experiences divinely integrated into the message.
   b) writing done under induced trances.
   c) the God-given creative abilities of biblical writers put to optimal use.
   d) God's choice of literature from an array of religious writing.

4. The best evidence of divine anointing on a message is the
   a) grammatical quality and logical organization of the message.
   b) extent to which God works through the message to impact lives.
   c) emotional response of the congregation.
   d) length of the message.

5. Biblical exposition should avoid opinion and present what from the text?
   a) Original languages, current linguistic analysis
   b) Popular interpretations, widely accepted errors
   c) Immediate application, denominational understanding
   d) Original meaning, current application

6. Structurally, a sermon should give due attention to a text's
   a) alliteration and other poetic devices.
   b) original structure and original message.
   c) symbolic or allegorical implications.
   d) chronological placement in biblical history.

7. Illustrations contribute to the impact of a sermon by
   a) reminding the audience that personal experience shapes the meaning of the Bible's message.
   b) bringing clarity to the text and making the associated lessons and truths memorable.
   c) giving the audience comic relief.
   d) breaking the sermon into portions to avoid excessive reading of the text.

8. Corporate worship in a church service should
   a) increase awareness of God's presence and spiritually refresh the participants.
   b) make God feel good so that He will answer prayer.
   c) bring conviction to nonbelievers who cannot genuinely worship.
   d) shed light on believers' sin and stir conviction.

9. In today's church, the altar is best described as a
   a) liturgical device with no real value.
   b) designated place where people can offer themselves to God.
   c) symbolic vestige of the Law of Moses.
   d) metaphor for the believer's heart.

10. When dealing with a person at the altar, it is important to
    a) identify whether the person is seeking rededication or salvation for the first time.
    b) rebuke familiar spirits or signs of demonic oppression.
    c) refute spiritual errors the person has accepted.
    d) be positive and encouraging, assuring the person of God's working in his or her heart.

Responses to Interactive Questions
Chapter 12

Some of these responses may include information that is supplemental to the IST. These questions are intended to produce reflective thinking beyond the course content and your responses may vary from these examples.

1 What is the primary nature of evangelistic preaching?

Effective evangelistic preaching prioritizes biblical exposition.

2 What is the proper place of the Word in relation to the speaker of the Word?

Anyone sharing the Word must do so with a firm conviction that God's Word is above him- or herself and unassailable by personal opinion.

3 In light of the divine inspiration of God's Word, what function did its human writers play?

God divinely directed the writing of His Word but perfectly integrated the experiences, thoughts, and vocabulary of the writers.

4 What role does the Holy Spirit play in the proclamation of God's Word?

The Holy Spirit offers to the seeking minister clear guidance into the truth of God's Word beyond that person's natural ability to discern truth.

5 How does true anointing differ from the popular concept of anointing?

Anointing is not measured by human enthusiasm or effort but by the extent to which God works through a human agent to communicate His Word in a life-giving manner.

6 What danger must be avoided when expositing, or explaining, biblical truth?

The person offering an interpretation of Scripture must carefully identify its original meaning and its intended application without taint of personal opinion.

7 Why is simplification of a text not to be confused with dumbing it down?

God's Word must be connected with people's contemporary language and experience, but its truths are not to be simplistically summarized or shared incompletely.

8 What must be the preacher's focus when organizing a sermon's structure?

The intended purpose of the original text's structure and the text's original message must remain clear; they cannot be camouflaged or obliterated by artificial organization.

9 Illustration of a text serves what purpose?

Illustrations bring clarity to a text and make a lesson or truth more memorable to the audience.

10 How does the Holy Spirit assist in the integration of a salvation invitation with the presentation of any text?

The Holy Spirit must empower the preacher's words and their connection with the Word of God in order for people to be drawn to salvation.

11 What does worship accomplish in the context of a church service?

Corporate worship invites a spiritually tangible divine presence that refreshes believers and influences nonbelievers.

12 What is the altar's significance?

Historically, God established altars as designated places for sacrifice where His presence would be particularly manifested. Today, churches continue to designate places where believers can place themselves in a position of consecration to receive what God would do in their lives.

13 What four components come into play when a pastor cooperates with the Holy Spirit in structuring an invitation to the altar?

The pastor must exercise faith, give a clear invitation, create an environment where respondents can easily access the altar, and position counselors to quickly assist those who respond.

14 What caution must be taken when interviewing those who are making spiritual decisions at an altar?

Care must be taken in the questions asked so that the person's true spiritual state can be discerned.

15 In the final analysis, why is it more important to focus at the altar on the fact of response rather than on the exact nature of a response?

Recognizing that God is the One who is at work in the person's heart, the altar worker should focus on encouraging the respondent to be obedient to the Spirit's leading.

CHAPTER 13

From Decision to Disciple

An Assemblies of God leader and his wife prayed daily for their son-in-law, Rick, from the time he married their daughter. First, Rick came to believe that God exists. When his wife received a divine healing, he progressed to believing in miracles. Although he was convinced the healing was divine, he still was not ready to receive Christ. Eventually, after coming to believe in the fulfillment of Old Testament prophecies concerning Christ, he received Jesus as His Savior and Lord on Good Friday. His commitment to Christ came after a thirteen-year spiritual journey.

Few nonbelievers are ready to receive Christ just because a Christian knocks on their door, presents them with a gospel tract or video, and challenges them to a salvation decision. Effective witness, especially with people we know well, requires faithful prayer, patience, and genuine love. For many, it can mean years of witnessing and discipling before they come to faith.

Following Christ is a journey, and it begins before the decision takes place. The Holy Spirit prepares a person's heart for the gospel message. The decision to follow Christ is not the finish line, but an open door to a life devoted to following Jesus. The goal of evangelism is not just a salvation decision but also a life of discipleship.

Lesson 13.1   Initial Follow-Up

Objectives

13.1.1 Outline how to communicate to new believers the Bible's central teaching role in their life of faith.

13.1.2 Explain the role of prayer in the believer's communication with God.

13.1.3 Identify the church as the believer's spiritual family and the lost as the believer's responsibility.

13.1.4 Describe how to focus the new believer's attention on the Holy Spirit as the source of help in all of Christian living.

Lesson 13.2   Discipling

Objectives

13.2.1 Define discipleship *in terms of its New Testament usage.*

13.2.2 Identify the interwoven functions of evangelism and discipleship.

13.2.3 Describe the relational goals of Christ's disciples.

13.2.4 Acknowledge the ongoing process and phases of discipleship.

Lesson 13.3   Components and Means of Discipling

Objectives

13.3.1 Cite the need to direct new believers toward character development through targeted Bible study and personal submission to the Holy Spirit.

13.3.2 Describe how to connect new believers with ministry opportunities and spiritual needs beyond their own.

13.3.3 Promote an array of discipleship vehicles within the church.

13.3.4 Explain the role of the character of each mature believer involved in discipling a new believer.

From Decision to Disciple

LESSON 13.1

13.1.1 OBJECTIVE
Outline how to communicate to new believers the Bible's central teaching role in their life of faith.

1 What three components work together to ground the believer in God's Word?

13.1.2 OBJECTIVE
Explain the role of prayer in the believer's communication with God.

Initial Follow-Up

After a person receives Christ, the local church is accountable to the Lord for his or her spiritual care and nurture. Just as a newborn baby needs care, the same is true of someone who has been born again spiritually through the Holy Spirit.

After making a decision for Christ, either in a witnessing context or at an altar, new believers should immediately be given instruction to help them begin their new life. To continue following Jesus, they need to be encouraged in regular Bible reading, prayer, local church participation, witnessing, and water and Holy Spirit baptisms. Each of these is essential to the spiritual growth and health of new believers.

When time at an altar is limited, it may be best to present a Bible reading, prayer, and belonging to a church and address other issues later.

The Bible, Our Spiritual Food

Encourage new believers to establish three regular practices concerning God's Word:

1. Bible Reading

Daily Bible reading is a powerful source of spiritual strength to the Christian. Most of us eat food every day to keep our physical bodies from becoming weak. We are spiritual, as well as, physical beings. Jesus said, "'Man shall not live on bread alone, but on every word that proceeds out of the mouth of God'" (Matthew 4:4). Just as we eat food more than once each day, we need spiritual bread more than once a day. New believers should be encouraged to start and end each day with Bible reading and prayer.

2. Bible Study

We need to go beyond Bible reading to studying God's Word. The Jews at Berea believed that Jesus was the true Savior from God, because their minds and hearts were prepared for the truth. This is why they were called "noble-minded" (Acts 17:11). They examined the Scriptures daily and received the truth with great joy. Their habit was to daily study God's Word.

God speaks to us as He guides us through His Word. Peter said in 2 Peter 1:20, "No prophecy of Scripture is a matter of one's own interpretation." We should not approach God's Word to get approval of our personal inclinations and desires. Instead, we should study His Word to understand what He is saying to us and to become obedient "doers of the Word" (Romans 2:13; James 1:22).

3. Bible Meditation

Meditation is taking time to think about what we've read in the Bible. As we make it a priority to concentrate on the Word, the Holy Spirit brings its truths to our memory. Paul said, "Let the word of Christ richly dwell within you" (Colossians 3:16). God's words should live in and be at home in our minds and hearts. Jesus said, "'If you remain in me and my words remain in you, ask whatever you wish, and it will be given you'" (John 15:7, NIV).

Prayer

Following Jesus is a relationship. In all the most important relationships of life, communication is necessary. No relationship stays the same. A relationship improves as two people come to know each other and share things that are important to them. People cannot get to know each other if they do not talk.

New believers should be taught that prayer is not a ritual but a conversation that involves both talking and listening. They need to be aware that God is everywhere and always hears when they pray. They also need to learn that the Bible teaches important conditions to receiving answers to prayer.

- Pray for God's purposes. The apostle John wrote, "This is the confidence we have in approaching God: that if we ask anything according to his will, he hears us" (1 John 5:14, NIV). God is able to work more effectively in life circumstances for those who are committed to His will.

- Pray in faith. "Without faith it is impossible to please God, because anyone who comes to him must believe that he exists and that he rewards those who earnestly seek him" (Hebrews 11:6, NIV). "'Therefore I say to you, all things for which you pray and ask, believe that you have received them, and they will be granted you'" (Mark 11:24).

- Pray in Jesus' name. In John 14:13 Jesus said, "'Whatever you ask in My name, that will I do, so that the Father may be glorified in the Son.'" Paul wrote in 1 Timothy 2:5, "There is one God, and one mediator also between God and men, the man Christ Jesus." We can come directly to God; that privilege is provided to us through the sacrifice of Christ on the cross. Praying in Jesus' name is not a formal ritual but a significant factor in having a right relationship with God through Jesus Christ.

A Spiritual Family

One of a person's greatest needs in life is to be part of a family. This is true in a spiritual sense, also. New believers should be encouraged to become a part of a church family. Explain the need to join with other Christians in worshiping God. As part of a church where spiritual brothers and sisters encourage them and help them, believers grow in faith. Being a part of a church will also give them the opportunity to serve Jesus by serving others.

Encourage new believers to pray for God's guidance concerning the church to which they should belong. They should be part of a church where salvation through faith in Jesus Christ is preached, a church where the Bible is believed, taught, and obeyed.

Letting Others Know

When something wonderful happens, we want to tell other people about it. Explain to new believers that the new life Jesus has given them is the greatest thing that has ever happened to them. They can let others know what Christ has done for them through their actions and their words.

Water Baptism

One of the most important things people can do in their new life in Christ is to follow Him in water baptism. Baptism shows that our old life is dead. The action of being put under the water symbolizes the old spiritual life being buried. When we come out of the water again, we show that we are new people in Christ.

Jesus commanded us to be baptized to show people that our life is changed. Encourage new believers to be baptized as soon as possible.

Witnessing

Explain to new believers that another part of God's plan for our lives is that He will use us to tell others about Jesus. God has chosen believers to have a part in building His everlasting kingdom. He commands us to tell others what He has done for us and what He will do for them.

From Decision to Disciple 169

13.1.4 OBJECTIVE
Describe how to focus the new believer's attention on the Holy Spirit as the source of help in all of Christian living.

The Helper

New believers should understand that they can do nothing to pay for their sins, but it will cost them something to follow Jesus. Some things in their old lives were wrong and caused them to sin. These things must change. Jesus commanded us in Luke 13:3 to turn away from our sins and put anything out of our lives that causes us to sin. (See Mark 9:43–48.) A person might think it will be difficult to banish some sins from their lives. Explain that when Jesus gave His life to free us from the penalty for sin, He also freed us from the power of sin. He sent the Holy Spirit to help us.

Jesus told His first followers, "'But you will receive power when the Holy Spirit comes on you; and you will be my witnesses in Jerusalem, and in all Judea and Samaria, and to the ends of the earth'" (Acts 1:8, NIV).

5 How does the Holy Spirit help new believers to live for Christ?

We need the Holy Spirit's help just as Jesus' first followers did. The Holy Spirit gives us the ability to be what God wants us to be—a witness for Jesus Christ in what we do, what we say, and who we are.

Encourage new believers to immediately seek to be filled with the Holy Spirit. Jesus promised this gift to all believers. As Peter said on the Day of Pentecost, "The promise is for you and your children and for all who are far off—for all whom the Lord our God will call" (Acts 2:39, NIV).

In Paul's first letter to the Corinthians, he refers to believers as being "God's building" (3:9). In the lifelong process of becoming what God has destined believers to be, the stones placed first in the foundation of a new believer's life are the strength of his or her future. Help a new believer establish the right spiritual disciplines by immediately seeking the Spirit's empowerment. The early spiritual care in the believer's life is critical to forming lifelong habits that will influence his or her future development.

LESSON 13.2

Discipling

What Is Discipleship?

The terms *evangelism* and *discipleship* do not have exact counterparts in the Greek language. *Evangelism* comes from the word for "gospel." *Discipleship* comes from the noun for "disciple" and the verb "to disciple."

13.2.1 OBJECTIVE
Define discipleship *in terms of its New Testament usage.*

In New Testament times, the Greek word *mathetes* generally referred to a style of education in which the disciple appropriated specific knowledge or conduct according to a set plan. It was the usual word for an apprentice in professions such as music, medicine, or rhetoric. A disciple was dependent upon an authority with superior knowledge in an ongoing relationship. The word could also apply to an intellectual link between people considerably removed in time. Socrates was considered to be a disciple of Homer, even though Socrates lived at least four hundred years after Homer (Kittel 1967, 416–417).

6 What two functions does the verb form of the word *disciple* serve?

The verb form of *disciple*, *matheteuo*, is used only four times in the New Testament—in the Great Commission (Matthew 28:19), two other times in Matthew, and once in Acts. Three relevant verses follow here.

"And Jesus said to them, 'Therefore every scribe who has *become a disciple* of the kingdom of heaven is like a head of a household, who brings out of his treasure things new and old'" (Matthew 13:52, emphasis added).

"When it was evening, there came a rich man from Arimathea, named Joseph, who himself had also *become a disciple* of Jesus" (Matthew 27:57, emphasis added).

"After they had preached the gospel to that city and had *made many disciples*, they returned to Lystra and to Iconium and to Antioch" (Acts 14:21, emphasis added).

The phrases "become a disciple" and "made many disciples" are both translations of a single Greek verb for disciple, *matheteuo*. Notice that the verb is used twice in the New Testament in reference to becoming a disciple and twice in reference to making disciples.

The Relationship of Discipleship With Evangelism

Discipleship Includes Evangelism

Discipleship is not just a follow-up to evangelism. In Matthew 28:19, when Jesus commanded His disciples concerning their mission, the imperative verb *matheteuo* had to include the proclamation of the gospel, because the command Jesus gave was to make disciples from among the spiritually lost multitudes of all nations. Discipleship includes both reaching spiritually lost people with the message of Christ and establishing them as His committed followers.

Evangelism Includes Discipleship

Evangelism is not merely the proclamation of the gospel with the objective of leading people to a decision to receive Christ. It includes the entire process of reaching and discipling spiritually lost people.

The good news always has a person's eternal destiny in view. The goal of evangelism is not only a salvation decision but also the formation of a devoted follower of Christ. In the context of Jesus' teaching concerning the Kingdom, evangelism's goal is to produce disciples who are committed to follow Christ for a lifetime.

The Disciple's Goal

The ultimate goal of a disciple is to become like his or her master. Paul wrote to the Romans in 8:29, "Those whom He foreknew, He also predestined to become conformed to the image of His Son." To the Corinthians Paul wrote, "We, who with unveiled faces all reflect the Lord's glory, are being transformed into his likeness with ever-increasing glory" (2 Corinthians 3:18).

Becoming like Christ in our character, thoughts, words, and actions affects our relationships with God and with other people. Paul identified those relationships in his epistles to the churches at Ephesus and Colosse. To the Ephesians, he wrote, "He chose us in Him before the foundation of the world, that we would be holy and blameless before Him" (Ephesians 1:4). To the Colossians, "He has now reconciled you in His fleshly body through death, in order to present you before Him holy and blameless and beyond reproach" (Colossians 1:22).

Being *holy* has to do with our relationship with God—being separated to Him. Being *blameless* relates to our standing before the world—our relationship with other people, both believers and nonbelievers.

Our relationships with God and others should be characteristic of how Jesus related to His heavenly Father and to people. The writer to the Hebrews echoes

---

13.2.2 OBJECTIVE
Identify the interwoven functions of evangelism and discipleship.

7 What is the relationship between discipleship and evangelism?

13.2.3 OBJECTIVE
Describe the relational goals of Christ's disciples.

8 What should be the goal of the disciple?

Ephesians and Colossians, "Make every effort to live in peace with all men and to be holy; without holiness no one will see the Lord" (Hebrews 12:14, NIV).

The Ongoing Process of Discipleship

13.2.4 OBJECTIVE
Acknowledge the ongoing process and phases of discipleship.

The Role of Leaders in the Church

Examine Paul's instructions to the Ephesians:

And He gave some as apostles, and some as prophets, and some as evangelists, and some as pastors and teachers, for the equipping of the saints for the work of service, to the building up of the body of Christ; until we all attain to the unity of the faith, and of the knowledge of the Son of God, to a mature man, to the measure of the stature which belongs to the fullness of Christ . . . we are to grow up in all aspects into Him who is the head, even Christ, from whom the whole body, being fitted and held together by what every joint supplies, according to the proper working of each individual part, causes the growth of the body for the building up of itself in love. (Ephesians 4:11–16)

9   What is the relationship between discipleship and personal responsibility?

We who are being saved by grace are responsible for our own spiritual condition. We will stand alone before the Judgment Seat of Christ. (See 2 Corinthians 5:10.) Jesus does not mean for believers to make the discipleship journey without help from others. He has sovereignly placed spiritual leaders in the Church both to help others become mature disciples and to equip members of the Body to disciple others.

Continual Discipline and Dependence

In 2 Peter 1:3–11, the apostle expressed the importance of ongoing personal spiritual development.

His divine power has granted to us everything pertaining to life and godliness, through the true knowledge of Him who called us by His own glory and excellence. For by these He has granted to us His precious and magnificent promises, so that by them you may become partakers of the divine nature, having escaped the corruption that is in the world by lust. Now for this very reason also, applying all diligence, in your faith supply moral excellence, and in your moral excellence, knowledge, and in your knowledge, self-control, and in your self-control, perseverance, and in your perseverance, godliness, and in your godliness, brotherly kindness, and in your brotherly kindness, love. For if these qualities are yours and are increasing, they render you neither useless nor unfruitful in the true knowledge of our Lord Jesus Christ. For he who lacks these qualities is blind or short-sighted, having forgotten his purification from his former sins. Therefore, brethren, be all the more diligent to make certain about His calling and choosing you; for as long as you practice these things, you will never stumble; for in this way the entrance into the eternal kingdom of our Lord and Savior Jesus Christ will be abundantly supplied to you.

Peter's exhortation helps us to understand the practical objectives for local church leadership. The discipleship process he describes will result in the formation of devoted followers of Christ.

As Paul did, Peter reinforces the essential need of believers for both discipline and dependence in discipleship. He specifies in 2 Peter 1:5 that development happens by "applying all diligence" when we "make every effort" (NIV). This indicates discipline on the part of the disciple. That discipline depends on what is stated in verse 3, that "his divine power has granted to us everything pertaining to life and godliness."

Continuing Growth

Being born again—regeneration—is not the finish line of evangelism. It is the starting point for an effective life in Christ. The disciple of Jesus Christ is predestined by God "to become conformed to the image of His Son, so that He would be the firstborn among many brethren; and these whom He predestined, He also called; and these whom He called, He also justified; and these whom He justified, He also glorified" (Romans 8:29–30).

A believer who is predestined, called, and justified by grace is in the process of being glorified. Unlike justification, glorification does not happen instantaneously. It is a progressive work. Paul wrote to the Corinthians, "We all, with unveiled face, beholding as in a mirror the glory of the Lord, are being transformed into the same image from glory to glory" (2 Corinthians 3:18). Spiritual growth happens in stages, "from glory to glory," as God works in us. Paul said to the believers at Philippi, "It is God who is at work in you, both to will and to work for His good pleasure" (Philippians 2:13). In the same epistle, he expressed his confidence that "He who began a good work in you will perfect it until the day of Christ Jesus" (1:6).

Notice that in 2 Peter 1:8, Peter says that if these qualities are the possession of the believer, and if they are increasing, they render the believer to be neither "useless nor unfruitful in the true knowledge of our Lord Jesus Christ." In other words, having these spiritual qualities is vital, but their continuing development is essential.

It is spiritually tragic for any Christian to believe he or she has arrived spiritually. Like Jesus' first followers, we are to be constantly growing, not only in knowledge but also in character and ministry. As Peter says in 2 Peter 1:10, the promise that we need "never stumble" is contingent on us being diligent in our calling and practicing the things he lists.

Growing in Grace

The 2 Peter passage speaks of three phases of God's grace:

1. In 1:1, we have received the faith by which we live.
2. In 1:3, His divine power has "granted to us everything pertaining to life and godliness."
3. In 1:11, entrance into our Lord's eternal kingdom "will be abundantly supplied" to us.

Our spiritual life *begins* with a gift from God. It is *sustained* by the power He continues to give. At the end of this life, entrance into His eternal kingdom *will be given* to us. Our past, present, and future are all results of God's grace.

10 What spiritual delusion does the reality of discipleship thoroughly refute?

LESSON 13.3

Components and Means of Discipling

Comprehensive and Integrated Discipleship

When Dr. Deborah Gill was discipleship commissioner for the Assemblies of God, she coined this insightful slogan, "*Knowing* is not enough. It's *living the life* that counts."

Discipleship is formation. Paul expressed it well in Galatians 4:19, "My children, with whom I am again in labor until Christ is formed in you." Having Christ formed in us is much more than acquiring biblical truth. Discipleship should be comprehensive, touching every area of Christian life. The passage from 2 Peter 1:5–8 expresses the importance of integrating spiritual qualities and practices. Faith, moral excellence (or virtue), knowledge, self-control, perseverance, godliness, kindness, and love are all essential to living the life.

13.3.1
OBJECTIVE
Cite the need to direct new believers toward character development through targeted Bible study and personal submission to the Holy Spirit.

The most effective discipleship ministry I have seen is in Victory Family Centre in Singapore. This church began in 1978 with eighteen people—six believers and twelve visitors—in a rented room in the Mandarin Hotel. At the time of this writing, it has grown to more than five thousand members. Through an aggressive missions program, the church has given more than sixty million dollars to missions in its twenty-seven-year history and fully supported more than 1,500 missionaries.

One reason this church has produced such a large number of committed people for the mission field is its commitment to intensive discipleship. Early in the church's formation, the missionary-pastor designed a discipleship program that incorporates these three major components: Bible knowledge, personal character development, and ministry involvement. This model offers a comprehensive, balanced, and integrated approach to personal discipleship.

Bible Knowledge

The foundation for a believer's growth in "the true knowledge of our Lord Jesus Christ" (2 Peter 1:8) is the spiritual discipline of daily reading God's Word. Jesus said, "'Man does not live on bread alone, but on every word that comes from the mouth of God'" (Matthew 4:4, NIV). Just as we need food every day for physical health, we need spiritual bread each day.

Encourage a systematic reading plan.

11 What disciplines in Bible reading help to convey the full benefit of Scripture to the reader?

I recommend that new believers begin reading in the Gospel of Mark, the shortest and most direct presentation of our Lord's life. Next, it is helpful for them to read through Acts and several Epistles, especially 1 John, 1 Peter, Philippians, Colossians, Ephesians, and Romans. New believers should use a simple, easy-to-read translation. As soon as possible, they should also study the sixteen foundational truths of the Assemblies of God.

Read complete books of the Bible.

Unfortunately, believers often take a promise-box approach to God's Word and pick out a verse or a chapter for the day. The Holy Spirit can use a small portion of Scripture to great benefit. Many Christians take a fragmented approach to studying the Scriptures. The Holy Spirit gave God's Word to us in separate but complete documents (books). These books should be studied as complete units. Studying Scripture in paragraphs of complete thoughts is better than doing so by chapters or verses. Reading the Bible a book at a time is extremely beneficial.

Focus on personal needs.

Some new believers also need focused Bible teaching concerning particular issues, such as family relationships or binding habits. This is especially true if they face crises in their family or are struggling with personal addictions.

Direct reading to subjects of personal interest.

New believers can also be directed to biblical subjects for which they have a specific interest. For example, in a survey of thousands of believers concerning a variety of subjects, the two topics of highest interest were *divine guidance*—how a person can know God's will for his or her life—and *where we are today in Bible prophecy* (Blair 1968).

Character Development

Personal character is developed only as God works in us by His Spirit. In his turning point in Romans, Paul wrote, "Therefore I urge you, brethren, by the mercies of God, to *present* your bodies a living and holy sacrifice, acceptable to God, which is your spiritual service of worship. And *do not be conformed* to this world, but *be transformed* by the renewing of your mind, so that you may prove what the will of God is, that which is good and acceptable and perfect" (Romans 12:1–2, emphasis added).

The Greek verb forms in these verses are instructive concerning the process of personal character development.

- The first verb is an imperative active: "present your bodies." Consecrating ourselves to God's purposes as living sacrifices is something we are capable of doing, which is why this verb is in the active voice.

- The second verb, translated "do not be conformed," is in the Greek middle voice. The subject performs or experiences the action of the verb in such a way that emphasizes the subject's participation in or determination of the action. The action of this verb implies that the world will conform us to itself, unless we take responsibility to determine that conformity does not happen.

- The third verb, "be transformed," is an imperative passive. Transformation is passive because we are not capable of changing ourselves. Only God by His grace and power can change us. The Greek word translated "transformed" here is *metamorphoo*, from which we get the English word *metamorphosis*. It implies an extreme change from one kind of thing to a completely different kind of thing, a change we are not capable of making ourselves. We are responsible to present our bodies as living sacrifices and not allow the world to conform us to itself, but the transformation of our character is something only God can do. We can present ourselves to Him, but He must change us.

Ministry Involvement

Helping believers become involved in ministry, both within the Body and among nonbelievers, will encourage them to become doers rather than mere hearers of the Word, as James 1:22 encourages. It will help them apply Bible knowledge to everyday life and translate that knowledge into character development.

Church leaders need to be cautious not to push new believers into ministries before they are ready. Paul instructed Timothy, "Do not lay hands upon anyone too hastily and thereby share responsibility for the sins of others" (1 Timothy 5:22). People should not be quickly placed into leadership. Similarly, while new believers need to begin serving the Lord in His church, they should not be placed in positions of responsibility that require teaching and experience.

Lesson 13.1 emphasizes that new believers can begin witnessing immediately and should be encouraged to do so. They should also get involved in ministries of the church that help them learn to serve God by serving others.

The Bible teaches that God gives spiritual gifts to each member of the Body, and it is His will for every believer to be involved in ministry. While spiritual gifts are just that—gifts—they must be used to develop further spiritual maturity.

Paul wrote, "Since you are eager to have spiritual gifts, try to excel in gifts that build up the church" (1 Corinthians 14:12, NIV).

Means of Discipling

13.3.3 OBJECTIVE
Promote an array of discipleship vehicles within the church.

The Bible teaches that "he who endures to the end shall be saved" (Matthew 24:13, NKJV). When Paul speaks in 1 Corinthians 9 of "saving" people "by all means," the context implies leading people to decisions and helping them to become devoted followers of Jesus presented before God "complete in Christ" (Colossians 1:28).

The proclamation of the gospel should be done by all means. So should discipleship. The primary focus of discipleship should not be on a particular aspect of the process but on the ultimate goal of who a person will become.

By examining what Scripture reveals about how God works, we discover that He providentially brings people into our lives to help our spiritual development. Certain people affect our lives more than others; we are influenced by many people, not just one. The Holy Spirit orchestrates relationships from among the diversity of gifts within the Body.

We can learn essential principles by observing Jesus' discipling methods. In his book, *The Master Plan of Evangelism*, Robert Coleman provides a definitive work on discipleship and an analysis of Jesus' discipleship methods.

Jesus' disciples were with Him for more than three years. (See Mark 3:14.) Few believers today could leave their jobs and families to the extent Jesus' first disciples seemed to. Also, a pastor doesn't travel with a group of people he or she is discipling. Jesus' methods must be applied practically in a variety of ways, timeframes, and social contexts.

14 What are five common components in church ministry that act as means to discipleship?

Following are some of the most common means of discipleship in the American church context.

Pulpit Ministry

Pastors disciple their congregations as they teach the Word. In Ephesians 4:11, pastors and teachers are not separate offices. Instead, the responsibilities are grouped together, because they are governed by one article (*the* occurs before *pastors* but not before *teachers*), and because the word *and* (*kai*) differs from the other form of *and* (*de*) in the verse. The titles seem to indicate two characteristics of the same person who is giving pastoral care to believers and instructing them in God's ways (Walvoord 1983, 635). Support for this perspective is found in Timothy and Titus, where Paul says that overseers or elders should be "able to teach" (1 Timothy 3:2; Titus 1:9).

Sunday School

For many years, Sunday school has provided a context for discipleship. Not only does Sunday school offer systematic study of God's Word, but it also provides opportunities for small-group ministry. Long before the emphasis in recent decades on various small-group ministries, Sunday school classes filled this role by hosting social events for fellowship and fostering close relationships. Groups studied God's Word together as they followed the Lord in Christian living.

New Believer's Classes

A class for new believers is an essential ministry in any church that is committed to evangelism. The purpose of this class is to acquaint people with the spiritual issues addressed in Lesson 13.1 and to share Assemblies of God history and foundational doctrines in brief, simple terms. New believers can also become familiar with the local church's core values and vision.

Small Groups

Small groups are increasing in church ministry. Small groups often meet at various times throughout the week. Groups can be organized either geographically for people from the same neighborhood or area of town, or they can be interest-centered to focus on a common topic that all participants enjoy.

One-on-One Discipling

Jesus took time for people, one at a time and in small groups. He did not concentrate only on the masses. Even among His twelve disciples, He seemed to spend more time with Peter, James, and John than the others. Later, after the Day of Pentecost, these disciples appear to have had the greatest influence in the Early Church.

At Victory Family Centre in Singapore, every person who comes to Christ is immediately assigned to a personal discipler. They meet together one-on-one once a week for two hours during the first six months and then for one hour each week for the second six months. Committing such a large amount of time to a person produces effective spiritual results. Having the right person doing the discipling is even more important than the time spent.

The Person More than the Process

Paul said, "Be imitators of me, just as I also am of Christ" (1 Corinthians 11:1). The NIV translates this verse, "Follow my example, as I follow the example of Christ." A follower of Christ must be discipled by people who not only know biblical truth but also live godly lives with evidence of following Christ.

For effective discipleship, the person doing the discipling is much more important than the process, regardless of the context. Each discipleship method has advantages and disadvantages. Some means of discipling afford more time in personal relationships. In one-on-one discipling, a new believer can ask questions, allowing the discipler to address specific interests and concerns. Preaching and group teaching contexts lack this personal quality but provide biblical content and information. Whatever the method, the most important factor is the spiritual character of the teacher. A disciple is better served as part of a group taught by a pastor or teacher who possesses an accurate and practical knowledge of God's Word, wisdom, and godly character than if he or she is discipled one-on-one by a person who is immature or carnal.

Another significant factor in personal discipling is the unique relationship of the disciple and the teacher. Some people connect with particular people better than others. In two instances in Ephesians (2:21; 4:16), Paul uses the Greek word *sunarmologeo*, which is translated "fitted" in the NASB. The NIV translation of this word, "joined," does not convey the full meaning, since two things can be joined but still not fit. The King James Version translates *sunarmologeo* well as "fitly framed" and "fitly joined." This word is not used anywhere else in the New Testament.

Discipling relationships should be determined prayerfully for the right fit. The right connections or joints (*haphe*) in the Body cause it to be held together (*sumbibazo*) in such a way that the Body "grows with a growth which is from God" (Colossians 2:19). Discipleship is not a human process; although God uses people, He causes the growth (1 Corinthians 3:6).

13.3.4
OBJECTIVE
Explain the role of the character of each mature believer involved in discipling a new believer.

15 What is the non-negotiable element in the discipleship process?

Test Yourself

Circle the letter of the *best* answer.

1. A good analogy for Bible reading is
   a) physical nourishment and physical exercise.
   b) reading history and biography to learn about life.
   c) slow reading in order to increase understanding.
   d) spiritual nourishment being compared with physical nourishment.

2. The local church helps the new believer by
   a) serving as a necessary channel of God's grace.
   b) preserving him or her from interacting with a sinful world.
   c) giving him or her the social standing needed in order to earn community respect.
   d) offering opportunities for corporate worship, spiritual encouragement, and service to others.

3. New believers are to communicate the truth of the gospel through their
   a) church membership and public Bible reading.
   b) actions, public testimonies, words, and one-on-one communication.
   c) monogamous lifestyles and pro-life voting records.
   d) regular participation in communion and obedience in water baptism.

4. The believer should view the relationship between evangelism and discipleship as
   a) interactive, each including the other without specific sequence.
   b) distinct, evangelism needing completion before discipleship can commence.
   c) mutually exclusive, since some lost people require evangelism and others discipleship.
   d) gifts of the Spirit, each used exclusively by believers with that gift.

5. The ultimate goal of the disciple is to
   a) live a life of sinless perfection.
   b) become like his or her master.
   c) absorb the theological position statements of his or her church.
   d) achieve material blessing as proof of God's favor.

6. When considering personal responsibility in relationship to discipleship,
   a) each person is responsible to identify the discipler for his or her life.
   b) each person's soul is the responsibility of a specific believer.
   c) each person is responsible for his or her spiritual condition, but other believers are responsible to spiritually nurture him or her.
   d) God takes full responsibility to choose disciplers for His followers.

7. In the lifelong discipleship process, the moment of salvation is
   a) a spiritual starting point rather than a finish line.
   b) a partial act of regeneration that requires nurturing to inherit eternal life.
   c) symbolic, with discipleship creating the fullness of God's work of grace.
   d) irreversible, with discipleship following a pre-ordained path of spiritual growth.

8. When it comes to ministry, the new believer should
   a) be prohibited from involvement, due to immaturity.
   b) always be the target of ministry rather than the participant.
   c) be evaluated for specific spiritual gifts and given structured training.
   d) be given opportunities to serve others and, thus, grow spiritually.

9. Sunday school and small groups offer discipleship in the context of
   a) developing key relationships with other believers through regular interaction.
   b) a structured curriculum that adheres to a church's theological position.
   c) media presentations that bring the Bible to life.
   d) a comfortable environment that promotes seeker sensitivity.

10. Regardless of the discipleship method employed, it is vital that
    a) the person being discipled be baptized in the Holy Spirit.
    b) both the discipler and disciple belong to the same denomination.
    c) both the discipler and the disciple be close in age.
    d) the discipler is of reputable Christian character.

Responses to Interactive Questions
Chapter 13

Some of these responses may include information that is supplemental to the IST. These questions are intended to produce reflective thinking beyond the course content and your responses may vary from these examples.

1 What three components work together to ground the believer in God's Word?

Bible reading (preferably more than once a day), Bible study (taking additional time to discern the full application of Scripture), and Bible meditation (regular mental focus on Bible truth) work together to integrate Bible truth with life practice.

2 What three practices make prayer fully effective in the believer's life?

The believer who prays according to God's purposes, prays in faith, and prays in Jesus' name will experience the full benefits of prayer.

3 How does a local church encourage a new believer in his or her faith?

The local church gives the believer opportunities to worship God with other believers, to receive spiritual strength through others' encouragement, and to serve Christ by serving others.

4 The new believer's mandate to share his or her faith includes what two areas of responsibility?

The believer's actions (lifestyle in general and water baptism as a particular command) and words (telling people about the gospel) must communicate salvation's message to the lost.

5 How does the Holy Spirit help new believers to live for Christ?

The Holy Spirit gives new Christians power to shun the sins of their old lives and to share with others the joy of their new lives.

6 What two functions does the verb form of the word *disciple* serve?

The verb form of disciple, *matheteuo*, can refer to becoming a disciple and to making disciples.

7 What is the relationship between discipleship and evangelism?

Each activity includes the other. Neither can function in isolation, and one does not merely follow the other.

8 What should be the goal of the disciple?

Everything the disciple does should be a step in becoming more like the Master.

9 What is the relationship between discipleship and personal responsibility?

While each person remains responsible for his or her own spiritual condition, God intends that believers support one another in the discipleship journey.

10 What spiritual delusion does the reality of discipleship thoroughly refute?

The lifelong personal growth involved in discipleship effectively contradicts the perception that regeneration—salvation—is a spiritual finish line.

11 What disciplines in Bible reading help to convey the full benefit of Scripture to the reader?

The believer should read the Word systematically, moving from short, clear presentations of the gospel to longer scriptural treatments of theology. To preserve the context in which biblical truth was originally communicated, it is best to read entire books of the Bible rather than focus on small groups of verses. A thematic reading of the Bible—highlighting personal needs or life issues—and connecting the Bible with an individual's interests help the reader bring to light the Bible's personal relevance.

12 What truths do the various Greek verb forms in Romans 12:1–2 convey?

The imperative active tense identifies actions to be taken by the reader. The middle voice points to actions carried out on the reader (in this case, something to be avoided). The imperative passive references an action to be carried out on the reader that the reader cannot carry out through personal ability (in this case, something the reader should allow). Taken together, the verbs describe personal character development in terms of the believer's allowing God to bring about miraculous inner change and reject the otherwise inevitable influence of the world.

13 Why is ministry involvement vital in the discipleship process?

The new believer who is led into personal ministry learns to apply the principles of God's Word rather than simply study them.

14 What are five common components in church ministry that act as means to discipleship?

Pulpit ministry offers discipleship in the Word through teaching. Sunday school connects systematic study of the Word with interpersonal relationships. A new believers' class gives new Christians a concentrated presentation of key truths aimed at spiritual formation. Small groups help believers stay connected with the church outside the standard schedule of services. One-on-one discipleship allows a new believer to benefit from the personal guidance of a mature believer.

15 What is the non-negotiable element in the discipleship process?

While the details of the discipleship process methods may vary, the believer entrusted with carrying out that process must be a person of spiritual character.

CHAPTER 14

World Missions

His fireplace told a story. The picture over the mantle was of a simple white farmhouse, the one in which Bob Schmidgall grew up. The mantle held a collection of models, all miniature John Deere tractors. One of eight children in a northern Illinois farm family, Bob was raised observing the laws of sowing and reaping. Plowing, planting, cultivating, and harvesting teach principles that well-equip a pastor.

From the beginning of his ministry, Bob taught his congregation to sow to reach the world. He believed in missions faith promise giving. He made it a high priority in the spiritual life of his congregation by scheduling annual fall and spring missions conventions.

Bob Schmidgall left a legacy of giving when he went to be with the Lord in 1998 at age fifty-five.

Subsequent leadership continues Bob's legacy at Calvary Church in Naperville, Illinois. Calvary Church has a passionate vision for reaching a lost world. As a result, the church's missions giving has escalated. In its first thirty years, the church gave more than sixteen million dollars to Assemblies of God World Missions. From 2000 to 2005, the church has already given more than nine million dollars.

What a pastor is, the congregation, in time, becomes. The reason Calvary Church is such an unwavering example of a church with a missions heart is its leadership. The pastors have kept a continuous, clear vision for reaching a lost world before the congregation.

Lesson 14.1   Our Worldwide Mission

Objectives
14.1.1 Identify the Assemblies of God's cooperative nature and its distinction as a Fellowship.
14.1.2 Describe the Fellowship's commitment to worldwide evangelization.
14.1.3 Explain the fourfold strategy of Assemblies of God World Missions (AGWM).
14.1.4 Explain the comprehensive methodology of AGWM.

Lesson 14.2   World Missions in the Local Church

Objectives
14.2.1 Embrace the practice of observing Missions Sunday.
14.2.2 Prioritize at least one, preferably two, missions conventions each year.
14.2.3 Explain the biblical foundation for faith-promise giving.
14.2.4 Outline the integration of the practice of faith-promise giving with the church's commitment to tithes and offerings.

World Missions

LESSON 14.1

Our Worldwide Mission

Evangelism is about souls—and eternity. It is about emptying hell and filling heaven. A local church that has a heart for the lost of its community will also have a heart for the lost of our nation as well as throughout the world. Every resource God has entrusted to us must be used wisely to maximize the spiritual harvest.

A Foundation of Cooperation

When delegates formed the Assemblies of God in 1914, they defined the Fellowship's missionary character and priority. The General Council minutes that first year describe world evangelization as "the chief concern of the church." Even in the resolution concerning tithes, the Council resolved that after the local ministry was supported, any surplus funds should be spent for "the spread of the gospel throughout the world."

Our founders stated that they saw a "great need of cooperation, fellowship and unity, according to the Scriptures," especially in "home and foreign mission work." Although Pentecostal believers had attempted to cooperate in missions efforts in various parts of the country, the Assemblies of God leaders said, "Seemingly God has a more scriptural basis and method and a broader field and a greater work than has been accomplished."

The word *cooperation* was especially prominent in the deliberations. As a result, the following resolution passed.

> Whereas, in the providence of God there have sprung up spontaneously in this movement throughout the country, Pentecostal centers, and . . . monies for missionary purposes are being sent to these centers and distributed upon the missionary field, therefore be it resolved, that the presbytery be instructed to seek to bring about a more perfect cooperation among these centers, in the matter of distribution of missionary funds, and the sending out of missionaries, with a view to greater efficiency. (*General Council Minutes*, 1914)

Later in that meeting, this declaration was made, "We commit ourselves and the movement to Him for the greatest evangelism that the world has ever seen. We pledge our hearty cooperation, prayers and help to this end."

"More perfect cooperation" related to efficiency. "Hearty cooperation" related to effectiveness.

The apostle Paul describes the church's nature and function in terms of a physical body. Cooperation is the natural and necessary way in which a body must function. These early Pentecostal leaders stated their objective to pursue more perfect cooperation. This implies that they wanted *more* perfect cooperation to increase their efficiency in sending and supporting missionaries.

The powerful result of cooperation is that we can accomplish much more in Christ's kingdom united in a common cause than our best individual efforts can produce.

The greatest example of this principle is found in the local church. We were not designed to live isolated Christian lives. God planned for those who follow Him to do so together with other believers.

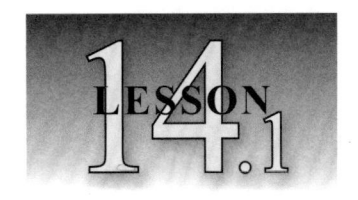

The same principle that applies on the local church level also is true in the larger context. As individual believers are more effective in ministry when they are part of a congregation, a congregation maximizes its impact on a lost world when it is part of a cooperative fellowship.

14.1.1 OBJECTIVE
Identify the Assemblies of God's cooperative nature and its distinction as a Fellowship.

1 What was "the chief concern of the church" identified in the formative gathering of Assemblies of God delegates?

14.1.2 OBJECTIVE
Describe the Fellowship's commitment to worldwide evangelization

2 How is the power of cooperation demonstrated throughout the structure of the church?

When our founders established the Assemblies of God, they specifically affirmed that they were not establishing a new sect. They avoided calling this new entity a *denomination*. Instead, they first called it a *movement* and later a *fellowship*; more specifically, a **voluntary cooperative fellowship.**

Our Mission—A Fourfold Strategy

14.1.3 OBJECTIVE
Explain the fourfold strategy of Assemblies of God World Missions (AGWM).

An examination of Assemblies of God statistics reveals incredible, progressive, exponential growth in our fraternal fellowships abroad. The primary reason for this growth in most of the world has been our longstanding commitment to establishing **indigenous**, New Testament churches.

The word *indigenous* describes something that begins, grows, and lives in its natural setting or environment. We do not transplant the American church. From the beginning, our missionaries have planted indigenous churches and invested their lives in national men and women whom God uses to establish the ministry. Our mission is to plant local bodies of believers who will live and grow without dependency on the Fellowship that sent the missionaries. Indigenous churches should be **self-supporting**, **self-governing**, and **self-propagating**.

Assemblies of God missionary outreach around the world is extensive in geographic scope and encompassing in breadth of ministry. The reason is simple; our strategy was formulated by the Spirit of God. Our early leaders set us on a course of obedience—first, to our Lord's command to preach the gospel and make disciples in all the world, and second, to the biblical principles that enable us to maximize the harvest.

3 What does an indigenous-ministry focus mean for those involved in ministry partnership?

4 What is the fourfold strategy of Assemblies of God World Missions?

The foundational pillars of our mission are summarized in these four words: *reaching*, *planting*, *training*, and *touching*. All four pillars—evangelism, church planting, education and compassion ministries—support our primary objective to establish churches that will endure. A firmly established church not only conserves the harvest of souls reached through evangelism but also becomes an expanding base for ongoing evangelism.

The following distinctives of our mission are not formulations of a strategy committee. Each is a biblical command, an observation of what the Spirit of God led our early missionary leadership to do and what successive leadership has affirmed and maintained. We must continue to obey these biblical mandates until Jesus returns to gather His bride from the four corners of the earth. (See Revelation 7:1.)

Reaching

We proclaim the message of Jesus Christ to the spiritually lost in all the world through every available means.

The cutting edge of our mission has always been evangelism—to penetrate the darkness with the light of Christ's gospel. Jesus made this compelling point in Matthew 18:13. He is happier about the one lost sheep that is found than about the ninety-nine that did not wander off.

Our missionaries are challenged to exemplify evangelism in their personal lives on the mission field regardless of their specialization, whether it be preaching, teaching, construction, or compassion ministry. Our missionaries must always personally share the light of the gospel with people in spiritual darkness.

Planting

We establish churches following the New Testament pattern.

Unless people reached through evangelism are discipled, most will be lost. The Great Commission is to "'go into all the world and preach the gospel to all creation'" (Mark 16:15). Our Lord also commanded, "'Go and make disciples of all nations . . . teaching them to obey everything I have commanded you'" (Matthew 28:19–20, NIV).

In obedience to our Lord's command to make disciples, we are establishing churches in more than two hundred nations and territories. We are called to reap a worldwide harvest and to help conserve it.

Training

We train leaders throughout the world to proclaim the message of Jesus Christ to their own people and to other nations.

Paul told Timothy, "The things which you have heard from me in the presence of many witnesses, entrust these to faithful men who will be able to teach others also" (2 Timothy 2:2).

From the beginning, the Assemblies of God has focused on training national believers. Because the heart of our mission is to establish churches that will endure, pastors are needed to care for those reached through evangelism.

Touching

We touch poor and suffering people with the compassion of Jesus Christ and invite them to become His followers.

Rather than establishing a centralized relief agency, Assemblies of God World Missions promotes localized ministries of compassion, led by people who have been called by the Holy Spirit to a specific area. The most effective distribution network for compassion ministries is the hundreds of thousands of local churches around the world. They are prepared not only to touch the needy in their areas with the compassion of Christ but also to share the gospel and offer a church—a spiritual family where they can grow in the Lord.

Our Method

All the Church

Many years ago, I dialogued with a professor of missions history who had served as a Lutheran missionary for thirty-four years in China and Japan. He was fascinated by the scope of Assemblies of God missions distinctives. I was intrigued by what provoked his interest and admiration the most—Speed the Light and Boys and Girls Missionary Crusade (now called Boys and Girls Missionary Challenge).

"Do you mean children and teenagers are involved in your world mission?" he asked.

When I explained that children supply translation services and educational literature for our missionaries and that teenagers supply vehicles and a variety of equipment, he was amazed.

In the Assemblies of God, the whole church is mobilized in our worldwide mission. This has been true for so long that we often fail to appreciate its uniqueness. Men, women, children, and teenagers work together to supply literature, personal and household goods, vehicles, and equipment to our missionary force throughout the world.

14.1.4 OBJECTIVE
Explain the comprehensive methodology of AGWM.

5 What is the Assemblies of God's threefold method for implementing its missions ministry?

Taking All the Gospel

Early in the Pentecostal movement many of our churches were described as **full gospel**. The full-gospel message assumes that what God promised to the New Testament church is still true for the church today. Our statement of foundational truths reflects this. As many denominations drift away from dependence upon the sovereign activity of God in building His church throughout the world, we steadfastly depend on His supernatural working. The full-gospel message proclaims salvation by grace alone through faith, the baptism in the Holy Spirit, the equipping of the saints through spiritual gifts, divine healing, and the promised return of Jesus Christ.

Into All the World

Most of the reasons our founders gave for forming the Assemblies of God related to reaching the world with the gospel. Unlike many church bodies whose missions focused on just certain parts of the world, our early leaders were compelled by the Spirit to obey our Lord's command to "go into *all* the world and preach the gospel" (Mark 16:15, emphasis added).

Our founding leaders' bold response to our Lord's command is astounding. How could such a small group of Christians even consider attempting to preach the gospel in *all* the world? Because they were truly Pentecostal. They believed both Jesus' command to reach the whole world and also His promise that they would receive the Holy Spirit's power to do it.

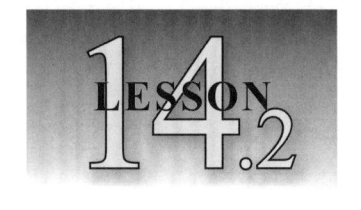

LESSON 14.2

World Missions in the Local Church

God blesses churches that have a heart for missions. Studies conducted by Assemblies of God World Missions confirm that churches holding missions conventions and other missions services throughout the year enjoy not only increased missions giving but also increased local evangelism and financial support. A local church's heart for the lost in its own community directly relates to its burden for the spiritually lost of the nation and the world. The church that commits to supporting missionaries throughout the United States and around the world will have an increased vision for reaching its immediate surroundings.

Like frontline soldiers in war, missionaries have a critical dependence on the support ministry of our home base. We also hold up their hands with faithful intercessory prayer. Through our giving we enjoy (as the apostle Paul beautifully describes) the "favor of participation in the support of the saints" (2 Corinthians 8:4). The strength of missions support in the Assemblies of God is not a centralized missions fund, but it is the designated giving by local churches to specific missionaries and ministries. In recent decades, other sources of funding have surfaced, such as legacies and missions funding organizations. These entities are minor compared with the primary Assemblies of God missions support base, the local church.

Three regular practices will help a local church motivate its congregation to be active in missions beyond its own community—**Missions Sunday**, the **missions convention**, and the missions faith promise.

14.2.1 OBJECTIVE
Embrace the practice of observing Missions Sunday

6   What is the primary source of support in the Assemblies of God for missions ministry?

Missions Sunday

7 What purpose does Missions Sunday serve?

Since 1916, the Assemblies of God has designated the first Sunday of every month as Missions Sunday. Missions Sundays afford a variety of opportunities.

- Many churches choose this day to receive monthly faith promise offerings and keep before the people the needs of missions.
- Some churches also choose Missions Sunday as a time to receive special offerings for missions projects.
- Audio or video messages from missionaries the church supports can be featured on Missions Sunday.
- Each Missions Sunday, special prayer can be offered for a particular missionary the church supports.

Some useful tools are available to help inspire a congregation's missionary vision on a monthly basis.

- Since 1998, the first *Today's Pentecostal Evangel* of each month has been devoted to world missions.
- Monthly missions videos provide regular missions updates for three age groups—adults, youth, and children.
- Each year, Assemblies of God World Missions selects a theme to promote missions awareness and produces a variety of items for local church use. These include banners, bulletin covers and inserts, placemats, faith promise cards, offering envelopes, letterhead stationery, thank-you cards, and an activity book for children. Also available are informational brochures that can help educate congregations concerning Assemblies of God missions.
- An annual missions musical can be presented in missions banquets and services by a choir, as a video presentation, or both. Though the musicals are most often presented in a missions convention, they are also designed so that single songs can be presented. Consequently, they can help highlight Missions Sundays throughout the year.

The Missions Convention

14.2.2
OBJECTIVE
Prioritize at least one, preferably two, missions conventions each year.

Missions conventions focus a congregation's attention on a worldwide missionary vision and remind believers of their responsibility in fulfilling the Great Commission. A major missions emphasis once a year, or preferably twice a year, will keep the cause of missions before the congregation. With prayer and planning, a missions convention can be a dynamic means God uses to inspire, enlist, challenge, and motivate the local church.

8 What purpose does a missions convention serve?

Each church, regardless of size, can have a missions convention. A church's first missions convention can be simple, with new features added in subsequent years. Increasingly, the missions convention will become a highlight of a local church's year.

The number of churches holding missions conventions is increasing. A growing number of churches have two missions conventions each year, one in the spring and one in the fall.

Faith-promise Sunday is the highlight of most missions conventions when each church participant is given the opportunity to make a commitment to the missions program of the local church. From these combined commitments, churches provide ongoing support to missionaries. This regular, faithful, monthly support is the supply lifeline to the missionary.

The Missions Faith Promise

14.2.3 OBJECTIVE
Explain the biblical foundation for faith-promise giving.

The most vital tool in missions funding has been the missions faith promise. For those who participate, it can be a life-changing experience. Two ongoing major missions events that facilitate and interrelate with faith promise giving are the missions convention and Missions Sunday. The missions convention is the time when believers are motivated to make six-month or one-year commitments to regular missions giving. Missions Sunday is a time each month when faith promises are collected, although it is better to encourage people to contribute their faith promises weekly when possible.

9 What is a faith promise?

The faith promise concept was born in the heart of Pastor Oswald Smith of People's Church in Toronto, Canada. When Pastor Smith was a young man, the Lord dealt with him in a missions convention concerning promising more than he thought he could give. As a step of faith, he obeyed the Lord's voice. Later, he shared a great testimony about God's miraculous provision that enabled him to keep that financial commitment to missions.

The Biblical Foundation

10 What is the biblical foundation for making a faith promise?

Although Pastor Oswald Smith popularized the term *faith promise*, the concept is taught in Scripture by the apostle Paul. In 2 Corinthians 8 and 9, Paul shares the inspiring testimony of the sacrificial faith giving of the churches in Macedonia.

Paul taught that the Macedonian churches gave in two ways: according to their ability, and beyond their ability. (See 2 Corinthians 8:3.) Because of their joy and liberality, the Macedonians gave according to their ability, even though they were in deep poverty. Their values and priorities were demonstrated by their commitment to the needs of their fellow saints. Paul emphasized that God provides "sufficiency in everything" so that believers may have an abundance for "every good deed" (2 Corinthians 9:8). We should always be ready to give and work so that we will have resources to help those in need.

Paul also said that the Macedonian Christians gave beyond their ability. How can people give beyond their ability? Because God is personally involved in their finances. While we are repeatedly warned in Scripture not to test God, the opposite is true concerning our finances. Instead, we are told, "'Test me in this,' says the Lord Almighty, 'and see if I will not throw open the floodgates of heaven and pour out so much blessing that you will not have room enough for it'" (Malachi 3:10, NIV).

A faith promise is an opportunity for believers to experience God's financial blessing in and through their lives.

Preparing the Congregation

14.2.4 OBJECTIVE
Outline the integration of the practice of faith-promise giving with the church's commitment to tithes and offerings.

In the weeks prior to the convention, it is essential that the pastor educates, or re-educates, the congregation concerning missions faith promises. Faith Promise Sunday is not the best time to educate people. That time should be used to motivate believers and call them to commitment. Thought and prayer concerning missions faith promises should take place before Faith Promise Sunday. Faith promises can be promoted in several ways during the weeks leading up to the missions convention.

Have a meeting with your adult and youth Sunday school teachers to convey your vision for total involvement concerning faith promises. A week or two before Faith Promise Sunday, teachers can allow five or ten minutes during class to challenge their students to personal missions involvement.

If possible, ask people from the congregation to share brief testimonies concerning how the Lord enabled them to give to missions and how their lives were blessed.

Presenting the Faith Promise Challenge

Training people to give regularly to missions is the most effective method of missions funding in the local church. Missions giving should be a regular part of worship, just as is giving tithes and offerings. Traditionally, most churches encourage people to make faith promise commitments for a year at a time. Six-month commitments may be more effective, for the following reasons:

- Generally, most people will trust God in faith to give more per week or per month for a six-month period than they will for a year. A year may seem long, so people commit more conservatively.

- Since we know that the missions pledge program works and that God honors people's faith in this way, most people will pledge again six months later. Many will increase their pledge. The result is greater missions giving over the twelve-month period.

- If you have a twelve-month program, new people coming into the church after the missions convention will wait before they have the opportunity to make a faith promise. If missions pledges are made every six months, they will have an opportunity to participate sooner. This serves two valuable purposes.

    1. New believers will get involved in missions giving early in their experience, when they tend to be most zealous and responsive.
    2. It increases the church's missions income for the year, giving the budget a boost during the second six-month period.

Maintaining Faith Promise Giving

When receiving Sunday morning tithes and offerings, say, "Now it is time to receive God's tithes, our offerings, and faith promises." Mentioning faith promises every time the Sunday morning offering is received keeps the concept before the people in only seconds per week.

God will give much more through us than He will ever give to us. This truth echoes Paul in 2 Corinthians 9:10–11, "Now he who supplies seed to the sower and bread for food will also supply and increase your store of seed and will enlarge the harvest of your righteousness. You will be made rich in every way so that you can be generous on every occasion, and through us your generosity will result in thanksgiving to God" (NIV). Notice that it is not consumable bread for food that is increased but our seed for sowing.

A farmer sows seed in the springtime with faith for a harvest in the fall. He trusts the soil, the weather, the seed, and God's laws to produce a harvest. We do the same with the seed of the gospel. As we do what we can to personally have a part in fulfilling the Great Commission, we demonstrate faith in the power of the gospel to bear a harvest in the world.

Test Yourself

Circle the letter of the *best* answer.

1. Assemblies of God founders identified what as the "chief concern of the church"?
   a) Speaking in tongues
   b) Divine healing
   c) Prosperity
   d) World evangelization

2. The relationship of the local believer to the local church and the local church to other churches illustrates the
   a) power of cooperation to multiply ministry effectiveness.
   b) modern embodiment of the twelve tribes of Israel.
   c) true interpretation of the Parable of the Ninety-Nine Sheep.
   d) validity of irresistible grace.

3. The Assemblies of God's focus on indigenous ministry gives primary attention to
   a) maintaining a chain of command between the U.S. Fellowship and foreign groups.
   b) establishing self-supporting, self-governing, and self-propagating churches in foreign nations.
   c) raising funds from around the world for relief projects.
   d) translating the Bible into every known language.

4. The fourfold strategy of Assemblies of God World Missions can be summarized as
   a) visiting, evangelizing, building, and administrating.
   b) loving, training, leading, and growing.
   c) reaching, planting, training, and touching.
   d) convicting, disciplining, guiding, and multiplying.

5. The Assemblies of God's threefold method for implementing missions ministry involves
   a) all local churches giving all available finances to support all missionaries.
   b) all Assemblies of God members tithing all their income to underwrite all departments.
   c) all adults committing to guide all children in praying for all nations.
   d) all the church in communicating all the gospel to all the world.

6. The primary source for mission support in the Assemblies of God is
   a) the local church.
   b) a centralized missions fund.
   c) a system of trusts and legacies.
   d) district councils.

7. Missions Sundays help local church congregations by
   a) motivating them to compete for various plaques and prizes at the next General Council.
   b) presenting them with needs from around the world and giving them an opportunity to respond.
   c) convicting them of spiritual complacency and reminding them of their material blessings.
   d) maintaining their affiliation with the Assemblies of God.

8. Churches find that using what tool once or twice a year can increase missions support?
   a) Offering a seminar on stewardship and financial planning
   b) Calling for a church-wide week of fasting
   c) Holding a missions convention that connects the congregation with missionaries and missions needs
   d) Sending the pastoral staff on a short-term missions trip

9. A missions faith promise
   a) gives the believer the opportunity to support missions regularly, trusting God to enable him or her to give.
   b) is a vow before God that carries serious repercussions if the amount promised is not given.
   c) should be honored at all costs, even if a loan is required.
   d) is a confession of faith that becomes a seed for gaining personal wealth.

10. Experience has shown that it is most effective to ask for new faith promises every
    a) year.
    b) six months.
    c) Missions Sunday.
    d) General Council.

Responses to Interactive Questions
Chapter 14

Some of these responses may include information that is supplemental to the IST. These questions are intended to produce reflective thinking beyond the course content and your responses may vary from these examples.

1 What was "the chief concern of the church" identified in the formative gathering of Assemblies of God delegates?

The delegates to the 1914 General Council identified world evangelization as "the chief concern of the church."

2 How is the power of cooperation demonstrated throughout the structure of the church?

Individual believers find their faith strengthened and experience greater personal effectiveness as they fellowship with a local body of believers. Local church bodies enjoy multiplied ministry effectiveness in cooperation with other local churches.

3 What does an indigenous-ministry focus mean for those involved in ministry partnership?

Those initiating the ministry seek to establish a church that is born, lives, and thrives in its own natural setting. The established church utilizes the strengths of the mother church without becoming dependent on that church for continued effective outreach.

4 What is the fourfold strategy of Assemblies of God World Missions?

The Assemblies of God is committed to reaching the lost with the gospel, planting local churches, training both leadership and lay ministers, and touching poor and suffering people with the compassion of Christ.

5 What is the Assemblies of God's threefold method for implementing its missions ministry?

All of the church is committed to communicating all of the gospel to all of the world.

6 What is the primary source of support in the Assemblies of God for missions ministry?

The local church, rather than a centralized missions fund, is the strength of Assemblies of God missions support.

7 What purpose does Missions Sunday serve?

Missions Sunday gives churches a monthly opportunity to receive missions offerings, feature missions speakers or multimedia events, and offer targeted prayer for missions needs.

8 What purpose does a missions convention serve?

Missions conventions create a sharper focus on worldwide missionary vision each year (preferably twice a year), remind the local congregation of their responsibility in fulfilling the Great Commission, and give opportunity to support missions regularly.

9 What is a faith promise?

A faith promise is an acknowledgement of God's desire to give through a believer even beyond that believer's resources. A faith promise exercises faith in God's ability to provide the funds needed.

10 What is the biblical foundation for making a faith promise?

The apostle Paul wrote of the believers in Macedonia who gave out of poverty and gave beyond their ability.

CHAPTER 15

The Church in Mission

Jesus came not only to rescue the lost from eternal punishment but also to give value to each person. Mary, Jesus' mother, prophesied before His birth that He would lift up the humble (Luke 1:52).

A local church is not an exclusive club, open to only the community's elite. Jesus consistently revealed His heart for the rejected and disenfranchised. God redeems lives from destruction (Psalm 103:4); He redeems them for a purpose.

When Steve Dodson assumed the pastorate of Hazel River Assembly of God in Rixeyville, Virginia, in 1995, the church had twenty-one members. Occasionally, Pastor Steve went to an apple orchard in the nearby mountains to pray. One day, the harvesters came through while he was there. As they completed their tasks, one said to Steve, "Feel free to take any apples left on the ground."

Many apples were left behind. Some had fallen out of the bucket when the harvesters came through. Others were discarded, because they were damaged and had scars or bruises. Steve gave the apples to some of the women in the church. They peeled and canned the apples. Later, they made beautiful pies.

Through this experience, God revealed to Steve that many people in the community were like those apples, waiting to be gathered. Neglected people are passed over by Christians who look on the outside and conclude that the people are unreachable.

Steve shared his experience with his congregation. It energized the church. Believers began gathering neglected people, and a variety of newcomers visited the church. Some were neglected as children. Some were addicts and alcoholics. They were scarred and bruised by sin and suffering. God made something beautiful of them. They began to take part in the life of the church. Some are now deacons in the church, because God saw their hidden potential.

During a decade starting in the mid-nineties, the church grew from the original twenty-one members to more than 350.

The mission of a church is to enter into God's redemptive mission in the lives of lost people, bringing the message of Jesus, forgiveness of sin, and the gift of everlasting life. It is the Lord's joy to accept the rejected and lift up the humble.

Lesson 15.1   The Redemptive Mission of the Church

Objectives

15.1.1 Describe the nature of Christ's redemptive mission.
15.1.2 Summarize Christ's commitment to empower His church to fulfill its mission.
15.1.3 Explain the interconnected functions of evangelism, worship, discipleship, and demonstrating compassion.
15.1.4 Identify the comprehensive role of evangelism.

Lesson 15.2   Fulfilling the Mission

Objectives

15.2.1 Identify faithful prayer as the foundation on which a church fulfills its mission.
15.2.2 Prepare sermons using biblical principles to motivate the congregation.
15.2.3 Dedicate money and time to the church's priority mission of evangelism.
15.2.4 Integrate dependence and discipline whenever the church acts in ministry.

LESSON 15.1

The Redemptive Mission of the Church

Jesus' Mission

When John the Baptist saw Jesus coming to him, he prophesied, "'Behold, the Lamb of God who takes away the sin of the world!'" (John 1:29). The apostle Peter wrote, "It was not with perishable things such as silver or gold that you were redeemed from the empty way of life handed down to you from your forefathers, but with the precious blood of Christ, a lamb without blemish or defect" (1 Peter 1:18–19, NIV).

The apostle Paul said, "In Him we have redemption through His blood, the forgiveness of our trespasses, according to the riches of His grace" (Ephesians 1:7). He told the Romans we are "being justified as a gift by His grace through the redemption which is in Christ Jesus" (Romans 3:24).

Jesus' **mission** on earth was to redeem and reconcile sinful humanity to the heavenly Father. Once He accomplished that mission, He committed His followers to a new mission. When Jesus appeared to His disciples after His resurrection, John 20:21 says He instructed them, "'As the Father has sent Me, I also send you.'" Jesus purchased the redemption for whoever will call upon His name. (See Romans 10:13.) Our task is to take the message of His forgiveness and gift of everlasting life to the world, so the lost can believe on Jesus, confess Him as Savior, and serve Him as Lord.

Paul wrote, "If anyone is in Christ, he is a new creation; the old has gone, the new has come! All this is from God, who reconciled us to himself through Christ and gave us the ministry of reconciliation: that God was reconciling the world to himself in Christ, not counting men's sins against them. And he has committed to us the message of reconciliation. We are therefore Christ's ambassadors, as though God were making his appeal through us" (2 Corinthians 5:17–20, NIV).

As Christ's ambassadors, we are His voice to reconcile a lost world to Him.

The Church's Fourfold Mission

The mission of Christ's church is integrally related to the reason Jesus came to Earth. He came "to seek and to save that which was lost" (Luke 19:10) and "give His life a ransom for many" (Matthew 20:28; Mark 10:45). Jesus' purpose in coming to the world and His command to us to carry on His work outlines our mission—a redemptive mission.

The terms *mission* and *missionary* do not appear in the Bible. The word *mission* comes from the Latin word *missio*, which means "sent." The purpose of a mission is to extend something beyond where it is, to send its message and activity somewhere else, to new territory.

Consider the following dictionary definitions:
- "a ministry commissioned by a religious organization to propagate its faith"
- "assignment to or work in a field of missionary enterprise"
- "a body of persons sent to perform a service or carry on an activity"
- "a group sent to a foreign country to conduct diplomatic or political negotiations"

In popular use, the term *mission* also implies an organization's reason for being or, simply put, its purpose. The most common practical usage of this word is found in the mission statement of an organization.

15.1.1 OBJECTIVE
Describe the nature of Christ's redemptive mission.

1 If Jesus completed His mission on earth, what role could His followers play in its fulfillment?

15.1.2 OBJECTIVE
Summarize Christ's commitment to empower His church to fulfill its mission.

2 What four elements comprise the Assemblies of God's description of the mission of the church?

The mission statement of the Assemblies of God includes a commitment for the organization to fulfill a fourfold mission:

1. To be an agency of God for evangelizing the world.
2. To be a corporate body in which man may worship God.
3. To be a channel of God's purpose to build a body of saints being perfected in the image of His Son (*General Council* 2003, 93).
4. To be a people who demonstrate God's love and compassion for all the world (Psalms 112:9; Galatians 2:10; 6:10; James 1:27). (General Council 2009, 94)

James River Assembly in Ozark, Missouri, expresses this fourfold purpose in its mission statement: "Upward in worship, Inward in commitment, Outward in evangelism." The fourfold mission must be understood in light of the difference between **exegetical theology** (interpretation of Bible passages) and **systematic theology** (belief and doctrine statements). Our mission statement is a systematization of biblical truth, which contributes to our comprehension. It can help our thinking processes and memories, as long as the systematic structure neither distorts nor artificially compartmentalizes. Because of the nature of God's revealed truth, systematic theology should always be guided by exegetical theology. The fourfold mission can only be accurately analyzed by examining how each component relates to the others as revealed in God's inspired Word. The weight and congruity of Scripture verifies the redemptive nature of the Church's mission.

15.1.3 OBJECTIVE

Explain the interconnected functions of evangelism, worship, discipleship, and demonstrating compassion.

Notice that the fourfold mission—evangelism, worship, discipleship, and demonstrating compassion—is considered a single reason-for-being. In a rainbow, each color is distinguishable, but lines cannot be drawn between the colors. Similarly, the four facets of God's redemptive mission are inseparable. Each aspect of the church's mission is necessary to the other three. Discipleship, evangelism, and compassionate service are also forms of worship. Worship, evangelism, and compassionate service should produce spiritual growth. Evangelism, worship, and discipleship should lead to compassionate service. Worship, compassionate service, and discipleship should result in evangelism. These four dimensions of the mission of the church are intertwined and interrelated.

3 What is the relationship between the four components of the church's mission?

How are discipleship, evangelism, and demonstrating compassion forms of worship? Children bring honor and respect to their parents by becoming what the parents have taught them to be. We bring honor and glory to God when we become in character what our Lord has destined for us and when we perform the good works He has prepared for us (Ephesians 2:10). Leading people to Christ, making disciples, and demonstrating compassion bring glory to God and are forms of worship to Him.

How do worship, works of compassion, and evangelism produce spiritual growth? Worshipping God, both in spirit and in truth, and being in His presence will open our lives to His influence and change us. The disciples grew and developed spiritually in Jesus' presence. In the same way, as we live in devotion and worship, we will be changed by His presence and power, resulting in spiritual growth. Spiritual growth will be inhibited in a person who is not involved in sharing Christ with nonbelievers, compassionate ministry to those in need, and ministry to other believers.

How do worship, spiritual growth, and compassionate, practical ministry result in evangelism? We cannot worship God and grow in Him while we ignore the eternal needs of the spiritually lost around us. We also cannot ignore the present needs of the poor, the starving, and the homeless. The effect of worshipping God in His presence and becoming in character what He has called us to be should cause our lives to have an impact on others, both believers and nonbelievers. Ministering to practical needs can also open up rich opportunities to share your faith in Christ with others.

How do worship, evangelism, and discipleship lead to compassionate ministry? When it is done for Christ, serving others becomes a dimension of our worship. Also, evangelism brings people to Christ and lays the foundation for a person's future Christian life. Discipleship builds upon that foundation, and helps shape us into more Christ-like people. As Christ-like people, we will become involved in compassionate ministry to the needy, the hungry, the homeless, the hurting. As Christ-like people we will also be able to share "a word in season" and lead people along the path to accepting Christ. In this way the cycle continues and grows, and God is glorified through His work upon the earth.

The book of Jonah gives a clear example of the problem of separating worship from obedience and mission.

Then the sailors said to each other, "Come, let us cast lots to find out who is responsible for this calamity." They cast lots and the lot fell on Jonah. So they asked him, "Tell us, who is responsible for making all this trouble for us? What do you do? Where do you come from? What is your country? From what people are you?" He answered, "I am a Hebrew and I worship the Lord, the God of heaven, who made the sea and the land" (Jonah 1:7–9, NIV).

Although Jonah claimed to be a worshipper of God, he was living in disobedience to God. He also didn't seem to care about the spiritual need of the people in Nineveh. Jonah illustrates how someone can believe he or she is a worshipper but is not being a true disciple and evangelist.

The connection between worship, discipleship, evangelism, and demonstrating compassion is well-expressed in the worship chorus, "Amazing love, how can it be that you, my King, would die for me? Amazing love, I know it's true, and it's my joy to honor you. In all I do, I honor you" (Foote 1997). The love manifested by our Lord's sacrifice should evoke the commitment, consecration, and compassion of a disciple. Our desire is to be patterned after our Master—devoted and passionate about sharing the message of Jesus with the spiritually lost.

The Comprehensive Role of Evangelism in the Mission

15.1.4 OBJECTIVE
Identify the comprehensive role of evangelism.

Many believers' understanding of evangelism is limited. Most Christians understand evangelism to be one or both of two objectives:

1. proclaiming the gospel
2. persuading nonbelievers to become Christians

4 In what way do most people misunderstand evangelism?

Most people's conceptions of evangelism are human-centered, focusing on human persuasion. True evangelism is God-centered, a work of the Holy Spirit in which we cooperate. Evangelism is not something believers do for God, but something the Holy Spirit does, allowing us the privilege of participating.

A simple but comprehensive definition of evangelism was written by William Temple, archbishop of Canterbury (1881-1944). His definition of evangelism is "… to so present Jesus Christ in the power of the Holy Spirit that men might come to trust Him as Savior and serve Him as Lord in the fellowship of His church."

Evangelism is more than a separate aspect of the church's mission. It is interrelated with our worship and personal development as followers of Christ.

The redemptive mission of the Church is to reach and disciple worshippers throughout the whole world. One day "he will send his angels with a loud trumpet call, and they will gather his elect from the four winds, from one end of the heavens to the other" (Matthew 24:31, NIV). The twenty-four elders will declare to Jesus, "You are worthy to take the scroll and to open its seals, because you were slain, and with your blood you purchased men for God from every tribe and language and people and nation" (Revelation 5:9, NIV). Notice that the subject of the twenty-four elders' worship is redemption, and the object of their worship is the Redeemer.

The Westminster Shorter Catechism, completed in 1647, states that "man's chief end is to glorify God and to enjoy him forever." Glorifying God involves much more than what is commonly termed *worship*. We bring glory to God through worship, of course; we also worship by becoming what He has in store for us and by influencing others. Worshipping God with words but not actions is what the Bible terms "lip service" (Isaiah 29:13, NASB). God wants worship from our lips but also from our lives. Evangelism, worship, discipleship, and works of compassion are four aspects of one purpose—glorifying God by entering into His mission of reconciling lost humanity to himself.

Our Lord committed His Church to a redemptive mission. He promised, "'I will build my church; and the gates of hell shall not prevail against it'" (Matthew 16:18, KJV). We are not attacked by gates! Rather, the Church is to be attacking the strongholds of the enemy to set free those who are in bondage. We are anointed and empowered by the same Spirit as Jesus. We are called in His name and by the power of His Spirit to His mission, which He announced in fulfillment of Isaiah's prophecy, "'The Spirit of the Lord God is upon me, because the Lord has anointed me to bring good news to the afflicted; He has sent me to bind up the brokenhearted, to proclaim liberty to captives and freedom to prisoners'" (Isaiah 61:1).

We who have been redeemed are to proclaim the gospel of Christ so that others can be rescued from the domain of darkness and transferred to the kingdom of God's beloved Son. (See Colossians 1:13–14.) The critical issue for all worshippers and disciples is our eternal destiny. Our business is to empty hell and fill heaven. It is entering into our Lord's mission of "bringing many sons to glory" (Hebrews 2:10).

The redemptive mission of the Church is to proclaim Christ's salvation and make disciples who will worship God "in spirit and truth" (John 4:23–24).

5 Is it more accurate to understand the church as being on the offensive or on the defensive as its people carry out its mission in the world?

LESSON 15.2

Fulfilling the Mission

What results will a spiritual leader see in ministry? My former pastor, Charles Crabtree, summarized it this way:

- We get what we *pray* for.
- We get what we *preach*.
- We get what we *prioritize*.

Prayer

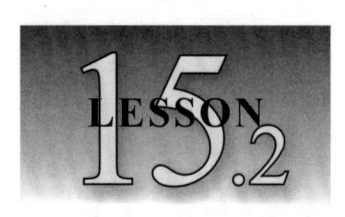

15.2.1 OBJECTIVE
Identify faithful prayer as the foundation on which a church fulfills its mission.

This course has highlighted how the apostle Paul emphasized the importance of our dependence on God's supernatural work. As Pentecostals, we know that God's purposes are not accomplished merely by human power or ability but by His Spirit (Zechariah 4:6). We can be obedient to the Word and live a disciplined life, but if God does not act in and through His Church, we will fail.

A spiritual leader will not see God's purposes accomplished through his or her ministry apart from prayer. An often-quoted Scripture is, "You do not have because

6 How does prayer connect with life experience?

you do not ask" (James 4:2). It is quoted often because it is true. Another familiar text is Paul's admonition to the Philippians, "Do not be anxious about anything, but in everything, by prayer and petition, with thanksgiving, present your requests to God. And the peace of God, which transcends all understanding, will guard your hearts and your minds in Christ Jesus" (Philippians 4:6–7, NIV). Notice that Paul's exhortation encompasses everything we do. We are not to be anxious about anything. We are to pray about everything! Prayer should pervade our lives.

To mobilize a congregation to prayer, specific opportunities must be part of the church's regular schedule. Many churches that are effective in evangelism hold a weekly prayer meeting.

One of the most inspiring weekly prayer meetings I have attended is at Cornerstone Church in Bowie, Maryland, pastored by Mark Lehmann at the time of this writing. The Saturday-night prayer meeting often has thirty percent of the church's Sunday morning congregation in attendance. The church has a heart for the lost, and a focus of the prayer meeting is evangelism. Believers pray fervently for nonbelievers to come to Christ in the Sunday services and for the missionaries the church supports. Pictures of missionaries line the sanctuary walls. This prayer meeting has continued since 1997. A mission-focused church makes developing a lifestyle of prayer a priority.

Preaching

John Williams was raised in a Christian home but turned away from God during his youth. Then he heard a sermon that changed his life. Called to missionary service in the South Pacific, he sailed for Tahiti. He evangelized Rarotonga, Samoa and other islands. He was martyred November 20, 1839, on the island of Erromanga in the New Hebrides. Most of the inhabited islands of the South Pacific were first reached with the gospel by this man whose life was changed by one sermon. A preacher may never know what the lasting and multiplying impact of God's Word will be.

A pastor should always preach at least one sermon a week in a progressive expository series through a book of the Bible. First Thessalonians 2:13 says that the Word of God "performs its work" in people's lives. For this reason, a pastor should make expository preaching a priority. God's Word is alive, Hebrews 4:12 says. The most important issues and topics in Christian living will arise while systematically preaching through the biblical text because the Bible is comprehensive and universal in its application.

A pastor also should plan to cover relevant life topics on a regular basis. Our physical bodies need a balanced diet of the right nutrition; a congregation needs spiritual nutrition from the pulpit to produce spiritual health translated into effective living as devoted followers of Christ.

An intentional aspect of this course's presentation is facilitation of Scripture retention; pastors should preach these Scriptures and their application to evangelism. The truths in the Great Commission, the Parable of the Sower, Jesus' example in evangelism, Peter's preaching, and Paul's teaching should be taught from the pulpit to help motivate and educate a congregation to have a heart for evangelism.

A church where many people are filled with the Holy Spirit is a church where the Holy Spirit baptism is preached and taught from the pulpit. If love is preached, love will be manifested in the congregation. Preach missions, and people will give to reach the lost. Preach witnessing, and people will be motivated to share their faith. Proclaiming Christ must be foremost in our preaching. When Christ is exalted, souls will be born into His kingdom.

15.2.2
OBJECTIVE

Prepare sermons using biblical principles to motivate the congregation.

7   Which two structures should characterize long-term preaching plans?

Each aspect of God's redemptive mission will be evident in a congregation only if it is regularly taught from the pulpit. Pastors should evaluate if their sermon schedule integrates the fourfold mission of the church in a balanced way. Preaching should lead people into more devoted worship, more conscientious discipleship, and more fervent evangelism.

Priorities

Taking inventory of our personal priorities is a simple task of examining our checkbook and calendar. Our priorities are disclosed by how we spend our money and time. What is true for the individual is also true for a church.

Money

In Matthew 6:21, Jesus taught that our hearts will be where our treasures are. A church that is guided by the Holy Spirit will sow financially in ministry that is focused on reaching the lost and reaping a harvest of souls. A church that gives generously to world missions will invariably experience increased income in its general fund and increased passion in the congregation to reach the community's lost.

Time

A few years ago I interviewed Jean Pawentaore, the general superintendent of Burkina Faso Assemblies of God. In our conversation, he made an astute observation concerning challenges the church in Burkina Faso faces compared to the church in America. He said, "There are those who would say that because you in America have so much and we in Burkina Faso have so little that you need to give us more of your money. But then we would have your problems. We do not have as much money as you, but we have something much more valuable. We have time. We have time to pray. And we see miracles."

Christians in America have the same number of minutes each day as Christians in Africa. The difference is how we use those minutes. Paul told the Romans in 12:2, "Do not be conformed to this world." J.B. Phillips translates the verse this way, "Don't let the world around you squeeze you into its own mold." We should be different from the world in how we spend our time.

Benjamin Franklin said that time is the stuff life is made of. Time is too precious to be wasted. Spiritual leaders should prayerfully seek God's guidance concerning a church's schedule. The few hours each week that most people are involved in scheduled church activities need to be spent wisely.

Pastors and leaders should devote personal time to motivating and equipping people to become evangelists and disciplers. Jesus focused his attention on a select number of His closest followers, so He could spend more time with them in friendship and spiritual formation. Like Jesus, a spiritual leader should invest time in relationships with nonbelievers.

Two "Secrets" of Spiritual Success

People buy millions of books that promise to reveal secrets of success. Occasionally, pastors ask me to describe the secret of a well-known pastor's success. After years of observation, I have identified two keys to exceptionally effective ministry, in general as well as specific areas, including evangelism.

Seek the Lord

The lives of Saul and David reveal the importance of seeking the Lord in prayer. What was the difference between these two kings? Saul had great abilities and every probability of success. Yet, his life ended in disaster. David faced challenges, including his own sin and failures, but his life ended in success. One revealing difference is found in a biblical phrase that is used frequently to describe David's life but is almost totally missing in descriptions of Saul's life. In 1 and 2 Samuel the expression, *and David inquired of the Lord,* appears repeatedly. The word translated "inquired" is the Hebrew word (*sha'al / shawal*), which means "ask, seek, or consult." The phrase is written about Saul only once, on the day before his death. He was terrified of the Philistine army. Scripture records, "He inquired of the Lord, but the Lord did not answer him by dreams or Urim or prophets" (1 Samuel 28:6, NIV).

In interviews with more than a dozen Assemblies of God pastors, I asked about the significant growth in their churches and the wide variety of ministries. As significant as what these pastors said concerning their breakthroughs in reaching the lost of their communities, what they did not say was even more important. None referred to books read, conferences attended, or prominent pastors who teach seminars about the secrets of effective evangelism and church growth. Each pastor, in some way, revealed how need, even desperation, caused him or her to seek the Lord in prayer. In response, the Holy Spirit gave guidance and a specific vision for each church within its community and context.

To maintain vital, effective ministry, seek the Lord of the church!

Keep Doing the Right Things

This principle applies in every aspect of the church's ministry. In the context of evangelism, pastors need to keep encouraging and exhorting believers to love and reach the lost.

When I was a teenager, dealers at used car lots wrote *Factory Air* in large letters across windshields. We don't see that anymore, because air conditioning now comes standard in all vehicles. Back in the 1960s, air conditioning was an option. If it was not installed at the factory, a unit had to be added under the dashboard. Factory air had vents that distributed the air evenly throughout the car. Add-on air conditioners hung below the dash over the transmission hump and cooled the center of the front seat. It worked but not nearly as well as air conditioning that was designed properly and installed at the factory.

10 Why is it important to fully integrate evangelism into the life of the church?

For many churches, evangelism is merely bolted on rather than built in. A church tries a personal evangelism training approach or outreach program. When results don't come as quickly as people would like, they try something else. These bolted on approaches to evangelism may work; they just do not work as well as having evangelism built in as a regular focus of the congregation's prayer life, the pastor's preaching, and the church's budget and schedule. Sometimes the right things aren't sensational and dramatic. If they are indeed the right things and if a church will keep doing them, the right results will happen.

What are the right things? Some are obvious.

A pastor should regularly do his or her best to encourage, equip, motivate, and educate the congregation as to the most essential practices of a devoted follower of Christ. These practices include daily Bible reading, daily prayer, the Spirit's infilling, faithful church attendance, tithing, giving to missions, building friendships with nonbelievers, loving people, and sharing Christ. Other right things will be discovered through guidance from God's Word and the Holy Spirit as pastors seek the Lord.

The two secrets of success reflect the two principles found throughout Paul's teaching: *dependence* and *discipline*. In a continual spiritual posture of dependence, *seek the Lord*. Then discipline yourself to *keep doing the right things*.

Test Yourself

Circle the letter of the *best* answer.

1. The fulfillment of the Great Commission requires that believers
   a) are agents with Christ of the grace of God.
   b) partner with Christ to communicate His completed mission to a lost world.
   c) must carry out personal evangelism in order to experience salvation.
   d) are to identify among themselves the people God has called to be witnesses.

2. Which four terms or phrases summarize the mission of the church?
   a) Evangelism, worship, discipleship, demonstrating compassion
   b) Worship, tithing, spiritual gifts, demonstrating compassion
   c) Evangelism, discipleship, communion, spiritual gifts
   d) Water baptism, Pentecost, evangelism, prayer

3. Discipleship and evangelism are
   a) conditions for salvation and sanctification.
   b) gifts of the Spirit best evidenced by Pentecostals.
   c) represented in the New Jerusalem's foundations.
   d) worship, since both bring God glory.

4. Evangelism is best understood as a
   a) persuasive act that convinces the lost of the gospel's truth.
   b) God-centered work of the Holy Spirit in which the believer cooperates.
   c) divine gift available to all believers who ask for it.
   d) responsibility of specific church leaders who receive laity prayer support.

5. Jesus spoke of the "gates of hell" as a
   a) powerful enemy rampaging against the Church.
   b) target for successful attacks by the Church.
   c) symbol of the believer's inner struggle with sin.
   d) reminder of death and the Great White Throne judgment.

6. The believer who understands and acts upon prayer will connect prayer with
   a) all areas of life, especially to defeat anxiety.
   b) corporate worship and find a prayer partner.
   c) with personal repentance and begin each prayer with confession.
   d) personal prosperity and begin each prayer by claiming a blessing.

7. When planning annual sermon series, pastors are wise to include sermons that
   a) identify the congregation's besetting sins and spiritual gifts.
   b) rely on alliteration.
   c) proclaim the way of salvation, as well as sermons that promote spiritual growth.
   d) progress through books of the Bible, as well as sermons that give in-depth treatment to biblical themes.

8. The believer who takes a biblical approach to money will
   a) prioritize and appropriate the Bible's prosperity promises.
   b) remember that money is the root of all evil which compromises one's faith.
   c) give all available cash to the poor and pursue personal poverty.
   d) trust God to meet personal needs and use all personal resources as God leads.

9. The primary difference between King Saul and King David was that
   a) Saul lacked reliance on God, and David pursued God's guidance and help.
   b) Saul was from the tribe of Benjamin and David the tribe of Judah.
   c) Saul was the tallest man in Israel, and David was of unremarkable height.
   d) Saul was symbolic of Israel's rebellion, and David was part of God's plan of salvation.

10. The key to evangelistic success in the local church is to
    a) take regular offerings for missionaries who evangelize as the church's representatives.
    b) preach sermons that highlight evangelism and connect it with Christian living.
    c) integrate evangelism into every expression of the church's life.
    d) conduct prayer walks through the community surrounding the church.

Responses to Interactive Questions
Chapter 15

Some of these responses may include information that is supplemental to the IST. These questions are intended to produce reflective thinking beyond the course content and your responses may vary from these examples.

1 If Jesus completed His mission on earth, what role could His followers play in its fulfillment?

Jesus purchased the redemption of sinful humanity and reconciliation to His Father. His followers must communicate that truth to the lost so that they can receive the accomplished benefits of Christ's divine mission.

2 What four elements comprise the Assemblies of God's description of the mission of the church?

The mission statement of the Assemblies of God calls for evangelism, worship, discipleship, and demonstrating compassion.

3 What is the relationship between the four components of the church's mission?

They are inseparable, with each component involving the other three. They form a single reason for being.

4 In what way do most people misunderstand evangelism?

Evangelism is often misunderstood as human-centered action relying on human powers of persuasion.

5 Is it more accurate to understand the church as being on the offensive or on the defensive as its people carry out its mission in the world?

Too often, believers conceive of hell and its powers as being on the attack against Christians who must withstand that assault. Jesus stated that the "gates of hell" would not prevail against His church. The forces of evil are defeated when the church rescues lost souls.

6 How does prayer connect with life experience?

The believer should pray about every part of life and defeat anxiety in any area of life through trusting prayer.

7 Which two structures should characterize long-term preaching plans?

A pastor's sermons should include expository series that progress through books of the Bible, as well as selected biblical themes strategically chosen to meet specific needs.

8 How can money become a positive factor in the believer's life?

When money is dedicated to fulfilling God's purposes, it becomes a blessing both to the giver and to the recipient.

9 What is the primary key to success in any ministry or life endeavor?

Regardless of the ministry or endeavor, God's guidance and blessing should be sought.

10 Why is it important to fully integrate evangelism into the life of the church?

Evangelism, like any right action, becomes more effective when it is a regular expression of an individual or organization rather than a periodic activity.

> **UNIT PROGRESS EVALUATION 4 AND FINAL EXAMINATION**
>
> You have now concluded all of the work in this independent-study textbook. Review the lessons in this unit carefully, and then answer the questions in the last unit progress evaluation (UPE). When you have completed the UPE, check your answers with the answer key provided in Essential Course Materials at the back of this IST. Review any items you may have answered incorrectly. Review for the final examination by studying the course objectives, lesson objectives, self-tests, and UPEs. Review any lesson content necessary to refresh your memory. If you review carefully and are able to fulfill the objectives, you should have no difficulty passing the closed-book final examination.

Taking the Final Examination

1. **All final exams must be taken closed book.** You are not allowed to use any materials or outside help while taking a final exam. You will take the final examination online at www.globaluniversity.edu. If the online option is not available to you, you may request a printed final exam. If you did not request a printed final exam when you ordered your course, you must submit this request a few weeks before you are ready to take the exam. The Request for a Printed Final Examination is in the Forms section of Essential Course Materials at the back of this IST.

2. Review for the final examination in the same manner in which you prepared for the UPEs. Refer to the form Checklist of Study Methods in the front part of the IST for further helpful review hints.

3. After you complete and submit the online final examination, the results will be immediately available to you. Your final course grade report will be e-mailed to your Global University student e-mail account after your Service Learning Requirement (SLR) report has been processed.

4. If you complete the exam in printed form, you will send your final examination, your answer sheets, and your SLR report to Berean School of the Bible for grading. Your final course grade report will be sent to your GU student e-mail account. If you do not have access to the Internet, your grade will be sent to your mailing address.

Appendix A

Evangelistic Presentations/Salvation Plans

The following evangelistic presentations and plans of salvation are abridged and simplified. Most supply a basic outline of the major points in each of the longer presentations. To read full texts, contact the respective ministry or publisher to obtain the printed literature, or visit the Web site addresses of the ministries (when available) at the conclusion of each presentation.

Two Great Questions

Two Great Questions, by the author of this course, is a simple analysis of the apostolic preaching of Peter[1] which answers two questions:

1. *Who* was Jesus?
2. *Why* did He give His life?

Being prepared to discuss these two questions will equip a person to clearly and simply share the message of Christ with nonbelievers.

Who was Jesus?[2]

In recent years, cover stories about Jesus have appeared in almost all major national news magazines. Television programs and mini-series have been made about Him. But, accounts of Christ's life by secular media almost always present Jesus as a fictional character. Or, even when He is shown as a historical person, He is depicted as a great teacher, or even a prophet, but only a man.

Jesus was much more than a teacher and prophet. He was God in human form. He was conceived by the Holy Spirit, born of a virgin, lived a sinless life, died for our sins, and conquered death by rising again to offer us forgiveness of sin and the gift of everlasting life. He ascended to heaven and will return to earth again for all His followers.

If Jesus Christ was not who He claimed to be, if He is not the crucified and risen Son of God, then, as the apostle Paul declared, our faith is useless (1 Corinthians 15:17). Paul wrote, "For there is one God and one mediator between God and men, the man Christ Jesus" (1 Timothy 2:5, NIV).

Why did He give His life?

The Jews and Romans cannot be blamed for Jesus' death. His life was not taken from Him. He gave it. Jesus said, "The Father loves Me, because I lay down My life that I may take it again. No one has taken it away from Me, but I lay it down on My own initiative. I have the authority to lay it down, and I have authority to take it up again" (John 10:17–18).

Jesus gave His life for two essential reasons:

1. Because we're sinners.
2. Because there was nothing we could do about it.

John the Baptist clearly announced the purpose of Jesus' mission on earth when he said, "'Behold, the Lamb of God who takes away the sin of the world!'" (John 1:29). Each of us has sinned and is separated from God. The punishment for sin is death (Romans 6:23). The death about which the Bible speaks is not just physical death. It means a person's spirit will be in everlasting punishment in hell. Jesus explained that hell is like a "lake of fire," and that everyone who goes there is separated from God forever and burns in fire that never ends (Mark 9:47–48; Revelation 20:15).

But God sent His Son, Jesus Christ, to pay the penalty for our sins. Jesus was born as a man, but He lived His life without sin. Men lied about Him and judged Him guilty of things He had never done. Then they killed Him on a cross. Jesus never sinned, but He was punished for sin. So death had no power over Him, and He came back to life after three days (Mark 8:31; 9:31; 14:27–28). Now, He gives everlasting life to anyone who calls upon His name (Romans 10:13) and receives Him as Savior and Lord.

---

[1] See Acts 2:22–36; 3:12–26; 4:8–12; 5:29–32; 10:34–43.

[2] To nonbelievers with no Christian background, I suggest first focusing on the question "Who *was* Jesus?" in an historical context, speaking of Jesus incarnate in human form two thousand years ago, before progressing to "Who *is* Jesus?" — the living, resurrected Christ.

For more complete information, visit www.evangelism.ag.org.

The ABCs of Salvation

The ABCs of Salvation have been included in every issue of *Today's Pentecostal Evangel* for many years. Perhaps the simplest presentation of the plan of salvation, this was originally written by the late Richard Champion, who served as editor of the *Pentecostal Evangel*.

To know God and be ready for heaven, follow these steps:

A. Admit you are a sinner.

"There is no one righteous, not even one . . . . for all have sinned and fall short of the glory of God" (Romans 3:10, 23).

Ask God's forgiveness.

"Everyone who calls on the name of the Lord will be saved" (Romans 10:13).

B. Believe in Jesus.

"For God so loved the world that he gave his one and only Son, that whoever believes in him shall not perish but have eternal life" (John 3:16).

Become a child of God by receiving Christ.

"To all who received him, to those who believed in his name, he gave the right to become children of God" (John 1:12).

C. Confess that Jesus is your Lord.

"If you confess with your mouth, 'Jesus is Lord,' and believe in your heart that God raised him from the dead, you will be saved" (Romans 10:9).

For more complete information, visit www.pentecostalevangel.ag.org/Salvation.cfm.

The Romans Road to Salvation

Paul's epistle to the Romans offers the most complete biblical presentation of the saving work of Christ. Perhaps because Paul had never been to Rome at the time the epistle was written (and, consequently, Roman believers had never been exposed to Paul's teaching), he composed an epistle that is notable for its complete presentation concerning salvation through Jesus Christ.

The Romans Road, author unknown, progressively highlights certain key verses throughout Romans to establish essential truths relevant to receiving Christ as Savior.

Romans 3:23

"For all have sinned and fall short of the glory of God."

Romans 6:23 (the first part of the verse)

"For the wages of sin is death."

Romans 6:23 (the second part of the verse)

"But the gift of God is eternal life in Christ Jesus our Lord."

Romans 5:8

"But God demonstrates his own love for us in this: While we were still sinners, Christ died for us."

Romans 10:9–10

"If you confess with your mouth, 'Jesus is Lord,' and believe in your heart that God raised him from the dead, you will be saved. For it is with your heart that you believe and are justified, and it is with your mouth that you confess and are saved."

Romans 10:13

"'Everyone who calls on the name of the Lord will be saved.'"

Bible quotations are from the NIV.

The Bridge to Life

Step 1—God's Love and His Plan

God created us in His own image to be His friend and to experience a full life assured of his love, abundant and eternal (John 10:10b, Romans 5:1).

Step 2—Our Problem: Separation from God

God created us in His own image to have abundant (meaningful) life. He did not make us robots to automatically love and obey him, but He gave us a will and a freedom of choice (Romans 3:23; Isaiah 59:2).

Step 3—God's Remedy: The Cross

Jesus Christ is the only answer to this problem. He died on the cross and rose from the grave, paying the penalty for our sin and bridging the gap between God and people (1 Peter 3:18; 1 Timothy 2:5; Romans 5:8).

Step 4—Our Response

Believing means trust and commitment—acknowledging our sinfulness, trusting Christ's forgiveness, and letting Him control our life. Eternal, abundant life is a gift for us to receive (John 3:16; John 5:24).

For more complete information, access the Ministry Tools link at www.navigators.org.

Three Story Evangelism

Three Story Evangelism is a witnessing method that Campus Life teaches its student leaders about how to witness. The three stories are:

1. your story
2. His story (Jesus' story)
3. their story (the friend to whom you are witnessing)

The author of this course recommends simple sequence variation of the Campus Life plan, as follows, in keeping with the Response Evangelism approach in Chapter 5 of the course:

1. their story
2. your story
3. His story

First, listen to a nonbeliever, learning as much as you can about *him or her*; then share *your* personal testimony, including how your life was totally changed because of *Jesus Christ*.

For more complete information, visit www.yfccampuslife.com/3story.htm.

Evangelism Explosion

For several decades, Evangelism Explosion, a ministry founded by Dr. James Kennedy, has been used by thousands of churches. The basic approach to explaining salvation begins with two simple questions:

1. Do you know for sure that you are going to be with God in heaven?
2. If God were to ask you, "Why should I let you into my heaven," what would you say?

The Bible tells how you can *know for sure* that you have eternal life and will go to be with God in heaven (1 John 5:13).

1. Heaven (Eternal Life) is a Free Gift.

Romans 6:23; Ephesians 2:8–9

2. Man is a Sinner.

Romans 3:23; Matthew 5:48; James 2:10

3. God is Merciful and, Therefore, Doesn't Want to Punish Us.

1 John 4:8; Jeremiah 31:3; Exodus 34:7; Ezekiel 18:4

4. God Solved this Problem for Us in the Person of Jesus Christ.

John 1:1, 14; Isaiah 53:6

5. This Gift is Received by Faith.

Acts 16:31

For more complete information, visit www.eeinternational.org.

The Four Spiritual Laws

Possibly the most widely distributed plan of salvation is The Four Spiritual Laws, written by the late Dr. Bill Bright, founder of Campus Crusade for Christ International.

Just as there are physical laws that govern the physical universe, so are there spiritual laws which govern your relationship with God.

Law 1: God loves you, and offers a wonderful plan for your life.

John 3:16; 10:10

Law 2: Man is sinful and separated from God.

Romans 3:23; 6:23

Law 3: Jesus Christ is God's only provision for man's sin. Through Him you can know and experience God's love and plan for your life.

Romans 5:8; 1 Corinthians 15:3–6; John 14:6

Law 4: We must individually receive Jesus Christ as Savior and Lord; then we can know and experience God's love and plan for our lives.

John 1:12; 3:1–8; Ephesians 2:8–9

For more complete information, visit www.crusade.org/fourlaws.

Glossary

		Chapter
allegory	— Goes beyond a parable by making several points and assigning symbolic meaning to multiple elements in the story.	4
alliteration	— The repetition of beginning consonant sounds in a string of words, commonly used by preachers as an aid to the audience's memory when composing points in a sermon.	12
altar	— A place of consecration and personal sacrifice in which the believer is more fully aware of God's presence.	12
anointing	— The Holy Spirit's work in the lives of both the speaker and hearer of the Word, giving the first the ability to clearly communicate a message with inspired clarity and giving the second the ability to understand and apply that message to life.	12
Antioch	— One of the earliest centers of Christianity; it was here that the followers of Christ were first called *Christians*. Antioch served as the headquarters for Paul's missionary journeys.	1
Calvinism	— The theological system of John Calvin (1509-1564), a French pastor in Geneva, prominent reformer, and the first systematic theologian of the Protestant movement. Calvinists believe that God has determined in advance who will be saved and who will be condemned and that Jesus died only for the elect. All the elect will ultimately be saved and apostasy (the deliberate abandonment of salvation) is impossible.	2
ceremonially unclean	— A condition of societal exclusion called for in the Law of Moses when a person was considered contaminated (temporarily or long-term) by eating prohibited food, exhibiting evidence of certain diseases, coming in contact with human bodily fluids, or any number of minor violations of the Law. The condition was not necessarily a sign of moral failure but was usually intended as a reminder of the sinful nature of all people.	5
church planting model	— A structural relationship between a host church and a church plant that accounts for varying levels of assistance by the host church and varying levels of independence of the church plant.	11
Codex Vaticanus	— A Greek manuscript, possibly the most important of all the manuscripts of Holy Scripture. It is named such because it belongs to the Vatican Library.	1
Codex Sinaiticus	— A Greek manuscript of the Old and New Testaments, of great antiquity and value, found on Mount Sinai, in St. Catherine's Monastery, by Constantine Tischendorf.	1

		Chapter
dependence	— The believer's reliance on God to divinely influence the person with whom he or she is sharing the gospel.	8
disciple	— As a verb, the process of nurturing spiritual growth in another. As a noun, a follower of Christ who lives in obedience to Christ's teachings.	1
discipleship	— Developing spiritual growth in the believer with the end objective of spiritual multiplication.	2
discipline	— The believer's recognition of personal responsibility to prepare for evangelism through Bible study, prayer, and consistent Christian living.	8
evangelism	— The presentation of Jesus Christ in the power of the Holy Spirit so that people might come to trust Him as Savior and serve Him as Lord in the fellowship of His church.	2
exegesis	— The careful, systematic study of the Scriptures, including critical analysis, to discover the original intended meaning and bring the meaning out of Scripture; distinguished from the error of eisegesis, which is reading meaning into the text.	12
exegetical theology	— The study of theology as solely revealed through Scripture.	15
exponential	— Increasing at a consistent and usually rapid rate.	2
fruit of the Spirit	— Personal characteristics created and nurtured by the Holy Spirit in the believer who maintains fellowship with Him.	6
full gospel	— The ministry focus that assumes that what God promised to the New Testament church is still true for the church today.	14
Great Commission	— The summary term for Christ's commands and instructions to His followers to proclaim the gospel and make disciples in all nations.	1
Great Commission cycle	— The constant interchange between evangelism of the lost and discipleship of new believers in preparation for their own ministry as evangelists to the lost.	2
hermeneutics	— The rules, principles, and procedures of Bible interpretation, often with special attention given to current life-application of the text.	12
homogeneous principle	— The idea that a group will usually grow more quickly and easily if it is comprised primarily of one kind of people.	2
illumination	— The means by which the Holy Spirit enlightens or gives understanding of God's revelation in the Bible.	12
imperative mood	— Form of a verb that expresses a command.	1
indigenous	— Something that begins, grows, and lives in its natural setting or environment.	14
initial evidence	— The first outward sign that a believer has received the baptism in the Holy Spirit, namely, speaking in other tongues.	6
inspiration	— The extraordinary supernatural influence exerted by the Holy Spirit on the thought processes of the writers of Scripture so that their words were rendered the words of God and are infallible.	12
Irenaeus	— *ca.* 125–*ca.* 202, Greek theologian, Bishop of Lyons, and the church father who systematized Christian beliefs that would later be accepted as orthodox doctrine and cited frequently by theologians.	1

The Local Church in Evangelism

		Chapter
ependence	— The believer's reliance on God to divinely influence the person with whom he or she is sharing the gospel.	8
disciple	— As a verb, the process of nurturing spiritual growth in another. As a noun, a follower of Christ who lives in obedience to Christ's teachings.	1
discipleship	— Developing spiritual growth in the believer with the end objective of spiritual multiplication.	2
discipline	— The believer's recognition of personal responsibility to prepare for evangelism through Bible study, prayer, and consistent Christian living.	8
evangelism	— The presentation of Jesus Christ in the power of the Holy Spirit so that people might come to trust Him as Savior and serve Him as Lord in the fellowship of His church.	2
exegesis	— The careful, systematic study of the Scriptures, including critical analysis, to discover the original intended meaning and bring the meaning out of Scripture; distinguished from the error of eisegesis, which is reading meaning into the text.	12
exegetical theology	— The study of theology as solely revealed through Scripture.	15
exponential	— Increasing at a consistent and usually rapid rate.	2
fruit of the Spirit	— Personal characteristics created and nurtured by the Holy Spirit in the believer who maintains fellowship with Him.	6
full gospel	— The ministry focus that assumes that what God promised to the New Testament church is still true for the church today.	14
Great Commission	— The summary term for Christ's commands and instructions to His followers to proclaim the gospel and make disciples in all nations.	1
Great Commission cycle	— The constant interchange between evangelism of the lost and discipleship of new believers in preparation for their own ministry as evangelists to the lost.	2
hermeneutics	— The rules, principles, and procedures of Bible interpretation, often with special attention given to current life-application of the text.	12
homogeneous principle	— The idea that a group will usually grow more quickly and easily if it is comprised primarily of one kind of people.	2
illumination	— The means by which the Holy Spirit enlightens or gives understanding of God's revelation in the Bible.	12
imperative mood	— Form of a verb that expresses a command.	1
indigenous	— Something that begins, grows, and lives in its natural setting or environment.	14
initial evidence	— The first outward sign that a believer has received the baptism in the Holy Spirit, namely, speaking in other tongues.	6
inspiration	— The extraordinary supernatural influence exerted by the Holy Spirit on the thought processes of the writers of Scripture so that their words were rendered the words of God and are infallible.	12
Irenaeus	— *ca.* 125–*ca.* 202, Greek theologian, Bishop of Lyons, and the church father who systematized Christian beliefs that would later be accepted as orthodox doctrine and cited frequently by theologians.	1

Glossary

Term	Definition	Chapter
metaphor	A literary or poetic device in which one object is described as another. Example: Jesus is the Lion of Judah.	4
mission	A derived term not found in the Bible but based on the Latin word missio, which means "sent." The purpose of a mission, or missionary, is to extend a message and activity to new territory.	15
missions conventions	Coordinated services and associated activities in a local church that connect the congregation with missionaries, missions projects, and missions vision. Usually commitments are received for regular missions giving in the form of faith promises.	14
Missions Sunday	The first Sunday of the month, designated throughout the history of the Assemblies of God as an opportunity to promote vision for missions ministry within the local church.	14
neighbor	Translated from Greek meaning "near." Whoever is there—near enough to require a responsibility to relate with the person.	2
ontological argument	The argument that originated with Anselm (1033-1109) and was developed further by French philosopher René Descartes (1596-1650). The ontological argument basically postulates that it is illogical to say that God does not exist, so He must exist. It associates three concepts—the concepts of *God*, *perfection*, and *existence*. The ontological argument was rejected by Saint Thomas Aquinas, the brilliant thirteenth-century Dominican philosopher.	12
outsider	A biblical description of the nonbeliever emphasizing that person's inability to connect with the language and culture of the church.	9
perish	A description of the eternal judgment to be suffered by the lost; not a description of personal annihilation.	3
preaching	Publicly or personally sharing the truth of the gospel. Not intended to describe only pulpit activity.	1
prevenient grace	Activity of the Holy Spirit to bring people and circumstances to bear in a nonbeliever's life in preparation for salvation.	8
response evangelism	Acknowledging God's sovereignty and His work in people's lives and circumstances, then responding to people and their needs while relying on the Holy Spirit's guidance.	5
Samaria	A region in Israel occupied by a people group of mixed ethnicity, including Jewish, who practiced an altered form of Judaism. The Jews looked down on the Samaritans.	5
self-governing	A church in which leadership is raised up by the Holy Spirit from among converts within its own body and is not accountable to or controlled by an outside church organization.	14
self-propagating	A church that extends itself throughout and beyond its own region and is not dependent on outside influence to grow and multiply.	14
self-supporting	A church that does not subsist or depend on outside or foreign sources for finances.	14

		Chapter
Synoptic Gospels	— The Bible books of Matthew, Mark, and Luke which record many of the same events in Jesus' life offering a similar synopsis of His ministry—a beginning-to-end examination of Jesus' life—as distinct from the thematic approach of John.	1
systematic theology	— The branch of theology that deals with the logical categorization of biblical truths; examining the Scriptures doctrinally rather than sequentially.	15
voluntary cooperative fellowship	— The distinctive organizational nature of the Assemblies of God. The founding delegates intended to distinguish the newly formed Pentecostal group as nonsectarian.	14

Reference List

Blair, Charles E. 1968. *The Silent Thousands Suddenly Speak!* Grand Rapids: Zondervan.

Cole, Alan. 1961. *Mark.* Leicester, England: Inter-Varsity Press.

Foote, Billy James. 1997. "Passion/Better is One Day." http://www.worshiptogether.com. (compact disc).

General Council of the Assemblies of God. 2003. *Constitution and Bylaws.*

Hurtado, Larry W. 2001. *New International Biblical Commentary: Mark.* Peabody, MA: Hendrickson Publishers.

Kittel, Gerhard, ed. 1967. *Theological Dictionary of the New Testament Volume IV.* Grand Rapids: Eerdmans.

Lane, William L. 1974. *The Gospel According to Mark: The English Text With Introduction, Exposition, and Notes (New International Commentary on the New Testament).* Grand Rapids: Eerdmans.

———. 1978. *Highlights of the Bible.* Ventura, CA: Regal Books.

Mackay, William Paton. 1863. "Revive Us Again" in *Sing His Praises.* 1991. Springfield, MO: Gospel Publishing House.

Mounce, Robert H. 2002. *New International Biblical Commentary: Matthew.* Peabody, MA: Hendrickson Publishers.

Palmer, Ray. 1830. "My Faith Looks Up to Thee" in *Sing His Praises.* 1991. Springfield, MO: Gospel Publishing House.

Spencer, William A. 1886. "The Songs of the Reaper." http://www.cyberhymnal.org/htm/s/o/n/songreap.htm.

Tasker, R. V. G. 1961. *The Gospel According to St. Matthew.* Leicester, England: Inter-Varsity Press.

Walvoord, J. F., and R. B. Zuck, eds. 1983. *Bible Knowledge Commentary: New Testament (New Testament Edition Based on the New International Version).* Colorado Springs, CO: Victor Books.

Essential Course Materials

CONTENTS

Service Learning Requirement Assignment and Report Form 217
Unit Progress Evaluation Instructions..221
Unit Progress Evaluations 223
Answer Keys 239
    Test Yourself Quizzes..241
    Unit Progress Evaluations...242
Forms..243
    Round-Tripper...245
    Request for Printed Final Examination...247

CHECKLIST OF MATERIALS TO BE SUBMITTED TO BEREAN SCHOOL OF THE BIBLE

at Global University; 1211 South Glenstone Avenue; Springfield, Missouri, 65804; USA:

- ❑ Service Learning Requirement Report (required)
- ❑ Round-Tripper Forms (as needed)
- ❑ Request for a Printed Final Examination (if needed)

Service Learning Requirement Assignment

BEREAN SCHOOL OF THE BIBLE
SLR INSTRUCTIONS

This Service Learning Requirement (SLR) assignment requires you to apply something you have learned from this course in a ministry activity. Although this assignment does not receive a grade, it is required. You will not receive credit for this course until you submit the satisfactorily completed SLR Report Form. This form will not be returned to you.

Seriously consider how you can design and complete a meaningful ministry* activity as an investment in preparing to fulfill God's calling on your life. If you are already involved in active ministry, plan how you can incorporate and apply something from this course in your ongoing ministry activity. Whether or not full-time ministry is your goal, this assignment is required and designed to bring personal enrichment to all students. Ask the Holy Spirit to guide your planning and completion of this ministry exercise.

> * Meaningful ministry is defined as an act whereby you give of yourself in such a way as to meet the needs of another or to enhance the well-being of another (or others) in a way that exalts Christ and His kingdom.

You will complete the SLR by following these instructions:

1. Complete a ministry activity of your choice that you develop according to the following criteria:
   a. Your ministry activity must occur during your enrollment in this course. Do not report on activities or experiences in which you were involved prior to enrolling in this course.
   b. Your ministry activity must apply something you learned in this course, or it must incorporate something from this course's content in some way. Provide chapter, lesson, or page number(s) from the independent-study textbook on which the activity is based.
   c. Your ministry activity must include interacting with at least one other person. You may choose to interact with an individual or a group.
   d. The activity you complete must represent meaningful ministry*. You may develop your own ministry activity or choose from the list of suggestions provided in these instructions.
   e. Consider a ministry activity outside your comfort zone such as sharing the message of salvation with unbelievers or offering loving assistance to someone you do not know well.

2. Then fill out the SLR Report Form following these instructions OR online by accessing the online course. Students who will take the final exam online are encouraged to complete the online report form.

3. Sincere reflection is a key ingredient in valid ministry and especially in the growth and development of your ministry knowledge and effectiveness.

4. Global University faculty will evaluate your report. Although the SLR does not receive a grade, it must be completed to the faculty's satisfaction before a final grade for the course is released. The faculty may require you to resubmit an SLR Report Form for several reasons, including an incomplete form, apparent insincerity, failing to interact with others, and failure to incorporate course content.

Do NOT submit your SLR notes, essays, or other documents; only submit your completed SLR Report Form. No prior approval is needed as long as the activity fulfills the criteria from number one above.

Suggested SLR Ministry Activities

You may choose to engage in any valid and meaningful ministry experience that incorporates this specific course's content and interacts with other people. The following list of suggestions is provided to help you understand the possible activities that will fulfill this requirement. Choose an idea that will connect well with your course material. You may also develop a ministry activity that is not on this list or incorporate content from this course in ministry activity in which you are actively involved at this time:

- Teach a class or small group of any size.
- Preach a sermon to any size group.
- Share the gospel with non-believers; be prepared to develop new relationships to open doors to this ministry. We strongly encourage you to engage in ministry that may be outside your comfort zone.
- Lead a prayer group experience or pray with individual(s) in need, perhaps over an extended period.
- Disciple new believers in their walk with Jesus.
- Interview pastors, missionaries, or other leaders on a topic related to something in your course (do not post or publish interview content).
- Intervene to help resolve personal conflicts.
- Personally share encouragement and resources with those in need.
- Organize and/or administer a church program such as youth ministry, feeding homeless people, transporting people, visiting hospitals or shut-ins, nursing home services, etc.
- Assist with starting a new church.
- Publish an online blog or an article in a church newsletter (include a link in your report to the content of your article or blog).
- For MIN327 only: present a summary of risk management to a church board or other leadership group; interview community business people regarding their opinion of church business practices.

To review sample SLR Reports and to access an online report form, go to this Web address: library.globaluniversity.edu. Navigate to the Berean School of the Bible Students link under "Resources for You." Another helpful resource is our GlobalReach Web site: www.globalreach.org. From that site you can download materials free of charge from Global University's School for Evangelism and Discipleship. These proven evangelism tools are available in many languages.

Service Learning Requirement (SLR) Assignment 219

BSB SERVICE LEARNING REQUIREMENT (SLR) REPORT

Please print or type your responses on this form, and submit the form to Berean School of the Bible. Do not submit other documents. This report will not be returned to you.

MIN123 The Local Church in Evangelism, Third Edition

Your Name.......................... **Student Number** .... **Date** ....

1. Ministry activity date .... **Description of ministry activity and its content:** Briefly describe your ministry activity in the space provided. (You are encouraged to engage in ministry such as sharing your faith with unbelievers, or other activities that may be outside your comfort zone.)

....

....

....

Identify related course content by chapter, lesson, or page number. ....

....

2. Results: What resulted from your own participation in this activity? Include descriptions of people's reactions, decisions to accept Christ, confirmed miracles, Spirit and water baptisms, life changes, etc. Describe the individuals or group who benefited from or participated in your ministry activity. Use numbers to describe results when appropriate (approximate when unsure).

....

....

....

....

Record numbers here: Unbelievers witnessed to?.................. New decisions for Jesus?..................

Holy Spirit baptisms?................ Other?..

3. Reflection: Answer the following questions based on your experience in completing this assignment:

Did this activity satisfy an evident need in others? How so? ....

....

Were you adequately prepared to engage in this activity? Why or why not? ....

....

What positive or negative feelings were you aware of while you were completing this activity? ....

....

In what ways were you aware of the Holy Spirit's help during your ministry activity? ....

....

What would you change if you did this ministry activity again? ....

....

What strengths or weaknesses within yourself did this assignment reveal to you?......................

....

Did you receive feedback about this activity? If so, describe: ....

....

Unit Progress Evaluations

The unit progress evaluations (UPEs) are designed to indicate how well you learned the material in each unit. This may indicate how well prepared you are to take the closed-book final examination.

Taking Your Unit Progress Evaluations

1. Review the lessons of each unit before you take its unit progress evaluation (UPE). Refer to the form Checklist of Study Methods in the How to Use Berean Courses section at the front of the IST.

2. Answer the questions in each UPE without referring to your course materials, Bible, or notes.

3. Look over your answers carefully to avoid errors.

4. Check your answers with the answer keys provided in this section. Review lesson sections pertaining to questions you may have missed. Please note that the UPE scores do not count toward your course grade. They may indicate how well you are prepared to take the closed-book final examination.

5. Enter the date you completed each UPE on the Student Planner and Record form, located in the How to Use Berean Courses section in the front of this IST.

6. Request a printed final examination **if** you cannot take the final examination online. You should do this a few weeks before you take the last unit progress evaluation so that you will be able to take the final examination without delay when you complete the course.

UNIT PROGRESS EVALUATION 1
MIN123 The Local Church in Evangelism, Third Edition
(Unit 1—Chapter 1–3)

MULTIPLE CHOICE QUESTIONS

Select the best answer to each question.

1. Three elements that are common to the Great Commission in both Mark and Matthew are
   a) communicating the message orally, in written form, and by example.
   b) going, communicating the message orally, and speaking in tongues.
   c) going, teaching, and preaching.
   d) going, communicating the message orally, and baptizing.

2. Water baptism is
   a) an optional ritual.
   b) a sacrament whereby a person is saved.
   c) an integral part of the Great Commission.
   d) unnecessary.

3. An analysis of the Great Commission in Mark and Matthew reveals
   a) unfortunate contradictions between them.
   b) strong agreement in the areas of going, proclaiming, and baptizing.
   c) that they are written concurrently.
   d) evidence of multiple authors in each Gospel.

4. In the beginning of Acts, Jesus instructs His disciples to
   a) begin the work of evangelizing the whole world immediately.
   b) wait for the baptism of the Holy Spirit.
   c) study the Scriptures at a Jewish synagogue.
   d) fast and pray.

5. Luke and Acts are
   a) two parts of one whole, divided into components dictated by the limits of scroll length.
   b) theoretically connected by liberal theologians to undermine the texts' validity.
   c) contrasted as examples of theology (Luke) and history (Acts).
   d) the only two books in the Bible that are components of a larger whole.

6. Luke (in Acts) and John recorded Jesus' instruction to His disciples regarding evangelizing as dependent upon
   a) the Holy Spirit's empowerment.
   b) tithing.
   c) heeding end-time warnings.
   d) rebuking the Pharisees.

7. The central role of preaching in fulfilling the Great Commission
   a) proves that Christ has entrusted His mandate only to the clergy.
   b) reflects the needs of an illiterate society and no longer applies in the Information Age.
   c) is no longer in effect, since the death of the apostles.
   d) is a call for all believers to personally share the gospel with the lost.

8. Both Mark and Luke emphasize what as the means of making disciples?
   a) Baptism
   b) Speaking in tongues
   c) Prayer
   d) Preaching

9. The believer's role in personal evangelism is to
   a) offer irrefutable logical arguments for the existence of God and the deity of Jesus.
   b) confront the lost with their sin.
   c) clearly explain the gospel, allowing the Holy Spirit to convince the lost.
   d) assure the lost that God is love.

10. The end objective of evangelism is
    a) a salvation decision.
    b) increased Sunday morning attendance.
    c) a committed and faithful follower of Christ.
    d) improved community relations.

11. In order to see people make decisions for Christ, we should
    a) push for a quick commitment.
    b) convince them of their sinful condition.
    c) cooperate with the Holy Spirit.
    d) demonstrate to people the errors in their world view.

12. The cycle of evangelism and discipleship is completed when
    a) a person commits his or her life to Jesus.
    b) disciples become evangelists.
    c) a disciple is filled with the Holy Spirit.
    d) a disciple is baptized.

13. The ultimate goal of fulfilling the Great Commission is to
    a) eliminate poverty and illness and usher in the Millennium.
    b) present every kind of person to God complete in Christ.
    c) prove the inerrancy of Scripture beyond doubt.
    d) prove the continuing validity of the Ten Commandments.

14. The Great Commission is an expression of
    a) the totally inclusive nature of God's love.
    b) the exclusive nature of the gospel.
    c) the fact that every person will eventually be accepted into God's kingdom.
    d) God's anger against the Jewish people.

15. The concept of *both* in Acts 1:8 means that the disciples should
    a) ensure that everyone believes in their own communities before expanding to all the world.
    b) prioritize one region over others.
    c) contain their ministry to the Roman empire.
    d) be witnesses to all of the areas mentioned without prioritizing.

16. To say that the gospel is heterogeneous means that it
    a) seeks to draw every kind of person from every part of the world into fellowship with Christ.
    b) is targeted at a specific people group.
    c) supports the biblical understanding of marriage.
    d) is centered around others.

17. Targeting a homogenous group
    a) is always a bad idea because it tends to be overly exclusive.
    b) always leads to a homogenous church.
    c) can help a church to become more heterogeneous.
    d) is a sign of spiritual apathy in the church.

18. In the account of the Great Commission in all four Gospels, Jesus
    a) told His disciples what their mission was, but did not tell them how it would be accomplished.
    b) instructed His disciples on the nature of their mission as well as how and why it would be carried out.
    c) centered on the role of the Holy Spirit in fulfilling the commission.
    d) included discussion of end time events.

19. Jesus' disciples were able to undertake the task of making disciples of all nations because
    a) their education and training in public speaking uniquely qualified them.
    b) based on His divine authority they were extensions of Jesus' mission to this world.
    c) of the Roman roads system which allowed for convenient travel throughout the empire.
    d) a common language was spoken throughout the region.

20. Which three truths outline the spiritual state of humanity?
    a) All humanity is lost, facing eternal consequences, with Jesus Christ as the only hope.
    b) All people are created equal, invited to live good lives, and promised eventual salvation.
    c) Humans are comprised of spirit, soul, and body.
    d) The elect are born to be saved, and the lost are born to be damned; only God knows who is who.

21. The gospels of John and Luke
    a) establish a direct connection between the Holy Spirit's empowerment and the mission of the disciples.
    b) were written about the same time.
    c) do not include a version of the Great Commission.
    d) minimize the role of the Holy Spirit in the Great Commission.

22. Concerning His returning to the Father, Jesus told His disciples that
    a) He would prefer to stay with them, but His time on earth was limited.
    b) it was to their advantage that He go away, because He would send the Holy Spirit to them.
    c) He would return periodically to assess their progress.
    d) He would accomplish the Great Commission without their help.

23. The difference between the Spirit's relationship to believers in the Old and New Testaments is that
    a) God did not speak to people by His Holy Spirit in the Old Testament.
    b) the Holy Spirit is not mentioned until the coming of Christ.
    c) in the Old Testament the Spirit came on select individuals, but in the New Testament the Holy Spirit comes to be in God's people.
    d) only priests could be filled with the Holy Spirit in the Old Testament, but the Spirit is available to all believers in the New Testament.

24. When describing the Holy Spirit, Jesus emphasized the
   a) Spirit's convicting activity and the danger of offending Him.
   b) permanence and intimate nature of the Spirit's presence in the believer's life.
   c) Old Testament symbols of fire and wind.
   d) need to pray in tongues.

25. The fact that the Israelites were given manna to feed them in the wilderness illustrates
   a) that God will give the Holy Spirit only to those who are without sin.
   b) that God will miraculously provide the bread of His Word to all the nations without the involvement of the church.
   c) the sinfulness of the wilderness generation.
   d) the need to continually be filled with the Holy Spirit.

After answering all of the questions in this UPE, check your answers with the answer key. Review material related to questions you may have missed, and then proceed to the next unit.

UNIT PROGRESS EVALUATION 2
MIN123 The Local Church in Evangelism, Third Edition
(Unit 2—Chapter 4–6)

MULTIPLE CHOICE QUESTIONS

Select the best answer to each question.

1. During His ministry, Jesus shifted His parables from
   a) agricultural symbols to monetary principles.
   b) easily understood concepts to more obscure truths that He explained to the disciples.
   c) a Hebrew to Greek worldview.
   d) straight-forward symbolism to numerology.

2. What two themes emerge from the parables following the Parable of the Sower in the Synoptic Gospels?
   a) The Jews will return to the Promised Land, and the Antichrist will be revealed.
   b) The sheep will be separated from the goats and the tares from the wheat.
   c) Wise virgins will save their oil, and wise wedding guests will be properly attired.
   d) Every person's choice to belong to God's kingdom or Satan's; and the ultimate, eternal triumph of God's kingdom.

3. The Parable of the Sower
   a) presents two contrasting pairs: productive and unproductive soil.
   b) is impossible for modern interpreters to understand.
   c) was the first parable that Jesus ever told.
   d) represents Jesus' death and resurrection.

4. In the Parable of the Sower, the thorny ground emphasizes the need for
   a) medical missions.
   b) prayer and fasting.
   c) sowing the right kind of seed.
   d) the continued discipling process.

5. Today's affluent and materialistic society is represented by what in the Parable of the Sower?
   a) Sand
   b) Stony ground
   c) Shallow ground
   d) Thorny ground

6. Jesus told the Parable of the Sower to His disciples
   a) to teach them about the inadequacy of the Old Testament law.
   b) because He understood the hardships the disciples would face in spreading the gospel.
   c) to illustrate the hypocrisy of the Pharisees.
   d) because He was concerned that they would be caught up with the cares of the world.

7. The focus in the Parable of the Sower is the
   a) sower.
   b) abundant harvest.
   c) unproductive soils.
   d) proof of predestination.

8. Jesus used salt as an example, indicating that His disciples should be
   a) a moral preservative and stimulate a desire for God and a hunger for truth and righteousness.
   b) an agent of change in their communities, a force for justice, and a healing salve to the hurting.
   c) crossing the seas to evangelize the nations.
   d) valued by their communities, as salt was a valuable commodity.

9. Believers are the light of the world because
   a) they reveal the true nature of things through God's truth, and they guide others.
   b) their prayers travel to God's throne at the speed of light.
   c) they act as a mirror for the souls of men.
   d) there is a natural spark of divinity within each of us.

10. The most complete recorded account of an encounter Jesus had with a nonbeliever is Jesus' conversation with
    a) Nicodemus.
    b) the widow at Nain.
    c) Andrew.
    d) the Samaritan woman.

11. The circumstance by which Jesus had opportunity to speak with the Samaritan woman reminds all believers to
    a) strategically plan opportunities to be in the presence of non-believers.
    b) be ready to seize the moment for witnessing, when God ordains it.
    c) be prepared to discuss the inadequacy of false religion.
    d) seek out the most sinful member in order to reach a community for Christ.

12. A social barrier that was not represented at the meeting between Jesus and the Samaritan woman was a
    a) racial barrier.
    b) language barrier.
    c) gender barrier.
    d) religious barrier.

13. Usually, the most effective means of witness is
    a) passing out gospel tracts.
    b) a predetermined evangelistic routine.
    c) condemning nonbelievers of their sinfulness.
    d) a personalized message that responds to the interest and needs of a nonbeliever.

14. Effective communication requires
    a) listening more than speaking.
    b) speaking with appropriate facial expressions.
    c) body language and vocal emphasis.
    d) a thorough knowledge of current events.

15. When witnessing, the believer should
    a) focus on a personal approach that emphasizes relationship with Jesus.
    b) emphasize propositional statements about the nature of God.
    c) persuade unbelievers about the social advantage of being a part of a church.
    d) try to avoid the subject of sin altogether.

16. To worship God in spirit is best explained as
    a) speaking in tongues.
    b) meditating during personal devotions.
    c) worship expressions that communicate directly with God.
    d) observing the sacrament of communion.

17. To worship God in truth is best explained as
    a) memorizing and quoting the truth of God's Word.
    b) demonstrating one's relationship with God through a righteous lifestyle.
    c) exercising the gift of knowledge.
    d) the moment of salvation when Jesus, who is Truth, is accepted as Lord.

18. When the disciples asked Jesus if He was about to restore His kingdom in Israel, Jesus replied by
    a) redirecting their attention to the Great Whore of Babylon.
    b) rebuking them for asking for signs and wonders.
    c) shifting their focus from the End Times to their need to be filled with the Spirit.
    d) predicting the fall of Jerusalem and warnings of earthquakes and wars.

19. Jesus used much of His final hours before the Crucifixion with the disciples to
    a) remind them of His parables and the meanings He had shared with them.
    b) rebuke them for constantly seeking high positions in His kingdom.
    c) teach in detail about the promised Holy Spirit's empowerment.
    d) warn them of the leaven of the Pharisees.

20. The promise of power in Acts 1:8
    a) indicates that great miracles should always accompany the presentation of the gospel.
    b) refers primarily to the gift of healing.
    c) means that the Spirit will supply what we need to accomplish the work God has assigned us.
    d) referred to the power with which Jesus will reign during the millennium.

21. In the Gospels, Jesus
    a) encourages His followers to seek after signs and wonders.
    b) warned His followers not to be deceived by signs and wonders.
    c) did not perform signs or wonders.
    d) taught that signs and wonders were only for a limited period of time.

22. Human desires can be changed
    a) by a disciplined and focused lifestyle.
    b) only by the power of God.
    c) in a group of supporting believers.
    d) only at the Second Coming.

23. When people are seeking Spirit baptism,
    a) instruct them to beware of a false experience.
    b) it is best not to become involved.
    c) encourage them not to worry that they will have a false experience.
    d) tell them they are not truly saved until they are filled with the Spirit.

24. When the believer speaks in tongues, it is a sign that
    a) the Holy Spirit has taken complete control of the believer.
    b) the Holy Spirit has enabled the believer with a gift that is being experienced.
    c) he or she has achieved a higher plane of spiritual existence.
    d) the Holy Spirit has endowed a lifelong infilling in that believer.

25. After a person has been filled with the Holy Spirit, he or she
    a) can be content with a one time experience.
    b) should continue to seek a fresh infilling.
    c) no longer needs to study languages for missions work.
    d) should enter full time vocational ministry.

After answering all of the questions in this UPE, check your answers with the answer key. Review material related to questions you may have missed, and then proceed to the next unit.

UNIT PROGRESS EVALUATION 3
MIN123 The Local Church in Evangelism, Third Edition
(Unit 3—Chapter 7–10)

MULTIPLE CHOICE QUESTIONS

Select the best answer to each question.

1. When witnessing to nonbelievers with no Christian background, it is best to focus on
   a) who Jesus was, in a historical context.
   b) who Jesus is, the living and resurrected Christ.
   c) separating the facts of Jesus' life from the myths that were later attached by the Gospel writers.
   d) yourself, and the successful life you live as a result of your faith.

2. Who was/were ultimately responsible for the death of Jesus?
   a) The Jews
   b) The Romans
   c) Jesus
   d) Pilate

3. The Gospel of Mark is
   a) a poor starting place for new converts because it is especially complex.
   b) the last Gospel to be written.
   c) an excellent starting place for new converts because of its brevity and clarity.
   d) the longest of the Gospels.

4. What is the most important validation of our witness?
   a) Membership in a credible organization
   b) Our degree of social acceptance
   c) The quality of the seed.
   d) The credibility of our lives.

5. Those who intend to specialize in evangelizing a specific niche group of people must remember that
   a) believers are called to share the gospel far and wide.
   b) the tactic is ineffective unless age, gender, and ethnicity are given equal weight.
   c) Jesus' practice of ministering predominantly to Gentiles must not be violated.
   d) specialization precludes the role of the Holy Spirit.

6. Regeneration, sanctification, transformation, and multiplication are all aspects of the power of the
   a) fruit of the Spirit.
   b) Word of God.
   c) effective evangelist.
   d) local church.

7. Two aspects of the method of Paul's preaching are
   a) encouraging and persuading.
   b) warning and teaching.
   c) exposition and application.
   d) condemnation and enlightenment.

8. Understanding what in evangelism is essential to having the faith to be witnesses?
   a) Our responsibility
   b) The church's role
   c) The satisfaction
   d) God's work

9. Jesus' prayer life was characterized by its
   a) careful observance of ceremony and ritual.
   b) use of rabbinical logic.
   c) lengthy incorporation of scriptural quotation.
   d) demonstration of an active and constant relationship with God.

10. The Holy Spirit is vital to evangelism because He
    a) influences both the speaker and the listener during witnessing opportunities.
    b) helps the believer identify who God has ordained to be saved and avoid those predestined to hell.
    c) supernaturally guarantees that the listener will come to Christ.
    d) dictates the believer's exact words.

11. When witnessing to nonbelievers, believers should
    a) be careful not to use terms that may not be understood by those outside of the Christian faith.
    b) introduce them to key terms such as salvation and justification.
    c) be careful not to bring up the subject of sin.
    d) push for an immediate decision.

12. When sharing the good news, the believer's focus on Jesus should be in terms of
    a) His identity as a Person and as the Savior and Lord.
    b) His teachings and His good life.
    c) God's plan to judge the world and condemn sinners to hell.
    d) His return to earth to rule with a rod of iron.

13. The believer's verbal witness must clearly connect with
    a) a consistent personal relationship with Christ.
    b) a sinless life.
    c) daily miracles.
    d) the liturgy of the church.

14. The term *missionary* applies only to those who
    a) go overseas.
    b) deliver the message of the gospel to other cultures.
    c) share the gospel to those around them in any context.
    d) are appointed by the Assemblies of God World Missions.

15. A biblical understanding of the missionary's ministry is that it is
    a) outreach by people specifically called to carry the gospel to other countries.
    b) a fruit of the Spirit.
    c) every believer's responsibility to take the gospel to his or her corner of the world.
    d) no longer needed, now that mass communications takes the gospel around the world.

16. When pursuing opportunities for personal evangelism, the believer should
    a) memorize John 3:16.
    b) always have a supply of tracts.
    c) first inquire about the person's soul.
    d) be sensitive to divine appointments to witness to the lost.

17. The caution in Ecclesiastes against watching the wind and the clouds
    a) is a reminder that open-air crusades are a bad idea.
    b) applies to farmers.
    c) reminds believers that witnessing opportunities are sometimes inconvenient.
    d) is a warning against idolatry.

18. When addressing the topic of sin with unbelievers,
    a) believers should acknowledge the reality of sin in the context of Christ's offer of forgiveness and eternal life.
    b) every sin committed by the unbelievers should be confessed.
    c) the person considering Christ's forgiveness must swear to never sin again.
    d) believers must admit all past sins.

19. One significant hindrance to effective personal evangelism is
    a) a failure to connect with others' cultures.
    b) insincerity or inconsistency between the believer's lifestyle and message.
    c) forgetting to shower.
    d) a lack of theological education.

20. Believers who use acts of benevolence as tools to communicate the gospel
    a) have misunderstood the Great Commission's call to preach the gospel.
    b) are deluded by the world's social gospel.
    c) are obeying Christ's command to let the world see their good works.
    d) are too insecure to talk about their relationship with Christ.

21. When Paul wrote of presenting "every man complete in Christ," he was
    a) exhibiting Pharisaical prejudice against women.
    b) referencing the need to witness to both individuals and to all groups of people.
    c) contrasting Old Testament circumcision with New Testament grace.
    d) alluding to the marriage of Christ and the church.

22. The early church found their confidence to witness
    a) within themselves.
    b) with training and preparation.
    c) in their knowledge and relationship with God.
    d) from the encouragement of friends.

23. Paul's sense of obligation to spread the gospel
    a) was unique to him because of his apostolic role.
    b) was based on a false expectation of the immediate return of Christ.
    c) applies to all believers because Christ's love compels us to reach the lost.
    d) is inappropriate for modern believers because it conflicts with current standards of tolerance.

24. Paul was unashamed in his ministry because
    a) of his self-confidence.
    b) of his eloquence in rhetoric.
    c) of his confidence in the power of the gospel itself.
    d) he was trained by a prominent Jewish Rabbi.

25. It is to our benefit that Paul had not personally visited Rome before writing Romans, because
   a) it allowed Peter to come to prominence in Rome.
   b) it provided him an occasion to be especially thorough in his communication of the saving work of Jesus.
   c) he would have been angered by the practices of the Roman church.
   d) it allowed him to travel to more important regions of the world.

After answering all of the questions in this UPE, check your answers with the answer key. Review material related to questions you may have missed, and then proceed to the next unit.

UNIT PROGRESS EVALUATION 4
MIN123 The Local Church in Evangelism, Third Edition
(Unit 4—Chapter 11–15)

MULTIPLE CHOICE QUESTIONS

Select the best answer to each question.

1. One of the most important ways a pastor can model evangelism in his or her church is by
   a) offering special incentives to church members who bring unsaved guests.
   b) giving regular public invitations to salvation.
   c) avoiding topics, like *sin*, that unbelievers may find uncomfortable.
   d) putting catchy phrases on the church sign.

2. Building relationships with nonbelievers
   a) is a waste of a pastor's valuable time.
   b) should be avoided by pastors because it may present "the appearance of evil."
   c) provides opportunities for a pastor to model evangelism.
   d) is unwise for pastors, since it sets a bad example for church members.

3. Evangelism is primarily
   a) a means of increasing church attendance.
   b) a work of the Spirit.
   c) the responsibility of those called to vocational ministry.
   d) centered around propositional statements of truth.

4. Most people who make decisions to follow Christ do so
   a) in a local church.
   b) as the result of personal evangelism.
   c) in large open air meetings.
   d) on their own accord, without anyone witnessing to them.

5. Certain seasons such as Christmas and Easter
   a) provide excellent opportunities for evangelism.
   b) demand that pastors preach seasonally appropriate messages that will not offend visitors.
   c) are unimportant because church visitors are usually insincere.
   d) are more trouble than they are worth.

6. Preaching a special sermon series and advertising to the community
   a) is a waste of time and money.
   b) only attracts believers.
   c) is appropriate only for pastors who are very well known in their communities.
   d) can be an effective means of evangelizing.

7. The only person who is named as an evangelist in the New Testament is
   a) Paul.
   b) Philip.
   c) Andrew.
   d) Peter.

8. In the Mother Church plant model,
   a) a host church releases people and resources as part of the initial startup for the new church.
   b) the church plant reproduces the ministries of the central church in another area.
   c) a number of churches agree to plant a church together.
   d) the church plant meets at different times or in a different part of the host church facility.

9. According to the course author, evangelistic preaching
   a) means delivering a sermon that is primarily directed to the nonbeliever.
   b) focuses on solid biblical exposition.
   c) is unnecessary in a Spirit-filled church.
   d) is not an effective means of reaching the lost.

10. In light of divine revelation, the writers of Scripture
    a) were possessed by the Holy Spirit and caused to write without their own understanding.
    b) wrote down the words that were spoken to them by the Holy Spirit.
    c) wrote, directed by the Holy Spirit, with their own thoughts, vocabulary, and experiences.
    d) often wrote only under their own authority without the guidance of the Holy Spirit.

11. To seek illumination when preparing to share God's Word, the preacher should rely on
    a) the time-tested resources of commentaries and lexicons.
    b) the Holy Spirit to reveal understanding, meaning, and application of a passage.
    c) current life experience to reveal the best illustrations for the text.
    d) personal spiritual disciplines and self-denial.

12. In order to impact people's lives, God's Word must be
    a) publicly read in the original languages before exposition.
    b) paraphrased into the latest jargon by the preacher.
    c) shared only with believers.
    d) connected with contemporary language and experience under the Spirit's anointing.

13. What is required to effectively preach and teach God's Word?
    a) Oratory skill and theological education
    b) Ministerial licensing and ordination
    c) Discipline and dependence
    d) A growing church and community outreach

14. The roles of "pastor and teacher" mentioned in Ephesians 4:11
    a) are grouped together as one.
    b) are distinctly separate according to Paul.
    c) are the most important roles in the church.
    d) come from the same Greek word roots.

15. The four components of a well-structured altar invitation are
    a) reading an appropriate Scripture, corporate recitation of the sinner's prayer, dismissal, allowing the Holy Spirit to lead specific people to the altar.
    b) prophecy, interpretation, word of wisdom, word of knowledge.
    c) faith in God to act, a clear message to the audience, an environment conducive to response, trained assistants ready to pray with those who respond.
    d) pronouncement of the lostness of man, announcement of the eternal duration of hell, description of God's grace, warning against accepting grace unworthily.

16. When asking an altar respondent to identify his or her need, it is important that he or she identify
    a) whether or not he or she has ever been a Christian.
    b) the nature and extent of sinful habits.
    c) whether he or she personally knows the Lord or has known the Lord.
    d) the four spiritual laws.

17. The three components that work together to ground the believer in God's Word are
    a) Bible reading, Scripture memorization, and Bible study.
    b) Bible reading, Bible study, and supplemental Christian reading.
    c) Bible study, Scripture memorization, and Bible meditation.
    d) Bible reading, Bible study, and Bible meditation.

18. Regarding water baptism, believers should
    a) be encouraged to be baptized as soon as possible.
    b) be baptized only after a thorough understanding of Scripture and the 16 Fundamental Truths.
    c) not be baptized again if they were baptized as infants.
    d) be baptized only after they have received the baptism of the Holy Spirit.

19. Small groups
    a) are unbiblical and cause divisions in the church.
    b) should be avoided because they tend to be overly homogenous.
    c) provide a means for discipleship in the local church.
    d) are a new age concept that should be rejected by the church.

20. One-on-one discipling
    a) was modeled by Jesus.
    b) can only be done in small churches.
    c) is an inefficient use of a pastor's time.
    d) should be done only by the pastor.

21. The Assemblies of God's threefold method for implementing its missions ministries is:
    a) all denominations reaching all the nations for all the kingdom.
    b) all the church communicating all the gospel to all the world.
    c) all people proclaiming all truth and meeting all needs.
    d) all pastors teaching all the laity to evangelize all their neighbors.

22. The best time to educate people about faith promises is
    a) Faith Promise Sunday.
    b) Easter Sunday.
    c) the weeks prior to missions convention.
    d) the first Sunday of the month.

23. The purpose of a missions convention is to
   a) highlight the local ministries of the church.
   b) show appreciation for workers within the congregation.
   c) focus on the life and ministry of a staff member.
   d) remind the congregation of their responsibility in fulfilling the Great Commission.

24. Money
   a) is the root of all evil.
   b) is much more important to give than time.
   c) can be a positive factor in the believer's life.
   d) always leads to corruption.

25. The two "secrets" of spiritual success are to
   a) seek the Lord and keep doing the right things.
   b) fast daily and read at least two chapters of the Bible every day.
   c) give regularly to missions and attend short term missions trips.
   d) read the right books and attend conferences led by prominent pastors.

After answering all of the questions in this UPE, check your answers with the answer key. Review material related to questions you may have missed. Review all materials in preparation for the final exam. Complete and submit your SLR assignment and take the closed-book final examination.

Taking the Final Examination

1. **All final exams must be taken closed book.** You are not allowed to use any materials or outside help while taking a final exam. You will take the final examination online at www.globaluniversity.edu. If the online option is not available to you, you may request a printed final exam. If you did not request a printed final exam when you ordered your course, you must submit this request a few weeks before you are ready to take the exam. The Request for a Printed Final Examination is in the Forms section of Essential Course Materials at the back of this IST.

2. Review for the final examination in the same manner in which you prepared for the UPEs. Refer to the form Checklist of Study Methods in the front part of the IST for further helpful review hints.

3. After you complete and submit the online final examination, the results will be immediately available to you. Your final course grade report will be e-mailed to your Global University student e-mail account after your Service Learning Requirement (SLR) report has been processed.

4. If you complete the exam in printed form, you will send your final examination, your answer sheets, and your SLR report to Berean School of the Bible for grading. Your final course grade report will be sent to your GU student e-mail account. If you do not have access to the Internet, your grade will be sent to your mailing address.

Answer Keys

- Compare your answers to the Test Yourself quizzes against those given in this section.
- Compare your answers to the UPE questions against the answer keys located in this section.
- Review the course content identified by your incorrect answers.

ANSWERS TO TEST YOURSELF

MIN123 The Local Church in Evangelism, Third Edition

Answers below are followed by the number of the objective being tested. For any questions you answered incorrectly, review the lesson content in preparation for your final exam.

Chapter 1
1. C 1.1.1
2. B 1.1.2
3. A 1.1.2
4. B 1.1.3
5. A 1.1.3
6. B 1.1.4
7. A 1.2.1
8. C 1.2.2
9. C 1.2.3
10. D 1.2.4

Chapter 2
1. A 2.1.1
2. D 2.1.2
3. C 2.1.2
4. B 2.1.3
5. B 2.1.4
6. C 2.2.1
7. A 2.2.2
8. D 2.2.3
9. A 2.2.3
10. D 2.2.4

Chapter 3
1. B 3.1.1
2. C 3.1.2
3. A 3.1.2
4. A 3.1.3
5. C 3.1.4
6. B 3.2.1
7. B 3.2.2
8. A 3.2.3
9. D 3.2.4
10. D 3.2.4

Chapter 4
1. A 4.1.1
2. B 4.1.4
3. C 4.2.1
4. A 4.2.2
5. A 4.2.3
6. D 4.2.4
7. B 4.3.2
8. B 4.3.4
9. C 4.4.1
10. D 4.4.3

Chapter 5
1. A 5.1.2
2. D 5.1.2
3. A 5.1.4
4. D 5.2.1
5. C 5.2.2
6. D 5.2.3
7. C 5.2.4
8. C 5.3.1
9. A 5.3.3
10. B 5.3.4

Chapter 6
1. A 6.1.1
2. A 6.1.3
3. B 6.1.4
4. B 6.2.1
5. A 6.2.1
6. B 6.2.3
7. C 6.2.4
8. C 6.3.1
9. A 6.3.3
10. C 6.3.4

Chapter 7
1. A 7.1.1
2. A 7.1.4
3. D 7.1.4
4. D 7.1.4
5. C 7.1.4
6. A 7.2.2
7. C 7.2.2
8. B 7.2.3
9. B 7.2.3
10. C 7.2.3

Chapter 8
1. A 8.1.1
2. B 8.1.2
3. C 8.1.3
4. A 8.1.4
5. B 8.2.1
6. D 8.2.2
7. C 8.2.4
8. C 8.3.1
9. A 8.3.2
10. C 8.3.4

Chapter 9
1. D 9.1.2
2. B 9.1.3
3. C 9.2.2
4. A 9.3.2
5. D 9.3.3
6. A 9.4.2
7. B 9.4.3
8. B 9.5.1
9. D 9.6.1
10. C 9.6.3

Chapter 10
1. D 10.1.1
2. A 10.1.1
3. B 10.1.2
4. C 10.1.3
5. C 10.1.4
6. A 10.2.1
7. B 10.2.3
8. D 10.2.3
9. A 10.2.3
10. C 10.2.4

Chapter 11
1. A 11.1.1
2. C 11.1.3
3. C 11.1.4
4. A 11.2.1
5. A 11.2.2
6. B 11.2.4
7. A 11.3.1
8. C 11.3.2
9. C 11.3.4
10. C 11.3.4

Chapter 12
1. A 12.1.1
2. A 12.1.1
3. A 12.1.2
4. B 12.1.4
5. D 12.2.1
6. B 12.2.3
7. B 12.2.4
8. A 12.3.1
9. B 12.3.1
10. D 12.3.4

Chapter 13
1. D 13.1.1
2. D 13.1.3
3. B 13.1.3
4. A 13.2.2
5. B 13.2.3
6. C 13.2.4
7. A 13.2.4
8. D 13.3.2
9. A 13.3.3
10. D 13.3.4

Chapter 14
1. D 14.1.1
2. A 14.1.2
3. B 14.1.3
4. C 14.1.3
5. D 14.1.4
6. A 14.2.1
7. B 14.2.1
8. C 14.2.2
9. A 14.2.3
10. B 14.2.4

Chapter 15
1. B 15.1.1
2. A 15.1.2
3. D 15.1.3
4. B 15.1.4
5. B 15.1.4
6. A 15.2.1
7. D 15.2.2
8. D 15.2.3
9. A 15.2.4
10. C 15.2.4

UNIT PROGRESS EVALUATION ANSWER KEYS
MIN123 The Local Church in Evangelism, Third Edition

Answers below are followed by the number of the objective being tested. For any questions you answered incorrectly, review the lesson content in preparation for your final exam.

UNIT PROGRESS EVALUATION 1	
1. D 1.1.4	14. A 2.2.1
2. C 1.1.4	15. D 2.2.1
3. B 1.1.4	16. A 2.2.3
4. B 1.2.1	17. C 2.2.2
5. A 1.2.1	18. B 3.1.1
6. A 1.2.3	19. B 3.1.2
7. D 1.2.4	20. A 3.1.3
8. D 1.2.4	21. A 3.2.3
9. C 2.1.2	22. B 3.2.1
10. C 2.1.4	23. C 3.2.2
11. C 2.1.2	24. B 3.2.2
12. B 2.1.3	25. D 3.2.4
13. B 2.1.4	

UNIT PROGRESS EVALUATION 2	
1. B 4.1.4	14. A 5.2.2
2. D 4.1.4	15. A 5.3.2
3. A 4.2.1	16. C 5.3.2
4. D 4.2.2	17. B 5.3.2
5. D 4.2.2	18. C 6.1.2
6. B 4.3.1	19. C 6.1.3
7. A 4.3.1	20. C 6.2.1
8. A 4.4.2	21. B 6.2.3
9. A 4.4.2	22. B 6.2.2
10. D 5.1.1	23. C 6.3.4
11. B 5.1.2	24. B 6.3.3
12. B 5.1.3	25. B 6.3.4
13. D 5.2.2	

UNIT PROGRESS EVALUATION 3	
1. A 7.1.4	14. C 9.3.4
2. C 7.1.4	15. C 9.3.4
3. C 7.2.1	16. D 9.4.1
4. D 8.1.3	17. C 9.4.4
5. A 8.2.1	18. A 9.5.2
6. B 8.2.4	19. B 9.5.1
7. B 8.3.1	20. C 9.5.3
8. D 8.3.3	21. B 9.6.3
9. D 9.1.1	22. C 10.1.1
10. A 9.1.4	23. C 10.1.2
11. A 9.3.2	24. C 10.1.4
12. A 9.2.3	25. B 10.1.1
13. A 9.2.4	

UNIT PROGRESS EVALUATION 4	
1. B 11.1.2	14. A 12.3.1
2. C 11.1.3	15. C 12.3.2
3. B 11.1.4	16. C 12.3.3
4. B 11.2.1	17. D 13.1.1
5. A 11.2.2	18. A 13.1.3
6. D 11.2.3	19. C 13.3.3
7. B 11.3.1	20. A 13.3.3
8. A 11.3.4	21. B 14.1.4
9. B 12.1.1	22. C 14.2.4
10. C 12.1.2	23. D 14.2.2
11. B 12.1.3	24. C 15.2.3
12. D 12.2.2	25. A 15.2.4
13. C 12.2.4	

Forms

The following pages contain two course forms: the Round-Tripper and the Request for a Printed Final Examination.

1. For students who do not have access to e-mail, we are including one **Round-Tripper** for your use if you have a question or comment related to your studies. If you do not have access to the Internet, you will want to make several photocopies of the Round-Tripper before you write on it. Retain the copies for submitting additional questions as needed. Students who have access to e-mail can submit questions at any time to bsbcontent@globaluniversity.edu.

2. Students who do not have access to the Internet-based tests may request a printed final examination. For faster service, please call Enrollment Services at 1-800-443-1083 or fax your **Request for a Printed Final Examination** to 417-862-0863.

ROUND-TRIPPER

MIN123 The Local Church in Evangelism, Third Edition   Date ....

Your Name .... Your Student Number ....

Send questions and comments by e-mail to bsbcontent@globaluniversity.edu. If you do not have access to e-mail, use this form to write to Berean School of the Bible with questions or comments related to your studies. Write your question in the space provided. Send this form to Berean School of the Bible. The form will make its return, or round-trip, as Berean School of the Bible responds.

YOUR QUESTION:

FOR BEREAN SCHOOL OF THE BIBLE'S RESPONSE: